The Capacity To Budget

ALLEN SCHICK

The Capacity To Budget

THE URBAN INSTITUTE PRESS
Washington, D.C.

Library of Congress Cataloging in Publication Data
    The capacity to budget/Allen Schick
    1. Budget—United States.   2. Government spending policy—United States.
    I. Title
HJ2051.S33 1990   336.73—dc20   89-25003
                                                                   CIP

ISBN 0-87766-439-0 (alk. paper)
ISBN 0-87766-438-2 (alk. paper; casebound)

Urban Institute books are printed on acid-free paper whenever possible.

Printed in the United States of America.

9   8   7   6   5   4   3   2   1

Distributed by:
        University Press of America
4720 Boston Way   3 Henrietta Street
Lanham, MD 20706   London WC2E 8LU ENGLAND

THE URBAN INSTITUTE is a nonprofit policy research and educational organization established in Washington, D.C., in 1968. Its staff investigates the social and economic problems confronting the nation and government policies and programs designed to alleviate such problems. The Institute disseminates significant findings of its research through the publications program of its Press. The Institute has two goals for work in each of its research areas: to help shape thinking about societal problems and efforts to solve them, and to improve government decisions and performance by providing better information and analytic tools.

Through work that ranges from broad conceptual studies to administrative and technical assistance, Institute researchers contribute to the stock of knowledge available to public officials and private individuals and groups concerned with formulating and implementing more efficient and effective government policy.

Conclusions or opinions expressed in Institute publications are those of the authors and do not necessarily reflect the views of other staff members, officers or trustees of the Institute, advisory groups, or any organizations that provide financial support to the Institute.

To Miriam,

whose capacity to love
surpasses her capacity to budget.

CONTENTS

Figures

FOREWORD

Ten years ago The Urban Institute commissioned Allen Schick to examine the effects of the Congressional Budget Act of 1974 on congressional behavior. His work resulted in *Congress and Money: Budgeting, Spending, and Taxing*, a prize-winning book that was the first study of legislative behavior issued under the auspices of the Institute. That act, heralded at the time as a major advance in the practice and accountability of the American government, purported to give Congress a comprehensive and consistent means of making fiscal choices and setting national priorities. The message of *Congress and Money* was that the process had limitations but that, on the whole, it provided a useful legislative tool for balancing budgetary and other interests and for managing budgetary conflict within Congress.

In the decade since publication of *Congress and Money*, the Reagan administration tried to recast national priorities and reduce the size of government. The decade has also been one of unprecedented and chronic deficits. And it has been a period during which established procedures broke down and new ones, centered around the reconciliation and Gramm-Rudman-Hollings process, were invented. The Institute once again invited Allen Schick to examine the impact of these changes and to give us his assessment of the current state of government budgeting. We are proud to present the results of his new examination, and hope that this book will contribute to the public debate on how to best bring order and effectiveness to the essential task of raising and expending public funds.

William Gorham
President

PREFACE

Each decade brands government with its own perspectives and possibilities. A decade ago, when The Urban Institute published a previous work of mine on the subject of federal budgeting, the congressional budget process was still in its infancy and there was a strong expectation that improvements in budget practices would lead to more favorable budget outcomes. That positive outlook was reflected in *Congress and Money: Budgeting, Spending, and Taxing* which was published by the Institute in 1980.

A few years ago, William Gorham and Steve Hitchner invited me to contribute a new book to the stockpile of published material on the federal budget. My first instinct was to rewrite and update *Congress and Money*. It didn't take much reflection, however, for me to conclude that trying to do so would be an exceedingly difficult and unproductive task. The federal budget generates many thousands of pages of official documents each year, along with an even larger supply of commentary and analysis. To compose a reasonably full account of budgeting in these times would take more time and patience than I could spend on this important subject.

But there was a more compelling reason for turning from an update to a different kind of work which came to be *The Capacity to Budget*. It has been a decade in which budgeting has dominated the political scene, and it has been a decade in which budgeting's weaknesses and limitations have been more exposed than ever before. If the previous work was suffused with the promise of congressional budgeting, the present one reflects the confusion and uncertainty of these times. Once there were answers, or at least many of us thought there were; today, there is doubt, or a babble of conflicting views about what went wrong and how things might be fixed. Because budgeting crowds out other matters and forces issues to be defined in fiscal terms does not mean that this process is as efficacious as it is often thought to be. Perhaps budgeting is most effective when it is prac-

ticed through the calming routines of bureaucratic review and legislative action rather than through the helter-skelter of political conflict.

In writing about the past decade, I've reached back to the 1960s
when I first began to observe and write about government budgeting.
A good deal of what I have watched and thought about over the past
quarter of a century is summed up in this work. I cannot possibly
recall the names of all of those who have helped me along the way.
I will mention only six, although hundreds more have been of assistance. Elizabeth Wharton provided valuable research assistance
and editorial advice during the preparation of this book. I drove her
almost as hard as I did myself to meet impossible deadlines and she
performed every task with skill and good cheer. I first met Bob Keith
and Richard Kogan when they were apprentice analysts at the
Congressional Research Service. Over the years, they have been a
willing source of data and advice. My gratitude for their assistance
is matched by my pride in what each has accomplished. This is the
second time that Bill Gorham has invested in me. Bill is a true patron
of scholarship. I value his friendship and hope that when, a decade
hence, he again turns to me for an accounting of the federal budget,
I will be able to repay his incurable confidence with a more favorable
verdict on the state of government finance. Steve Hitchner has been
my "handler" from the start of this project. He is what every re-
searcher needs but rarely gets: a supporter who makes sure that you
are always headed in the right direction. We all owe a debt to the
Lynde and Harry Bradley Foundation, the Andrew W. Mellon Foundation, and the Ford Foundation whose support to the Institute made
this book possible.

This book is dedicated to the woman I first met when my only
knowledge of budgeting was how to start a family while completing
graduate education. Miriam has never reconciled a bank statement,
but she has always reconciled the more important things in our lives.
Her love makes budgeting a manageable subject.

Allen Schick

Chapter 1

THE CRISIS IN BUDGETING

Budgeting is essential to the effective operation of modern government. It has become the closest thing to a national command and
control process, the means by which governments steer and finance
their vast ambitions. It is no exaggeration to state that the capacity
to govern depends on the capacity to budget. Without the capacity
to budget, central governments could not have grown so large or
come to exercise so much power. Big, active governments would be
unthinkable without the discipline and regularities of budgeting.

Over time, the U.S. budget has taken on functions so that it now
does much more than allocate money to federal programs and agencies. The federal government uses the budget to establish and pursue
national objectives, to promote favorable economic conditions, to
manage its diverse activities, to respond to the demands of citizens
and groups, to assess past performance, and to plan for the future.
In previous decades, the budget propelled the growth of the national
government; in the 1980s, it was the Reagan administration's prin-
ciple weapon in reshaping national priorities and downsizing domestic programs.

But just as budgeting once enhanced political and managerial capabilities, it now has the potential to weaken them. There is convincing evidence that the effectiveness of American budgeting has
been seriously eroded. The signs of breakdown are pervasive:

☐ Record deficits have tripled the national debt—which now ex-
ceeds $2.5 trillion—in the 1980s. For perhaps the first time in
U.S. history, economic growth has not sufficed to rein in the
deficit. After seven consecutive years of expansion—a peacetime record—the deficit remains well above the apex reached
in the last recession. Although the deficit has fallen by about
$70 billion from its peak level ($221 billion in the 1986 fiscal
year), much of the improvement has been due to the buildup of

balances in the Social Security trust funds.[1] Some critics have suggested that the huge deficits were planned by a canny president determined to deprive the government of funds that might be used to expand programs. But the persistence of big deficits suggests that inadequacies in budget capacity also have contributed to the problem.

□ An increasing portion of the budget is allocated to mandatory payments—one reason for the chronic deficits. Entitlements now account for about half of federal spending. With interest charges added in, mandatory costs constitute almost two-thirds of total spending. These expenditures rise automatically each year, regardless of the condition of the budget or the needs of other government programs. The automaticity of these expenditures has made the budget less flexible than it once was and more a means of accounting for past decisions than for making new ones.

□ A breakdown in budget procedure has accompanied the failure of budget policy. Congress rarely completes its budget work on schedule, and some recent fiscal years have started without a single appropriation bill enacted. When this occurs, Congress packages all of the regular appropriations, along with a substantial amount of extraneous and often controversial legislation, into an omnibus measure that sprawls across hundreds of pages of the statute books. These extraordinary measures are assembled under chaotic conditions, typically with few members of Congress knowing what is hidden in them. Sometimes, even affected interests are not aware of what is in store for them until the legislation has been enacted.

□ Malaise has spread from legislative chambers to executive offices. Recent presidential budgets have been labeled "dead on arrival," signaling that they have little influence on congressional actions. The problem goes a lot deeper, however, than presidential budgeting at the top of the executive branch. It also pervades the everyday budget work of federal agencies. Agencies often go through the motions of preparing budgets that are not used in making budget decisions. There is reason to believe that the vast amounts of material submitted by agencies in support of their budget requests are virtually disregarded in making presidential budget decisions, though the detailed submissions are used in routine negotiations between OMB examiners and agency staff to settle small but administratively important matters, such as the number of personnel. These justifications materials are also less influential in shaping congressional outcomes than once was the case.

□ A general loss of budgetary potency has enfeebled all major participants. The weakening of agency roles has not strengthened the president or his Office of Management and Budget. The erosion of the president's once-commanding position has not been counterbalanced by a gain in congressional budget prowess. In Congress, most authorizing committees have lost influence, as have the appropriations committees. The budget committees, established in 1974 to bring order to congressional budgeting, have not picked up the slack.

□ The basic rules of accounting for budget transactions have broken down. Without actually paring a single dollar from outlays, Congress and the president now use bookkeeping tricks to show that spending or the deficit has been cut. The president submits budgets grounded on untenable economic assumptions or on policy recommendations that have no chance of adoption. For its part, Congress adroitly advances or defers payment dates to reduce reported outlays, and it joins with the White House in promoting asset sales that are counted in the budget as negative expenditures. Although such budget gimmicks are not new, they appear to be more extensively and blatantly used than previously.[2] The widespread use of gimmicks has thwarted genuine deficit reduction while undermining public confidence in the federal government.

The contemporary crisis in budgeting has both policy and procedural dimensions. The policy crisis pertains to the rigidity of federal expenditures, the massive and persistent deficits, the uncertain role of the budget in economic policy, and the gap between resources and demands. The procedural crisis is manifested in the collapse of established budget methods, the strained relationship between the president and Congress, reliance on ad hoc arrangements to make the budget, and instability in budgetary roles.

Policy and process are two sides of the same budgetary coin. One should not expect the procedures to be in good working order if the substantive results are not. Thus, the interplay of policy and process is a recurring theme of this book. Significant changes in one are likely to be accompanied (or precipitated) by adjustments in the other. The particular relationship between process and policy that concerns us here is how growth or cutback affects the manner in which budgets are decided and the types of decisions made. There are adaptations in both the "how" and the "what" of federal budgeting.

BUDGETARY BREAKDOWN: FROM THE CONGRESSIONAL BUDGET ACT TO THE GRAMM-RUDMAN-HOLLINGS LAW

The crisis in federal budgeting is reflected in key differences between two laws passed less than a dozen years apart. The first was the Congressional Budget Act (CBA) of 1974; the second was the Gramm-Rudman-Hollings law (GRH) of 1985.[3] The two laws were spawned by similar problems, but they took different approaches and were suffused by different expectations. Both laws were prompted by chronic deficits and by the failure of Congress to complete its budget work on time. CBA's solution was to enlarge Congress's budget powers, GRH's to constrain them. CBA was animated by confidence that if Congress took control of the purse, it would act in a fiscally responsible manner; GRH is steeped in frustration over Congress's inability to come to grips with the nation's budgetary problems.

CBA created a neutral budget process in which each year's outcome would be shaped by a congressional majority. It neither ordained that revenue or spending should rise or decline each year nor prescribed the appropriate size of the deficit. These matters were left to the full discretion of Congress, to be decided in budget resolutions that would set forth the policies it wanted. CBA permitted Congress to take whatever action it wanted, provided it did so in the framework of the budget and was provided timely information on the budgetary implications of its decisions. With but one major exception—pertaining to *total* revenue and spending—the restrictions in the Budget Act were procedural, not substantive. Their purpose was to ensure that due process of budgeting was observed, not to prevent a congressional majority from enacting its budget preferences.[4]

GRH, conversely, is premised on the notion that if left to its own will, a congressional majority would not be able to control the deficit. It is necessary, therefore, to prescribe steadily declining deficits in law until a balanced budget is achieved. Although it preserves CBA's basic procedures, GRH bars Congress from adopting a budget resolution at variance with preset deficit targets. GRH also provides a number of substantive points of order that could be deployed (particularly in the Senate) to block legislation not conforming with the deficit target or other budget policies.[5] To enforce its deficit policies,

GRH establishes a sequestration process by means of which congressional appropriations could be superseded by automatic cutbacks that take place without legislative concurrence. In effect, GRH permits legislative enactments to be canceled by administrative actions.

The shift from CBA's permissiveness to GRH's restrictiveness was a reaction to the deficit history of the period between these laws. Table 1.1 shows the persistence of high deficits between the 1976 and the 1986 fiscal years. In fact, despite some improvement in the years immediately after CBA was enacted, the budget deficit soared in absolute size as well as in relation to the gross national product and total outlays. Not surprisingly, the deficit peaked in the fiscal year the Gramm-Rudman-Hollings law was enacted. Moreover, the years between the two enactments were ones in which Congress experienced a steady deterioration in the timeliness of its budget actions. After a promising start in which action on the budget and most appropriation bills was completed on or close to schedule, Congress regressed to a point where the budget resolution was adopted months behind schedule, and none of the appropriation bills were enacted by the start of the fiscal year.[6]

The intractable deficits and the erosion of budget procedures changed Congress's perception of its budgetary effectiveness. In 1974, the congressional budget process was seen as the solution; in 1985, it was perceived as a big part of the problem. Congress tied its own

Table 1.1 FEDERAL BUDGET DEFICIT, 1976–86

Fiscal year	Deficit ($ in millions)	Deficit as percentage of GNP	Deficit as percentage of outlays
1976[a]	73,719	4.3	19.8
1977	53,644	2.8	13.1
1978	59,168	2.7	12.9
1979	40,162	1.6	8.0
1980	73,808	2.8	12.5
1981	78,936	2.6	11.6
1982	127,940	4.1	17.2
1983	207,764	6.3	25.7
1984	185,324	5.0	21.8
1985	212,260	5.4	22.4
1986	221,167	5.3	22.3

Source: *Historical Tables, Budget of the United States Government, Fiscal Year 1989* (hereafter abbreviated as *Historical Tables* with year).
[a]Does not include the transition quarter between the 1976 and the 1977 fiscal years.

hands in 1985 because members felt that they could not be trusted to do the right or the effective thing. The budget had to be protected from Congress.

In 1974, members were confident that a new era in congressional responsibility was about to begin. Richard Bolling, who shepherded the budget reform legislation through the House, spoke of the new capacity it would give Congress: "We will be setting ceilings on spending. We will be deciding openly and clearly what we intend to do about any deficit. . . . If we find that we have exceeded our goals, then we will be required to reconcile those goals in a fashion that is responsible and open by providing for scaling down, perhaps, appropriations, increasing taxes, or a combination of the two."[7] Edmund Muskie, who would soon chair the new Senate Budget Committee, stressed that the reform "will give Congress the means to deal in an orderly and comprehensive fashion with our most important decisions—those of budget policy and national priorities."[8] The few dissenting voices were drowned out by a self-confident chorus of accolades.[9]

The confidence was long gone in 1985 when a fractious Congress voted for the GRH restrictions. Although some who opposed Gramm-Rudman-Hollings thought that the mess was a result of presidential policies, not of congressional processes, most members thought that Congress was to blame.[10] "We've bungled it as badly as it can be bungled," said House Republican leader Robert Michel of Congress's budget performance.[11] Senator John Chafee said simply, "We have failed, [and] there is little indication that we are serious enough about deficits to make choices."[12] One nettlesome congressman, Robert Walker, was blunter in his assessment: "The fact is the budget process has failed miserably. It is coming apart at the seams."[13] Hardly anyone said a nice word about the budget process.

CAUSES OF BREAKDOWN: POTENTIAL WILL OR BUDGET CAPACITY?

What went wrong? In assessing the crisis in budgeting, one cannot deny its inextricable linkage to big deficits. If deficits had been small, Congress probably would not be castigating itself for failing to stanch the flow of red ink. The budget process would also be much sturdier if Congress faced manageable deficits each year. Alas, the deficits have been truly gargantuan. Explaining why this has been the case is essential for assessing the causes of breakdown.

One popular explanation is that the unwillingness of politicians to make tough choices has undermined the process and generated the deficits. According to this view, if politicians were willing to cut spending or raise taxes, the deficit problem would abate, and the budget process would stabilize. But because politicians have not been willing to approve sufficient tax increases or spending cuts, the deficit has persisted. It follows from this argument that procedural fixes would not do much to remedy the problem.

Political actions obviously affect budgetary outcomes. The budgetary history of our times might have been a lot different if the Reagan administration had not seriously miscalculated the impact of its spending and tax policies in 1981.[14] The government might have made more headway in closing the budget gap if it had not been stalemated for so many years by political conflict between a Republican White House and a divided or Democratic Congress. Nevertheless, a strong case can be made that the problem is more durable and entrenched than the recent budgetary strife between the White House and Congress.

The behavior of politicians has a great bearing on the efficacy of the budget process, but the reverse is also true—the process influences the conduct of those who make budgets. A budget process can be organized to ease or complicate the task of cutback; it can sensitize politicians to the financial implications of their policies or hide the implications from them; it can stimulate or retard expectations of program expansion; it can embolden politicians to seek more tax revenue or discourage them from trying; it can alter the relative strength of claimants for public funds and guardians of the treasury. In these and many other ways, the will of politicians can be strengthened or weakened by the manner in which budgeting is practiced.

The adjustment of pensions for inflation illustrates how decisional rules can affect political behavior and budget outcomes. The issue facing politicians is quite different when pensions are adjusted by discretionary action than when they are automatically indexed to price changes. If inflation were running at 4 percent a year, a discretionary adjustment of 2 percent might be recorded as an increase, but if pensions have been indexed, the same 2 percent increase would be scored as a cutback. It requires little understanding of politics to sense that the decision is transformed from a popular into an unpopular action by indexation. The same politician who lacks the political will to lower indexed pensions might be quite willful if given the opportunity to raise unindexed ones, even if the increase does not fully compensate for inflation.

Just as indexation can undermine the capacity of politicians to act, other changes in the rules of budgeting can strengthen their will. Consider the change in the situation facing politicians wrought by the Gramm-Rudman-Hollings process. By limiting the size of the deficit and threatening sequestration, GRH has made it easier for politicians to demand cutbacks and oppose expansions. GRH has not drained budgeting of political choice, but it has altered the manner in which it is exercised. Politicians have proved politically willful in terminating two popular programs—revenue sharing in 1986 and urban development action grants in 1988. Probably both would still be funded if GRH had not changed political incentives.

Those who argue that the crisis in budgeting is due to the unwillingness of elected officials to make hard choices must explain why political judgment has been so much more seriously incapacitated in the 1980s than previously. Ours is not the first time in American history that citizens have wanted to be taxed less and benefited more. Public opinion polls have regularly shown this pattern over the past half-century.[15] Nor is ours the first time in which taxpayers have held inconsistent views, preferring to see the programs they favor expanded while demanding that the overall cost of government be held down. The institutional arrangements for governing are not all that different now than they once were. True, we have had a long stretch of divided government, but we have also had a president insisting on spending cuts.

If all it takes to balance the books is the exercise of political judgment, why hasn't presidential endorsement of cutbacks induced Congress to enact them? Why hasn't the professed desire of members of Congress to end deficit spending produced that result? And why hasn't citizen disapproval of big deficits (as reflected in public opinion polls) induced Congress to take the necessary steps to align federal revenue and expenditure? The answer is that over time, budgeting has been altered in ways that not only have produced huge deficits but also have complicated the task of politicians. Budgeting is a different process from what it once was. Indeed, the central theme of this book is that changes in the environment and conduct of budgeting have weakened the capacity of government to balance resources and demands. If today's politicians are less willful, it is partly because they have less effective tools to do the job.

On the surface, the federal government appears to have more than adequate machinery for budgeting. This is especially true of Congress, which now has greater institutional capacity to harmonize revenue and spending decisions than at any time in its 200-year history. It has budget committees to oversee and coordinate the numerous legislative actions on the budget and a budget resolution to plan revenue and spending totals for the next fiscal year and beyond. It also has a corps of experts in the Congressional Budget Office to provide timely data and analysis on budget policies and trends. Not long ago, Congress had none of these. Before the 1974 Budget Act, Congress did not even vote on total spending or on the size of the deficits. The totals just happened as the sum of dozens of separate actions taken each year.

Yet, somehow, without coordination, things were coordinated. The United States went through long periods during which the federal budget was balanced except in time of war or economic crisis. No one in Congress added up the totals, but generally they were in alignment. Why did the government have little or no deficit even though Congress had no budget process? And why is it that now that Congress has a budget process, the government has seemingly intractable deficits? Unless we can answer these questions, we cannot get to the heart of why the federal government's capacity to budget is so impaired.

This book provides part of the explanation. The postwar transformation of federal budgeting from a control process to one oriented to spending growth has upset the relation between available resources and demands on the budget. In the distant past, there was no deficit problem because demands on the budget were weak and controls on spending strong. The key control was the capacity to decide how much should be spent in the light of how much was available. Now, the reverse prevails: demands are strong and the controls weak. Demands have a dynamic of their own; they move upward regardless of the resources at hand. How this reversal occurred is one of the stories of this book. Telling this story requires attention to both the revenue and spending sides of the budget, to both presidential and congressional actions, and to both budget procedures and budget policies.

WHAT DETERMINES BUDGET CAPACITY?

Many factors go into determining how budgeting is conducted. Because it is so vital to government, budgeting's own effectiveness is largely dependent on the behavior of political and administrative institutions. One should not expect budgeting to be an oasis of strength and competence amidst governmental ineptitude and drift. In examining the determinants of capacity, it is necessary to venture a bit beyond the strict confines of budgeting, but unless one wants to broaden the question of budgeting into that of overall political capacity, it is also necessary to relate this study directly to the raising and spending of public money.[16]

The second paragraph of this chapter identified a variety of important functions associated with contemporary budgeting. Over decades, many managerial and financial tasks have been attached to budgeting to take advantage of its command of the public purse and its action-forcing characteristics. The capacity to budget can be assessed in terms of any of these contemporary functions; in fact, reformers typically concentrate on many of these features when they seek to change the process. But although functions such as economic management and program planning are quite important, they are ancillary purposes of budgeting. Budgeting can exist—and has—without them. To consider the basic capacity of budgeting—the characteristics that determine whether the budget produces the balance between resources and expenditures that politicians and citizens seek—it is useful to strip away the elective features and examine the irreducible elements of every budget system.

Wherever it is conducted, budgeting entails decisions on the amount of funds to be raised, a request for funds, and an allocation of funds.[17] Budgeting has three basic components: generating, claiming, and rationing resources. These are the fewest number of actions constituting a budget process. Budgeting does not occur if any elements are missing, but it can if these are the only processes at work. Producing, claiming, and rationing resources take place both when revenue and expenditures are rising and when they are being cut back. They occur in big governments with complex budget systems and in small ones with simple routines.

Budgeting is not the only means by which money (and other resources) are claimed and allocated. Markets perform these functions, as do other social exchanges. What distinguishes budgeting is that resources are claimed and rationed according to rules and procedures established for this purpose. Budgeting is the process that prescribes how, when, and by whom claims are made and resources rationed. Take away the rules and procedures, and budgeting does not exist in any recognizable or commonly understood form. The rules do not have to spell out every step, but they have to be sufficiently stable and detailed to determine how the money is asked for and distributed. In contrast to budgeting, markets lack allocative routines; goods and services are exchanged by whatever means are consented to by the participants.[18]

A budget claim is any demand for resources made according to the rules and procedures of the process. Claims typically are submitted by administrative agencies, but the process can provide for them to be submitted through other channels as well. There have to be claims for there to be a budget. If no one expresses a want for public funds, there is no need to allocate them through a budget.

The rationing function arises out of a common, perhaps universal, characteristic of budget claims: They add up to more than is available. Budgeting would not exist if all claims were satisfied. Simply asking for resources would suffice for getting them. If, on the other hand, no claims were satisfied, there also would be no budget process. Budgeting can occur at any point between these extremes; that is, whenever some—but not all—demanded resources are allocated.

The relative strength of the claiming and rationing functions varies as conditions under which budgeting is conducted change. One would expect claims to be relatively stronger when resources are plentiful, the government favors program expansion, the economy is buoyant, and new spending can be financed without a tax increase. On the other hand, claims would be relatively weaker when the budget is tight, political leaders favor contraction, and additional spending would generate pressure for a tax increase or a bigger deficit.

The process of budgeting also affects the relative strength of the claiming and rationing functions of budgeting. Changes in the process may intentionally or inadvertently alter the balance between these functions and thereby affect budget outcomes. Procedural adjustments may strengthen or weaken demands and make it easier or harder to ration resources. The two examples discussed earlier—indexation and the Gramm-Rudman-Hollings law—are changes in budget rules and procedures that affect the relative strength of claiming and rationing. Whereas indexation strengthens claims on the budget, the GRH process strengthens the rationing side of budgeting.

For government to have a capacity to budget, the relative strength of claiming and rationing must be such as to produce wanted outcomes. A government cannot have effective budget capacity if it seeks to expand programs but is thwarted because of an inability to generate new claims on resources or because powerful rationers turn down all claims for spending increases. This situation is thought uncommon because politicians can take steps to encourage claims or to tie the hands of rationers. The converse is likely to occur when claims are so powerful that they cannot be resisted, or guardians so weak that they cannot ration resources.

Even if politicians do not will deficits, they may cause them by altering the balance between the claiming and the rationing sides of budgeting. Big, unwanted, and persistent deficits indicate a serious imbalance in the relative strength of budgeting's key functions. These deficits persist when claims on the budget are so powerful that they cannot be denied despite the inadequacy of resources to pay for them or when guardians of the public purse are so weak that they cannot ration spending.

A government has the capacity to budget when it can adjust claims and rations to produce desired outcomes. If politicians want to end deficits or narrow the revenue-spending gap, they would have to pursue that objective by weakening claims on the budget or by strengthening those who guard the treasury. Suppose, however, that politicians castigate deficit spending but fail to back their words with appropriate actions. How are we to know whether the words or the deeds reflect their true preferences? This is precisely the situation that has confronted the federal government in the 1980s.

One clue to whether the deficits result from an impairment of budget capacity or from the real preferences of politicians is whether the process is functioning smoothly. If the budget process were to operate in an orderly manner, one would have some basis for concluding that the deficit was welcomed. This has been the case when deficits have been used to stimulate a weak economy or to provide nontax resources for expenditure. But when deficits hobble government, as they have in the 1980s, it is hard to conclude that they represent the will of politicians.

This is a book about how budgeting became a growth-oriented process in the decades after World War II and how it has struggled to adapt to less favorable conditions since the mid-1970s. Throughout the book, the interplay between substantive policy and budget procedures is examined in terms of the relative strength of the claiming and rationing functions. In a nutshell, the argument is that claims on the budget became stronger when budgeting was an expansionary process, and that it has not been easy for the federal government to reverse course as circumstances have become more constrained. The result has been a breakdown of established processes and a resort to improvisational budgeting—that is, to budgeting according to ad hoc arrangements rather than preset rules.

Proposals to restore budget capacity must reckon with the factors that have contributed to the breakdown. In line with the book's theme, every budget reform should be tested in terms of its effects on claimants and rationers of public funds. Regardless of the procedural adjustments made, budgeting will not be a sturdier process unless its several functions are brought into balance. The concluding chapter of this book suggests a package of reforms that would strengthen the capacity to budget. The task of making the budget into a more effective process must be given high priority, for on its success depends the future governing capacity of the United States.

Notes

1. The Congressional Budget Office has projected that without Social Security, the baseline deficit would rise from $194 billion in the 1988 fiscal year to $209 billion in fiscal 1990 and to $239 billion in the 1994 fiscal year. The annual surplus in the Social Security trust funds is projected to rise from $39 billion in fiscal 1988 to $117 billion in 1994. See Congressional Budget Office, *The Economic and Budget Outlook: Fiscal Years 1990–1994*, January 1989, p. 46.

2. For a fuller discussion of the use of budget gimmicks, see chapter 4, "Cutting Back and Spending More."

3. The Gramm-Rudman-Hollings law is the popular name of what is officially the Balanced Budget and Emergency Deficit Control Act of 1985 (PL 99-177).

4. As this author wrote almost a decade ago, what emerged in 1974 "is a process that is neutral on its face. It can be deployed in favor of higher or lower spending, bigger or smaller deficits. Its effects on budget outcomes will depend more on congressional preferences rather than on procedural limitations." See Allen Schick, *Congress and Money: Budgeting, Spending, and Taxing* (Washington, D.C.: Urban Institute, 1980), p. 73.

5. The GRH rules are exceptional in that enforcement is tougher in the Senate than in the House. Not only are there more substantive points of order in the Senate but waiving the GRH rules generally requires a three-fifths vote, unlike in the House, where waiver can be accomplished by majority vote.

6. See Sandy Streeter, *Regular Appropriations Enacted Separately and in Continuing Appropriations, Fiscal Years 1977–1987* CRS Report no. 87-826 (Washington, D.C.: Congressional Research Service, October 16, 1987).

7. Richard Bolling, *Congressional Record*, December 4, 1973, p. 39341.

8. Edmund Muskie, *Congressional Record*, June 21, 1974, p. 20468.

9. Old, crusty Rep. H.R. Gross, one of the few House members to vote against the Congressional Budget Act, entered a dissent that reads better as the years go by. "Yes, Mr. Speaker, with this bill, everything and everybody is going to be reformed. Everything is going to be hunky-dory and the goose is going to hang high. If we just pass this bill, we will have brought into play all the will, all of the restraint, and all of the discipline that is necessary to balance the budget, stop inflation, and restore fiscal sanity. Do not believe it. I will not be here when this alleged reform goes into

operation, but I predict Members of this House and the Members of the other body will quickly find ways to warp and bend the reform rules laid down here today. . . ." *Congressional Record*, June 18, 1974, p. 19684.

10. Thus, Senator Gary Hart protested: "The policies failed, not the budget process. The policies failed. If you change the basic fiscal policies of this country and it does not work, what are you doing back in here saying the process failed?. . . . Now, why come back here and lash Congress? Instead, let us lash ourselves for agreeing to do what the President told us to do." *Congressional Record*, October 5, 1985 (daily ed.), p. S12699.

11. Robert Michel, *Congressional Record*, November 6, 1985 (daily ed.), p. H9851.

12. John Chafee, *Congressional Record*, December 11, 1985 (daily ed.), p. S17432.

13. Robert Walker, *Congressional Record*, October 23, 1985 (daily ed.), p. H9091.

14. How and why this miscalculation came about is forthrightly discussed in David A. Stockman, *The Triumph of Politics: Why the Reagan Revolution Failed* (New York: Harper & Row, 1986).

15. See Royce Crocker, "Federal Government Spending and *Public Opinion*," *Public Budgeting and Finance* 1 (Autumn 1981), pp. 25–35.

16. Aaron Wildavsky once wrote: "Perhaps the 'study of budgeting' is just another expression for the 'study of politics'; yet one cannot study everything at once, and the vantage point offered by concentration on budgeting offers a useful and much-neglected perspective from which to analyze the making of public policy." Aaron Wildavsky, *The Politics of the Budgetary Process* (Boston: Little, Brown, 1964), p. 126.

17. Decisions refer both to policy changes and to "nondecisions" that continue current tax laws.

18. In specifying process as one of budgeting's defining elements, one comes perilously close to arguing that budgeting is whatever it is deemed to be. Yet the definition must be sufficiently loose to accommodate the many different ways budgeting is done, but sufficiently tight to differentiate it from other means of allocation. The concept of process is both elastic and differentiating.

Chapter 2

BUDGETING FOR GROWTH: FROM THE NEW DEAL THROUGH THE GREAT SOCIETY

The federal government spends more than $1 trillion each year, an amount exceeding one-fifth of the gross national product. The budget is much bigger than it once was, and it will be bigger yet in the future. Growth is built into the federal budget. It is incessant and often seems unstoppable. Spending rises from year to year, whether resources are plentiful or scarce, whether the economy is growing or stagnant, whether presidential power is in Republican or Democratic hands.

A glance at table 2.1 reveals the upward march of federal spending over the past sixty years. Adjusted for inflation, federal outlays were ten times greater in 1988 than they were before World War II, four times their postwar level, two and a half times the 1960 level, and close to double the 1970 amount. The rise in spending continued throughout the 1980s. At the end of the decade, real spending was about $200 billion higher than it had been at the start.

During part of the period displayed in table 2.1, the revenue trend kept pace with the similar rise in spending. From 1950 to 1970, both revenue and spending grew relative to GNP, the latter rising 3.8 percent, the former, 4.7 percent. Increased spending was propelled or financed by increased revenue. Since 1970, the two trends have diverged. Whereas spending has claimed another 3 percent relative to GNP, revenues have been flat.

For the past two decades, the rise in spending has been largely independent of the trend in revenue. Spending has had its own dynamics, procedures, and policies, which have pushed the level of expenditures upward. Budgeting has become a growth-oriented process in which demands on resources have been strong and capacity to deny these claims has been weak. This chapter discusses the transformation of budgeting from a process that once inhibited the spending of additional funds to one that now regularly produces that outcome.[1] The period covered by this chapter covers more than three

Table 2.1 FEDERAL OUTLAYS, RECEIPTS AND DEFICITS FOR SELECTED YEARS (billions of dollars)

Fiscal year	Federal outlays (current dollars)	Outlays (constant [1982] dollars)	Outlays as percentage of GNP	Federal receipts (current dollars)	Receipts as percentage of GNP	Number of years of balanced budgets in previous decade	Cumulative deficit as percentage of cumulative GNP in previous decade
1929	$ 3.1	—	3.0	$ 3.9	3.8	—	—
1940	9.5	$ 83.2	9.9	6.5	6.8	0	—
1950	42.6	220.5	16.0	39.4	14.8	3	9.9
1960	92.2	340.4	18.2	92.5	18.3	3	0.8
1970	195.6	509.4	19.8	192.8	19.5	2	1.0
1980	590.9	699.1	22.1	517.1	19.4	0	2.3
1988	1,064.0	879.2	22.3	909.0	19.0	0[a]	4.5[a]

Source: Historical Tables 1989, Tables 1.2, 1.3, and 1.4.

[a]1980–88.

decades, beginning with the New Deal response to the Depression and continuing beyond the Great Society and its legislative successes. The New Deal is a useful starting point because it significantly enlarged the federal government and led to more growth-oriented attitudes toward federal expenditure. It is difficult to pinpoint when the growth era ended, or—more accurately—faded away. Economic expansion persisted through the 1960s. However, fiscal stress appeared in the late 1960s as the government sought to balance the cost of war in Southeast Asia and demands for social expenditure. Spending and program growth also continued into the 1970s, aggravating budget tensions and fueling demands to reform the budget process.

THE WAYS AND MEANS OF GROWTH

The impulse to expand federal activities is a legacy of the New Deal that was legitimized after the war and given additional impetus in the 1960s. The wherewithal for bigger government came from tax increases enacted during World War II and from an economic boom in the quarter-century after the war. The New Deal spurred the government to behave expansively—that is, to view legislation and the budget as instruments for initiating or enlarging federal programs. The tax increases and economic growth gave it sufficient resources to finance its burgeoning ambitions.

The New Deal and Its Legacy

At the eve of the Great Depression, federal expenditures amounted to only 3 percent of the GNP, about the same percentage it had been at the turn of the century.[2] The Depression came at the end of a decade during which the new Bureau of the Budget (established in 1921) imposed strict controls that retrenched government. When the Depression arrived, federal outlays, receipts, and the public debt were lower than they had been at the start of the 1920s.

The New Deal reversed course by undertaking numerous spending commitments whose budgetary impact is still strongly felt more than a half-century later. The financial legacy of the New Deal includes farm price supports, unemployment insurance, Social Security, housing programs, and public assistance. Because of the durability of these programs, what started as emergency relief ended as a permanent enlargement in the scope and financial responsibility of the federal government. These and later transfer programs recast the main domestic role of the government from a provider of public services into a stabilizer and redistributor of private incomes.

When the New Deal was unfolding, one could not know the extent to which it would permanently alter the scope and role of government. Some of its principal innovations were controversial and were discarded before they took root.[3] After the war, enlarged government was made permanent and even extended. The conservative coalition of Republicans and southern Democrats that dominated Congress in the decade after the war did not roll back basic New Deal programs.[4] In fact, Congress added significantly to federal spending commitments. Americans came out of the war with pent-up demands for improved public facilities, and Congress responded by providing direct assistance to local governments for urban renewal, airport construction, and hospitals. Americans also remembered the Depression and did not want that tragedy repeated. In the 1948 presidential campaign, the Democrats promised to expand the New Deal, and Republicans pledged not to undo it. In marked contrast to their alarm when Social Security was established in 1935, the Republicans, in their 1948 platform, urged "extension of the federal old-age and survivors' insurance program and increase of the benefits to a more realistic level."[5] Congress followed suit by expanding Social Security in 1950 legislation that had strong bipartisan support.[6] The Republican platform also recommended federal assistance for slum clearance and low-income housing, and Congress authorized these programs in the 1949 Housing Act.[7] Republican me-tooism told Americans what they already knew and wanted—that the social safety net erected by the New Deal would continue to protect them.

Although there were important program expansions in the postwar decade, a number of issues were left unsettled. The fight for federal aid to education was lost in the 1950s but won in the 1960s. National health insurance was rejected, but less than two decades later, Congress enacted health care financing schemes that had less coverage and high costs. The later program expansions built on the New Deal, but they were more a product of postwar economic vigor than of prewar economic crisis.

World War II: Paying for Big Government by Taxing for War

The New Deal enlargement of government was reflected in the tripling of federal outlays from 3 percent of GNP in 1929 to almost 10 percent in 1940. But, as table 2.1 above shows, the New Deal was not able to pay its own way. When he ran for president in 1932, Franklin Roosevelt promised to balance the budget; when he mounted a successful reelection campaign four years later, Roosevelt had a budget deficit that exceeded total federal revenue. Big deficits were not a secure basis for enlarging government, but at the time they were regarded by New Dealers as unavoidable.

World War II came to the rescue. It gave the government a voracious need for vastly more revenue to finance mobilization, and Congress enacted the first mass income tax in U.S. history. Before the war, the lowest tax rate was 4 percent on income above $4,000; at the war's end, the lowest rate was 23 percent on taxable income above $2,000. The highest rate was boosted from 81 percent to 94 percent, and the taxable income on which it was levied dropped from $5 million to $200,000. Higher taxes were accompanied by a withholding scheme that took money out of each paycheck rather than in one lump payment at the end of the year. As a consequence of tax increases and the wartime economic boom, federal revenue soared from less than $7 billion in 1940 to more than $50 billion in 1945.

After the war, tax rates and federal revenue receded somewhat, but they did not return—or even come close—to prewar levels. The lowest rate was changed six times in the postwar decade before being stabilized at 20 percent, whereas the highest rate settled down at 91 percent. These high rates provided the government with a much bigger revenue base than it had before the war. In the 1950s, federal revenue ranged from about 16 to 18 percent of GNP, triple the prewar percentage.

The added funds paid for high defense spending, growing domestic programs, and curtailment of deficits. After the war, there was the usual displacement of defense spending by civilian expenditures, but both categories claimed much higher shares of GNP than they had before the war.[8] Defense spending was 9.5 percent of GNP in 1960, compared with only 1.7 percent in 1940. Spending on human resource programs ebbed during the war, partly because of the diversion of resources to the war effort and partly because the economic crisis vanished as the country rapidly shifted from high unemployment to a shortage of workers. However, human resource spending recovered after the war; at 5.2 percent of GNP in 1960, it was above the prewar level.

The additional funds not only paid for guns and butter but also took care of the deficit problem. The massive deficits racked up during the New Deal and World War II virtually disappeared after the war. The federal budget was balanced in half of the fiscal years from 1947, when most of the budgetary effects of the war had abated, through 1960, the last full year of the Eisenhower presidency. In the years in which there was a deficit, the shortfall was miniscule or a product of special circumstances, such as the Korean War and the 1958–59 recession. The federal debt was halved from 115 percent of GNP to 57 percent, while the amount of debt held by the public grew only slightly.[9]

The Fiscal Dividend

Federal outlays trended sharply higher in the postwar era. On an inflation-adjusted basis, they were about 60 percent higher in 1960 than they had been a decade earlier. As noted, this rise in real spending occurred during a period in which the budget was in or near balance and tax rates were stable or declining. How did the government manage to spend more while taxing and borrowing less? The simple answer is that most of the additional spending was financed by the incremental revenues produced by an expanding economy.

The economy exploded during World War II, with real growth averaging more than 12 percent a year. Demobilization brought an expected downturn, but what was not expected was the swiftness and durability of the subsequent expansion. The economy grew in twenty-two of the twenty-six years from 1948 through 1973, and it went through a full decade (1959–69) of uninterrupted annual growth. This sustained growth also was extraordinarily vigorous, averaging 4.0 percent in the 1950s and 4.1 percent in the 1960s.

The postwar success extended beyond general growth to other measures of economic performance. The pattern displayed in table 2.2 is of an economy on a roll. Prices were stable, unemployment low. Productivity advanced along with real wages, disposable income, and corporate profits. Unemployment averaged about 4.5 percent, only slightly above the 4 percent "full employment" level, and real disposable income doubled during the 1950s and 1960s.

These records compare favorably with the long-term performance of the U.S. economy. In the century from 1870, the beginning of industrial expansion after the Civil War, through 1969, annual GNP growth averaged 3.7 percent, just a bit below that achieved in the 1950s and 1960s.[10] But, as table 2.3 reports, viewed in terms of output per employee or per capita GNP, the post-World War II performance was far superior to the long-term pattern. In earlier periods, a substantial portion of the growth was due to expansion of the work force

Table 2.2 MEASURES OF ECONOMIC PERFORMANCE (Average Annual Percentages)

Period	Real GNP growth	Unemployment rate	Rise in consumer price index	Productivity growth[a]	Rise in real compensation per hour[b]	Growth in corporate profits[c]	Per capita real disposable income growth
1951–55	4.5	3.7	2.2	2.4	3.1	6.9	1.8
1956–60	2.2	5.1	2.0	1.8	2.8	1.8	1.1
1961–65	4.6	5.4	1.3	3.3	2.5	10.6	3.1
1966–70	3.0	3.8	4.3	1.4	2.1	−1.3	3.0

Source: *Economic Report of the President, 1988.*
[a]Output per hour of all persons, nonfarm business sector. Output refers to gross domestic product originating in the sector in 1982 dollars.
[b]Hourly compensation divided by the consumer price index for all urban consumers.
[c]Corporate profits with inventory valuation and capital consumption adjustments.

Table 2.3 GROWTH RATES OF GNP AND OUTPUT PER EMPLOYEE, 1871–1969
(Percentages)

Period	GNP growth rate	Output per employee growth rate	Per capita GNP growth rate
1871–1913	4.3	1.9	2.2
1913–1929	3.1	1.5	1.7
1929–1950	2.9	1.7	1.8
1950–1960	3.2	2.1	1.4
1960–1969	4.5	2.6	3.2
1871–1969	3.7	1.9	2.0

Source: U.S. Department of Commerce, Long Term Economic Growth 1860–1970 (June 1973), p. 99.

as the U.S. population was swelled by tides of immigrants. In more recent periods, most of the expansion was due to productivity gains.

Even more significant than the rate of economic growth was its stability. From the 1890s to the Depression, the United States experienced eleven business cycles during which there was a downturn followed by resumed growth in industrial production. Most of these cycles were short-lived; on average, each lasted only about three years.[11] Recollection of the previous downturn was always fresh, and expectations of the next one were usually strong. Business-cycle theory was a prominent field in economics, and it influenced the behavior of the government, which was careful not to overexpand in good times lest it be caught overspending when the cycle turned down. The postwar cycles were much longer, averaging more than five years; the long expansion in the 1960s continued for about nine years. With the economy on a steady upward course, the budget could follow suit confidently.

Economic growth and government growth went hand in hand. The public economy could grow because the private one also was expanding. As the economy advanced, budget receipts rose, though Congress periodically lowered income tax rates and provided incremental resources for programs. But because spending increases were virtually matched by economic expansion, outlays were about the same percentage of GNP in 1965 as they had been a decade earlier.

Economic growth provided an expedient solution to the chronic contradiction in American public opinion referred to in chapter 1. Over the decades, polls have shown that Americans are of two minds about the size and services of government. A majority has wanted the federal government to continue or, in some cases, increase its programs. Yet most Americans also favor lower taxes, balanced bud-

gets, and smaller government. Economic growth resolved this attitudinal quandary for politicians. Government would expand, not by
taking from the disposable incomes of Americans but by using growth
dividends of a buoyant economy. Growth was seen as a costless, pro
bono policy that benefited just about everyone.

In the exuberance of the times, growth was seen as a good that
could be sustained through skillful management of the economy. It
was appropriate, therefore, to spend not only current fiscal dividends
but future ones as well.

This was done principally by the Great Society harvest of legislation in 1964 and 1965. Medical care for the poor and elderly was
enacted; the federal government started to finance public education
in a big way; housing and community development programs were
expanded; the War on Poverty was launched; and hundreds of grant-
in-aid programs were established or enlarged. Spending on human
resource programs grew from 30 percent of total federal outlays in
1965 to more than 50 percent a decade later, and from less than
6 percent of GNP to more than 11 percent. Federal aid to states
and localities ballooned from $10 billion to $50 billion during the
1965–75 decade. Adjusted for inflation, the increase was smaller but
still spectacular—a 150 percent rise in just ten years.

The additional spending was authorized "in an atmosphere col-
ored by the notion of a fiscal dividend," and, as Herbert Stein has
pointed out, "policymakers were looking forward to the increasing
flow of revenue that would result from the growth of the economy."[12]
They did not foresee how the budget would fare a decade or more
later when the fiscal increment would not suffice to finance expanded government.

LEGITIMIZING GOVERNMENT EXPANSION: POLITICAL AND ECONOMIC THEORIES OF GROWTH

During the confident years of growth, the economy and the budget
were linked by more than revenue flows from one into the other.
They also were joined by a political theory that argued that a budget
process focused on spending increments is more rational than one
that strives to review all expenditure and by an economic theory that
showed how the growth of government could sustain favorable conditions. The incremental theory of budgeting legitimized the persistent uptrend in public expenditure; the Keynesian theory of economic

stabilization legitimized government spending to stimulate an economy operating below potential. The two theories complemented one
another. Incrementalism relates to microbudgeting, the growth of
programs and agencies. Keynesianism pertains to macrobudgeting,
the total pattern of revenue and expenditure. The parts of the budget
could not grow unless the totals also did, and the totals would not
grow unless there was justification for spending more on the parts.

Normative Incrementalism

During the high-growth era, incrementalism was the preeminent theory
of budgeting. It offered the leading explanation of how the process
works, and, as expressed in Wildavsky's *The Politics of the Budgetary Process*, it also offered a persuasive case for how a rational
process should work. On a descriptive level, Wildavsky saw incrementalism as simply a statement that budget makers concentrate on
proposed increases while allowing existing expenditures and programs—the base—generally to escape stringent review.[13]

Incrementalism's hold on budgeting stemmed more from its normative claims than from its usefulness as a description of how budgeting works.[14] Wildavsky vigorously argued that a process that
concentrates on the increment is preferable to one that attempts to
remake the entire budget. Incremental decisionmaking moderates
conflict, stabilizes budgetary roles and expectations, simplifies budget preparation and reduces the amount of time that busy officials
must invest in it, and increases the likelihood that important political
values will be taken into account. Incrementalism asserts that budget
makers cannot—and should not try to—reexamine each item every
year. Nor should they pit all claims on the budget against one another
in a competition for scarce funds. To try to behave in this seemingly
rational manner would overload the budget process, require more
data and decisions than could be managed in the limited time available, and trigger intense conflict over money and values. So rather
than being rational by being comprehensive, Wildavsky urged that
budget makers be rational by behaving incrementally.

Incrementalism is a pattern of behavior in which a continuing rise
in expenditures is welcomed and taken for granted. It is not just a
mechanistic process in which agencies ask for and get more money.
In an incremental environment, budgeting itself becomes an engine
of expansion, a means of providing bigger allocations in the next
budget. When incrementalism flourishes, spending growth is seen
as legitimate and not as simply something that occurs because gov-

ernment agencies outmaneuver the budget office. Everybody behaves in a growth-oriented manner, including those, as we shall see later in the chapter, whose job it is to guard the treasury. The budget is legitimized as the annual opportunity for agencies to ask for more money and for central officials to give them more.

Incrementalism provided budgeting with a built-in measure of the correctness of its outcomes. If the process is in good working order, incremental expenditures must be the right ones, else they would not have been approved. Moreover, incrementalism stresses that budgeting is a remedial process, that is, an error in this year's budget can be corrected next year. When budget changes are made at the margins, mistakes would be small and can be corrected easily the next time around.

These characteristics of incrementalism set it apart from analytic approaches, such as program budgeting and planning-programming-budgeting (PPB) systems. These innovations were inspired by a strong economy, but unlike incrementalism, which focused on marginal increases, PPB systems sought to make budgeting into a more objectively rational process. Analysis was to be systematic, covering the spending base as well as any increment. Only in this way, the PPB approach insisted, could the cost-effectiveness of expenditures be evaluated.

In design, results-oriented analysis had the potential to generate big changes in the pattern of expenditure and to enable the budget to spend sizable chunks of the fiscal dividend. In practice, PPB had the opposite effect. Its demand for more options, additional data, and more comprehensive analysis slowed the budget's responsiveness to opportunities for growth. By expanding the scope of review, systematic analysis provided more opportunities to block change. Many federal agencies found that PPB resulted in "paralysis by analysis," not in bigger budgets. Like the race in the fable of the hare and the tortoise, the budget could grow faster when the steps were smaller and more evenly paced than it might in the stop–go environment of systems analysis and program planning. Thus, increment by increment, the federal budget was expanded in the postwar decades, so that by 1975, outlays were 50 percent higher in real terms than they were a decade earlier and almost double what they were in 1955.

Although it narrowed budgeting to decisions at the margins, incrementalism enhanced budgeting's relevance and prominence. With claimants for resources fighting for a piece of the increment, budgeting was at the center of policy. Those who controlled the budget and allocated the increment determined spending trends and priorities. By concentrating on the matters that were actually decided and that claimants cared about, budget makers strengthened their role in resource allocation.

Applied Keynesianism

When the budget's share of GNP was modest, as it was before the New Deal, its relation to the economy was generally static. Revenues were more buoyant during booms and contracted somewhat during busts. The budget adjusted to these swings by moderating expenditure growth during economic downturns and stimulating growth when funds were more plentiful. The budget spent available revenues, but it was not seen as a critical influence in the overall performance of the economy. But with the budget's share of GNP spiraling to 10 percent before the war and stabilizing above 15 percent after the war, the government inevitably became more involved in steering the economy. With the federal government spending and transferring close to one-fifth of the national output, it could not be indifferent to the fiscal effects of its revenue and spending decisions.

Keynesian doctrine legitimized active fiscal policy by making a persuasive case that the country would be better off through use of the budget to spur economic growth while keeping unemployment low and prices stable. The rapid spread and startling success of Keynesianism in the 1960s gave the government confidence that it could do good by intervening in economic matters.

Effective use of the budget to guide the economy depended on the relation between revenue and expenditure on the one hand and the level of economic activity, jobs, and prices on the other. In the postwar era, this relation was explained in terms of the impact of the budget on aggregate demand. Applied Keynesian fiscal policy promised an optimal level of demand by adjusting the budget's balance to add or withdraw stimulus. (The term *applied Keynesianism* is used to sidestep controversy over what Keynes actually intended and whether policies carried out in his name are consonant with his views.)

Applied Keynesianism did not start out as expansionary budgeting, but it ended up that way. The Keynesians who advised President Kennedy intended that any actual or anticipated slackening in the demand be countered by compensatory budget action, but they wanted most of the added stimulus to be provided by tax reduction, not by spending increases. Whether because tax reduction would be more politically feasible or would provide a speedier fiscal response, they looked principally to tax policy for adjustments to changing economic conditions. Kennedy did request standby authority to increase construction expenditures, and he obtained new funds for area development and other purposes, but total spending did not increase significantly during his truncated presidency.[15] Nevertheless, Keynesian fiscal policy did lead to a weakening in spending control and expansionary budgeting.

Applied Keynesianism fostered expansionary budgeting by weakening the balanced budget norm, shifting from passive to active fiscal policy, defining fiscal objectives in terms of the potential of the economy, and fine-tuning the economy to achieve its potential.

Balancing the economy came to be viewed as more imperative than balancing the budget. Near the end of his administration, Dwight Eisenhower upheld the balanced budget norm; at the start of his presidency, John Kennedy subordinated this norm to the performance of the economy. President Eisenhower's 1960 economic report asserted that "in the economic circumstances now prevailing and expected in the near future, a budgetary surplus used to retire debt would be a powerful aid in helping to restrain inflationary pressure and to promote sound growth."[16] "The success of fiscal and budget policies," President Kennedy's economic advisors testified in 1961, "cannot be measured only by whether the budget is in the black or in the red. The true test is whether the economy is in balance."[17] Peacetime deficits were regarded as the by-products of a faltering economy, not of irresponsible budgets. "Recession and slack generate deficits; prosperity and growth balance budgets," the 1963 economic report proclaimed.[18] Instead of strict balance, the government now conditioned its budget stance on each year's perceived needs. In buoyant years, the government would budget according to the performance of the economy; in slack times, according to its potential. The confident expectation was that this policy would nudge performance closer to the potential of the economy and that budgetary balance therefore would be maintained over the course of a full business cycle.

Structural balance might have been more achievable if the government had relied on automatic stabilizers—principally tax receipts and transfer payments—to counter the swings in the economy. With the rise in withholding taxes and transfer payments, postwar budgets had built-in stabilizers that automatically adjusted revenue and spending to changing economic conditions. The budget could move from surplus to deficit and back without active intervention by the government. A self-correcting budget would yield cyclical deficits while preserving structural balance. In the 1960s, however, applied Keynesians were convinced that the economy also needed discretionary correction. "The economy cannot regulate itself," Walter Heller insisted. "We now take it for granted that the government must step in to provide the essential stability at high levels of employment and growth that the market mechanism, left alone, cannot deliver."[19] Discretionary action was necessary because the built-in stabilizers were insufficient. They would shut off stimulus before the economy had reached potential. The 1963 economic report labeled automatic stabilization "an ambiguous blessing," noting that "the protection it gives against cumulative downward movements of output and employment is all the more welcome. But its symmetrical 'protection' against upward movement becomes an obstacle on the path to full employment, throttling expansion before full employment is reached."[20]

Discretionary fiscal policy was intended to eliminate this fiscal drag and to spur the economy to perform closer to full potential than it would have if corrections had been limited to automatic stabilizers. To the postwar Keynesians, any shortfall in economic performance meant lost output and additional unemployment. But because potential is so difficult to reach—and can be redefined upward as performance improves—this fiscal objective virtually ensured expansionary policies. Budgeting according to the potential of the economy required continual monitoring of conditions and adjustments to keep on a full-employment course. Fine-tuning, as this posture came to be called, was intended to correct both for weak and excess demand, but the experience of the late 1960s demonstrated the political ease of providing additional stimulus and the political difficulty of trying to dampen an overheated economy.[21]

The practical effect of endorsing deficits in slack times was to make them more likely when the economy was strong. The withering of the balanced budget norm deprived budget officials of a tool they had used effectively for generations to constrain agency spending demands. The elasticity of Keynesian fiscal rules meant that budget claims could be advanced without a prior decision about what the budget totals would be. Expenditure totals became more adaptable to political judgment and to pressures facing the government. Detailed case studies on budget formulation during the postwar decades reveal a shift from the practice of setting firm totals at the start of the process in the Eisenhower presidency to making do with flexible totals that were not firmed up until the end of the process during later administrations. Under Kennedy, "budgetary targets had to remain malleable through most of the annual planning cycle in order to preserve flexibility and responsibleness to fiscal policy requirements, which themselves did not emerge until later in the planning cycle."[22] In the absence of strong, prior constraints on the totals, budgets were built up in a process that can be characterized as the *rising lid*. The total rose to accommodate spending pressures. If the increments supplied by the economy were not significant, the additional spending could be financed by borrowing the resources that would have been available if the economy were performing at a higher level. This turned out to be a sure prescription for the progressive enlargement of the public sector.

ADAPTING BUDGET POLICIES AND PROCESSES TO GROWTH

Postwar fiscal policy altered the manner in which budget totals are decided and enforced. The totals became more pliant; they could be altered at any time during the year to accommodate changes in economic conditions or spending demands. For spending to grow, it was also necessary to alter *microbudgeting*, decisions on particular items and programs. Spending could not grow unless financial controls were loosened and budget claims encouraged.

The federal government entered World War II with budget practices that restrained public expenditure. Financial control was centralized. Spending agencies often had to obtain prior approval from the Bureau of the Budget and the General Accounting Office before committing public funds. Appropriations were voted and controlled in numerous separate accounts, and the budget consisted of long lists of the items (personnel, supplies, equipment, etc.) purchased by agencies. Budgeting was conducted under generally accepted, though often violated principles, that prescribed annual, comprehensive, and balanced budgets.[23]

In the postwar era, centralized controls were relaxed, and claims on resources were encouraged as budgeting was recast into an expansionary process. Expansionary budgeting was a response to sustained economic growth as well as a powerful stimulus to program enlargement. It is unlikely that federal spending would have moved so steeply and persistently upward in the 1950–75 period if the budget controls used in the past had been retained. But with expansion the order of the day, budgeting adapted to the new reality.

Budgeting for growth differs from budgeting for stabilization or cutback. Claimants for public funds are more vigorous, guardians more subdued. Both executive and legislative processes and behavior were modified. So, too, was the composition of federal expenditures. Few of the changes were dramatic, but their cumulative effect was to make progressively higher spending the normal and expected outcome.

Some of the changes were technical. As federal expenditures soared, line items receded in importance and were consolidated into broad expense categories. After World War II, there was a steep reduction in the number of appropriation accounts, so that agencies now had greater flexibility in using the funds at their disposal.[24] Agencies also were liberated from most central spending controls. The GAO shifted from preaudits to postaudits and from maintaining external control to establishing standards for internal control by the agencies themselves. The Bureau of the Budget divested itself of most input controls and took a more programmatic view of agency requests. Once funds were appropriated, the Budget Bureau determined how they were to be apportioned, but it had little continuing involvement in the spendout of money.[25]

The Expectation of Growth

Although relaxed controls promoted expansion, changes in budget expectations were equally significant in promoting incremental outcomes. Expectations are the seedbed of budgetary growth. Agencies request more when they expect to get more. Policymakers in both the legislative and executive branches promote new programs when the market for them is favorable. The New Deal did more than merely enlarge the federal government. It also changed public attitudes toward public expenditure and paved the way for more active and expansive policies. Government now was expected to be much more than a caretaker and watchman. It would provide vital benefits to the American people. Through public expenditure, homes would be built, land reclaimed, personal income cushioned against economic and other shocks, health care improved.

In an era of positive government, budgeting could not persist as the process that held the spenders at bay. Instead, the budget came to be the annual opportunity for agencies to ask for more money and for central officials to give them more. Budgeting was the means of buying public goods with public money. It became customary for chief executives at all levels of American government to point to increased spending as evidence of the added benefits provided through the budget. More money in the budget for education demonstrated that more education was being provided.

The language of budgeting adapted to incremental expectations. What once were called estimates were often referred to in the postwar years as requests, signaling a more active and ambitious search for funds by government agencies. Deficiency appropriations faded away—the last was enacted in 1964—and all additional funds were now supplied in supplemental appropriations, a label that suggests vigor rather than failure. Over time, supplementals came to be recurring features of the annual budget cycle, as expected as the regular appropriation bills.[26]

Information Flows in Budgeting

Budgeting is a process of information exchanges. Agencies trade information with budget officials who also exchange data with congressional participants in the process. The form, content, and accessibility of the information has a great deal to do with the articulation and effectiveness of budgetary demands.

In pre-incremental budgeting, demands were inhibited by closing the process to outside review and influence. The budget was prepared in utmost secrecy, and its contents were not known until the document was released. Embargoes on premature disclosure were strictly enforced.[27] Even after the budget was published, it was hard to figure out what the recommendations meant. Well into the New Deal years, the budget was formatted as a "book of estimates." This book had column after column of line-item detail, but it lacked any explanation of what the money was to accomplish. The line-item details obscured the program implications of the budget and made it easy to constrain spending without stirring up opposition. There were few outside budget watchers, and few independent analyses of budget policy.

After World War II, the Budget Bureau began to clothe the numbers with explanations of what the funds were to accomplish. Spurred by the 1949 recommendation of the Hoover Commission that the federal government adopt a performance budget, the Bureau added some statistics on workload or output. It also classified expenditures in terms of their benefits and end results, but the general failure of these reforms limited the use to which new program classifications were put.

Political developments in the 1960s and 1970s made the budget more transparent. With increased resources available and additional spending welcomed because of its fiscal stimulus or program benefits, prerelease leaks became increasingly common, and affected groups became more active and vigilant in monitoring both budget preparation in the executive branch and legislative consideration in Congress. Agencies became more adept at disclosing their real preferences, and congressmen became more aggressive in prying the information from them.

By the late 1970s, it became customary for interest groups to distribute their own in-depth analyses of the annual budget. These typically treated the president's recommendations as "floors" and served as tools for the groups to lobby Congress for additional funds.

Congress became a more permeable institution, with more points of access and more opportunities for outsiders to influence outcomes. During the 1960s and continuing into the next decade, many authorizing committees strengthened their role as program advocates by switching from permanent to temporary, sometimes annual, authorizations. Some muscled their way to power by devising "backdoor" spending schemes that evade regular appropriations procedures. The appropriations committees became more responsive to outside influence by opening their markups, adding staff, hearing more outside witnesses, and adding members with propensities to spend.[28] But, like the president, they had more rivals for budgetary power and frequently found their recommendations challenged by floor amendments, especially when they tried to moderate the growth in spending.

The President's Budget Staff: From Controlling to Guiding

The president's budget office (the Bureau of the Budget, renamed the Office of Management and Budget in 1970) adapted to incremental expectations by divesting central controls and becoming active in developing the president's program. The adjustment was not easy. President Roosevelt inherited a small budget staff (about 45 employees) that took pride in tightly controlling federal expenditures. Lewis Douglas, his first budget director, was determined to balance the budget, but he resigned in 1934 when it became evident that the New Deal's emergency measures had evolved into expansionary policies. Douglas suggested that the president hire "someone who is in more complete accord with your budgetary policies."[29]

Roosevelt, however, needed more than a supportive budget director. He needed a budget staff with the vision and skill to manage the growing responsibilities and objectives of government. This he got through the work of the President's Committee on Administrative Management, chaired by Louis Brownlow. The committee recommended converting the Budget Bureau from a financial control agency into "the right arm of the President for the central fiscal management of the vast administrative machine."[30] Big government was here to stay, and it had to be managed effectively. The Bureau was moved into the new Executive Office of the President; its staff was increased more than tenfold; and the budget became an annual statement of presidential policy and program objectives.[31]

After World War II, the Bureau adapted to incremental expectations by taking a more positive attitude toward agency spending proposals. This evolution has been perceptively described by Philip S. Hughes, a civil servant who rose through the ranks to become the Bureau's highest career official in the 1960s:

It's very hard for me to say that . . . on "x" date we had a philosophical change. . . . [But] over the years, and I think it started in the middle or the later part of the Eisenhower Administration, the role of the Bureau has changed somewhat; as government grew . . . the Bureau . . . acquired a programming role that it did not have, at least to the same extent, before. The problem of choice among the programs has become increasingly important. And perhaps, to some extent, the negative role of the bureau has become less important, at least in relative terms. . . . In the old days . . . our initial answer was supposed to be no and everybody would have been surprised if we said yes the first time around. As time has passed, we're supposed to do something a little different than that. We can say no, perhaps in a fairly high percentage of cases, but in some of the more crucial ones we're supposed to give pretty serious consideration to the alternative and better ways of accomplishing an objective which the President or an agency head or a member of the majority party in the Congress thinks is a desirable objective.[32]

The Bureau's attitudinal shift was in step with the exuberance of the times. The Bureau was neither impervious to incremental expectations nor unaware that there was a lot more money to spend. It could not block program advocates merely by saying no to their ideas for new legislation. After all, these ideas were the stuff of which presidential dreams were made during the heady growth period.

The Bureau wanted to spend the increment through the budget apparatus it controlled. As custodian of the increment, it would have the lead role in deciding which programs would grow and by how much. In so doing, it could take care that legislative initiatives were integrated with budget requests and suited to available resources. But as the increment grew larger and expectations became more expansive, even a positive-thinking bureau was an impediment to presidential ambitions. During the Great Society's rush to legislate in the mid-1960s, program development and legislative action often were divorced from recurring budget decisions. The budget process was slow moving, and it was constrained by current resources. Legislative initiatives were more impulsive and opportunistic. They could be taken any time during the year, and they could spend future increments, not just those allocated through this or the next year's budget.

Separating Legislative Activity and Budget Control

The linkage of legislation and the budget began during the Budget Bureau's first year and reached its fullest development in the early postwar period. Bureau Circular 49 (December 19, 1921) required budgetary review of all legislative proposals that would "create a charge upon the public or commit the government to obligations which later require appropriations to meet them." Before the New Deal, legislative clearance had essentially a negative purpose, to prevent agencies from obtaining via legislation what they could not get through normal budget procedures. The New Deal broadened the scope of legislative clearance and gave it a more positive role by requiring all proposals to be cleared through the Bureau to ascertain whether they were in accord with the president's program. Significantly, however, the clearance process was hardly used for major New Deal legislation.[33]

After the war, President Truman expanded the clearance process by relying on it to prepare his annual legislative program. The broadened process entailed the solicitation of legislative proposals in tandem with the annual "call for estimates" and the submission of a comprehensive legislative program to Congress. This structured review ensured that legislative initiatives were consistent with the president's spending priorities and were funded by available resources. Legislative clearance, Richard Neustadt explained, "had been negative; it was to be made positive. It had interpreted policies and programs where it found them; it was to help create them."[34]

Legislative review through the budget process worked well during the early postwar period, when program expansion was still measured and relatively modest. But the expansionary thrust of the 1960s led to a divorce of legislating from budgeting. Budgeting was too slow, too vulnerable to blockage, and, presidential advisors thought, too distant from the White House to be in step with the president's program objectives and legislative agenda. President Kennedy preferred to work with close aides on major issues, drawing on the Budget Bureau's staff on an ad hoc basis. Lyndon Johnson set numerous task forces at devising proposals for submission to Congress without rigorous budgetary scrutiny. Costs often were carelessly projected, for presidential policymakers were confident that today's good ideas could be paid for by tomorrow's economic bounty. In any case, it was more productive for the president to reap his legislative harvest when it was there for the picking than to wait for budget experts to fit the new ideas into their spending plans.

Budget Bureau leaders adjusted to this practice by trying to make budgeting more relevant to presidential concerns. They sought to demonstrate that the bureau could contribute to the development of new programs not by outpromising the White House task forces but by devising more cost-effective solutions. They marketed PPB as a system that would make budgeting into a means of selecting the program options that would achieve presidential objectives while conserving scarce resources.[35] As its sequence of initials showed, PPB would tightly link plans and programs to budgets. In so doing, it would continue budgeting's dominant role in resource allocation and thereby increase the likelihood that programs were designed with an eye on prospective costs. However, PPB never lived up to its promise. It came on board after most of the Great Society legislation had been enacted. When money for new programs dried up under Vietnam War pressures in the late 1960s and less favorable economic conditions in the 1970s, so, too, did interest in PPB. It was futile to analyze program options when there was no money for them.

The changed relationship of legislation to budgets also affected Congress. In the period before incrementalism, the appropriations committees had almost complete jurisdiction over federal spending. The House Appropriations Committee guarded the treasury against expansive spending claims and its jurisdiction against encroachment by legislative committees. Although it and the Senate Appropriations Committee had numerous subcommittees and operated in a seemingly uncoordinated manner, in fact, both committees produced highly coordinated outcomes. They reviewed each in terms of the previous appropriation, as well as the president's request for the next year, in order to produce outcomes in which most appropriations were below the president's budget but above the previous level. In this way, the appropriations committees kept spending increases roughly in line with available resources.

Legislative committees had little influence over resource allocation before the New Deal. Most authorizing legislation was permanent; money was not even mentioned in them. Three developments, however, led to a substantial increase in the budgetary role of legislative committees and to a splintering of financial decisions in Congress. These were the switch to temporary authorizations, the increase in trust fund financing, and the growth in the prominence of entitlement expenditure. Unlike permanent authorizations, which are usually indefinite in amount—typically authorizing "such sums as may be necessary"—temporary authorizations almost always specify an amount for each fiscal year. Authorizing committees can stake their claim for resources without regard for the overall budget condition. Conventional authorizations usually are weak claims. They neither provide funds nor bind the appropriations committees. Nevertheless, they inject legislative committees into the budget process and sometimes enhance the budgetary role of these committees.[36]

Trust funds convert weak legislative claims on the budget into strong ones because they combine jurisdiction over earmarked revenue and expenditure in a single set of legislative committees. Before the establishment of social security in 1935, trust funds typically were small, and the funds were genuine trusts held by the United States for entities such as Indian tribes. Social Security started small, but it had built-in growth linked to demographic and employment trends. Its trust funds were really means of earmarking revenue, giving Social Security a permanent appropriation, and assigning jurisdiction to the House Ways and Means and Senate Finance Committees. Social Security also was established as an entitlement; eligible persons were given a legal right to payment from the treasury. Over time, as entitlements grew, legislative committees captured an increasing share of direct spending jurisdiction. By the early 1980s, the appropriations committees had direct jurisdiction over less than half of total spending.[37]

The separation of legislation and budgets characterizes growth spurts in the federal government. It occurred in the early New Deal and in the 1964–65 Great Society legislation. But unlike past instances in which the separation was temporary, now it was institutionalized. Congress had evolved to the point where it had two distinct spending processes, one driven by legislative decisions, the other by appropriations.

THE CHANGING COMPOSITION OF
FEDERAL EXPENDITURE

Most of the developments discussed thus far pertain to budgetary procedures or behavior. Parallel developments altered the substantive character of federal expenditures and made sustained growth more likely. In terms of the resources spent, the dominant role of the federal budget came to be transferring money to recipients outside the government rather than financing the operations of government.

Before the New Deal, the bulk of federal expenditures were spent by agencies on their own operations—salaries, supplies and equipment, travel costs, and other purchases of goods and services. Today, however, spending is predominantly in the form of transfers to "third" parties. Most of the money goes to state and local governments, bondholders, and recipients of transfer payments. Table 2.4 shows how the composition of the federal budget in the national income and product accounts has changed during the postwar decades. More than 60 percent of the budget was spent on goods and services (including defense purchases) in the 1957 fiscal year. These purchases

Table 2.4 COMPOSITION OF FEDERAL EXPENDITURES IN THE NATIONAL INCOME AND PRODUCT ACCOUNTS, FIVE-YEAR INTERVALS 1957–87
(Percentages of total expenditure)

Fiscal year	Goods and services	Transfer payments	Grants to states and localities	Net interest	Net subsidies[a]
1957	62.7	21.4	4.9	7.2	3.7
1962	57.2	25.6	7.1	6.4	3.6
1967	55.9	25.2	9.4	6.1	3.3
1972	44.0	33.5	13.7	5.9	2.7
1977	35.0	40.8	15.8	6.8	1.6
1982	35.0	41.4	11.0	10.9	1.7
1987	35.5	38.9	9.8	13.2	2.6

Source: 1957 and 1962 data are from the Economic Report of the President, 1967, p. 287. All remaining data are from Economic Report of the President, 1988, p. 343.
[a]Subsidies less current surplus of government enterprises.

now account for only 35 percent of the total. The share of the budget spent on transfer payments doubled during the past 30 years, from approximately one-fifth to almost two-fifths. Grants have had a more volatile record, tripling in relative size between 1958 and 1978 but declining as a share of total outlays since then. Significantly, however, the composition of these grants has shifted with the change in total federal expenditures. In 1978, less than one-third of the grants went for payments to individuals. Now, more than half of the grants passed through state and local governments are for these payments.[38]

But much more has been changed than the locus of expenditures. The process of claiming federal resources has also been altered. Some of the effects, such as the opening up of the budget process to outside influence, have already been discussed. The outsiders who receive federal checks are no less party to the budget than are the federal agencies that submit formal budget requests and spend appropriated funds. Recipients of transfers, states and localities, and other end-users of federal dollars cannot abide a situation in which only privileged insiders know what is happening while they must wait until the budget is published or funds are appropriated. Because they have a vital stake in budget outcomes, these outsiders make it their business to be informed.

Why did the composition of the federal budget change in the incremental era? Was it because the growth in federal resources made it possible to assist outsiders without reducing the funds provided to government agencies, or did pressure for higher transfer payments force the enlargement of the budget? In other words, were the transfer payments cause or effect in the transformation and growth of expenditures? Probably they were both. The budget would have been smaller if most of the money continued to be for agency operations rather than for transfers, and the transfers would have been smaller if increments were not sufficient to pay for them.

The changed composition of expenditure is reflected in four developments discussed below: (1) impoundment disputes between the president and Congress, (2) entitlements to public funds, (3) indexation of transfer payments, and (4) recourse to nonconventional forms of expenditure.

Impoundments

Impoundments are actions taken in the executive branch that delay or block the use of funds provided by Congress. Impoundment is an old practice that became an issue only when attitudes toward federal spending and the character of expenditure changed. Although funds have been withheld throughout U.S. history, they rarely occasioned strong protests from Congress before the 1940s. In 1921, for example, the newly appointed director of the budget ordered a cutback in spending previously approved by Congress.[39] There were no protests, despite the fact that this executive action pared sizable amounts from the budget. It was only pursuant to the New Deal that executive refusal to spend appropriated funds became a matter of contention. It was also only as a consequence of changed attitudes that the word "impoundment" entered budgetary vocabulary.[40]

Appropriations once were understood as limitations on expenditures. Hence, underspending was not deemed a problem. With the enlargement of government and the rise of transfer payments and other direct benefits provided through the budget, appropriations came to be viewed as mandates. Shortfalls in spending would mean that there also were shortfalls in performance. Hence, deliberate underspending would violate congressional intent. The traditional concept of appropriations was grounded in the constitutional provision that "no money shall be drawn from the treasury, but in consequence of appropriations made by law." The plain intent of this provision was to bar any expenditure without prior authorization of Congress. From time to time, the attorney general was called on to rule whether a particular appropriation was mandatory or permissive. An 1898 opinion held an appropriation to have been made "with the deliberate intention of leaving . . . the question whether any of the sum named should be expanded; and if so, how much" to the discretion of executive officers.[41]

Although it is impossible to reconstruct U.S. financial history to measure the extent to which appropriations were actually spent, probably virtually all available funds were used. Most appropriations were for operating expenses, and failure to spend the money would have impaired the capacity of federal agencies to perform their work. Public works were an exception to this pattern. This was the part of the budget that provided conspicuous external benefits. Therefore, Congress had the greatest interest in ensuring that appropriated funds would be used.

Public works also were the part of the budget that occasioned some of the early impoundment battles between the president and Congress. Writing shortly before the Great Depression, a leading budget expert noted that there are appropriations such "as those for the erection of a particular public building or the improvement of rivers and harbors which, if not put into effect would undoubtedly cause resentment on the part of Congress and action by it that would make the expenditure obligatory."[42] This prediction came to pass during World War II, when the Budget Bureau, acting with presidential approval, impounded $500 million appropriated for public works projects. The impoundments led to strong protests in Congress from members who wanted the funds released for projects in their state or district, as well as from those who thought that the Budget Bureau was acting without proper legal authority.

The impoundment disputes spilled over into the New Deal's anti-Depression programs, many of which were similar to public works in that they provided tangible benefits to particular groups or areas. Despite the onset of war and a substantial improvement in economic conditions, Congress still provided hundreds of millions of dollars in fiscal 1942 to the Civilian Conservation Corps, the National Youth Administration, and the Surplus Marketing Corporation. Even though it was wartime when the Budget Bureau impounded some of these funds, their benefits were lost, and some members of Congress sought to get the money released.

The wartime battles between the president's budget office and Congress opened the modern era of impoundment. In an age of expanded government, appropriations had become mandates to spend. Failure to spend meant that the intended benefits would not be provided. When those deprived of their benefits protested, Congress reacted by challenging the president's power to impound.

Congress sought to clarify the legal basis of impoundment in 1950 legislation that expanded the reasons for which the Budget Bureau could reserve funds from apportionment.[43] But this did not end interbranch conflict and most postwar presidents encountered objections when they refused to spend appropriated money. In 1974, Congress established procedures by means of which it could compel the release of impounded funds.[44] The new rules put into practice what Congress had been saying for a generation: When it appropriates, it intends that the funds be spent.[45]

Entitlements

The transformation of appropriations from limits into mandates did not assure would-be beneficiaries that they would receive any financial assistance. Congress still could refuse to appropriate, or it could provide less than beneficiaries wanted. This was a real possibility, because, as late as the 1960s, the appropriations committees were parsimonious in allocating increases. The size of discretionary appropriations, especially of the increases, depended on each year's circumstances. These included the economic outlook, the political lineup in Congress, the skill with which agencies advanced their spending claims, and the overall condition of the budget. There were good years and not so good ones, years in which the increases were quite substantial, and years in which the increases did not keep up with rising expenses. The variable fate of appropriations was well suited for boom-and-bust economic cycles, which had been the pattern through most of U.S. history. But postwar successes gave policymakers confidence that they could maintain the economy on an expansionary course and avoid cyclical recessions. If the economy could be stabilized on an upward track, it would be safe also to stabilize benefits by giving recipients the right to payments fixed in law. These *entitlements*, as the payments came to be known, were insulated from the vagaries of the annual budget go-round. With strong economic growth expected to continue, it was assumed that even after paying the entitlements, the budget would have incremental resources for discretionary appropriations.

Entitlements are easy to define but not always easy to identify. All entitlements have several common features: (1) eligible recipients have a legal right to payment from the government; (2) the size of the payments are determined by criteria, such as formulas, written into law; and (3) the federal government is obligated to make the mandated payment. A few entitlements are capped—their total cost is limited—regardless of the number of eligible recipients. Most, however, are open-ended, so that the total expenditure is the sum of the mandated payment. Some entitlements, such as Social Security and Medicare, have permanent appropriations, and payments are made without any annual action by Congress. Other entitlements, such as veterans' benefits and Medicaid, have annual appropriations, but Congress must provide the amounts to which recipients are entitled. If the appropriation turns out to be insufficient, Congress will have to provide supplemental funds.

The upsurge in entitlements occurred during the 1960s and the early 1970s, the postwar growth period.[46] Medicare for the elderly and Medicaid for low-income Americans were established in 1965. Coal miners afflicted with black lung disease were vested with benefits; the supplemental security program providing assistance to poor persons who are aged, blind, or disabled replaced a state-operated program; college students were given easy access to subsidized loans; and several child nutrition programs were made into entitlements. Older entitlements were expanded by raising benefits or lowering eligibility requirements. The rise in Social Security benefits outpaced inflation; participation in the Aid to Families with Dependent Children (AFDC) program more than doubled from 4.3 million in 1965 to 10.9 million in 1972; the period for receiving unemployment compensation was extended; and the food stamp program was liberalized.

The separation of policymaking and legislation from budgeting and appropriations spurred the rise in entitlements. Many entitlement schemes focused on the needs of the population to be benefited, not on the additional expenditures that would be required. Often, entitlements were inaugurated or expanded without reliable data on their prospective costs and without subjecting them to careful budget review. Insensitivity to future costs was partly fostered by the expectation that they would be paid for by economic growth, and partly by the manner in which these claims were advanced. Entitlements were enacted in substantive legislation, not in appropriation bills. The legislation did not usually mention money; instead, it specified the rights of those to be assisted.

Budgets have a way of sensitizing policymakers to costs, but by the time the new and expanded entitlements impacted on the budget, the added costs were already inscribed into law. Budgeting became a means of accounting for the rise in entitlement payments, not for deciding how much should be spent. Payments for individuals doubled from 5 percent of GNP in 1965 to 10 percent in 1975, and their share of total federal outlays escalated from 28 percent to 46 percent. Spending also rose in constant dollars; they were almost three times higher in 1975 than they had been a decade earlier. During that period, almost the entire real growth in spending occurred in transfer payments.[47] Entitlements had begun to crowd out other expenditures.

Indexation

In an expanding economy, it was considered the right thing to entitle beneficiaries to future payments. But the value of these benefits was not guaranteed. It depended on future inflation rates and on discretionary adjustments in payment levels. From time to time, Congress did raise various payments to compensate recipients for inflation. But these adjustments were discretionary and irregular, and they often lagged behind inflation. For example, there was no general increase in payments during the first ten years of Social Security. Moreover, more than four years elapsed after the 1954 increase, six years after the 1959 adjustment, and three years after the 1965 adjustment. These lags were of minor consequence when inflation was low, but when prices rose more steeply in the late 1960s, the lack of quick, reliable adjustments became a political headache. Robert Ball, former commissioner of Social Security, complained in 1969 testimony that "there have been substantial periods in which people have had to go a long time with benefits reduced in value," and he called for an automatic provision that would protect the purchasing power of the payments.[48]

The indexation of benefits occurred piecemeal, but, unlike the establishment of entitlements, it was concentrated in a relatively brief period. Food stamps were indexed in 1971, Social Security in 1972, various nutrition programs in 1973, and Supplemental Security Income in 1974. Some programs have built-in adjustments, so that payments rise even though they are not explicitly indexed. Thus, Medicare and Medicaid payments rise as the cost of health care increases.

There is evidence that indexation was sometimes adopted to eliminate pressure for discretionary increases above the inflation rate. Congress raised Social Security benefits 43 percent between 1965 and 1971, a period during which consumer prices rose 27 percent. It further increased benefits by 20 percent in the 1972 legislation that indexed future Social Security payments. But although pressure for above-inflation increases was a spur in the case of Social Security, the fact that indexation spread rapidly to programs where discretionary adjustments had been fairly modest suggests that broader considerations were at work. In a growth era, indexation was regarded as just and affordable. The economy was growing, and money would be available to protect the real value of benefits. Even after the economy began to slow down in the 1970s, momentum to index entitlements led to its application to other federal programs. Indeed, the right to have benefits protected against price increases came to be regarded almost as much an entitlement as the core benefits themselves.

By the late 1970s, approximately two dozen entitlements were indexed, and almost a dozen more were quasi-indexed—the term the Congressional Budget Office uses for programs that have automatic adjustment similar to indexation. As table 2.5 reveals, spending on these programs was approaching $300 billion a year, an amount equal to about 40 percent of total federal outlays.

Indexation was initiated under one set of circumstances, but its impact on the budget was most strongly felt when conditions had

Table 2.5 INDEXED ENTITLEMENT PROGRAMS

Program	Date of indexation	Estimated 1981 outlays (millions of dollars)
INDEXED ENTITLEMENT PROGRAMS		
1. Civil Service Retirement	1962	17,326
2. Military Retired Pay	1963	13,781
3. Social Security (OASDI)	1972 (eff. 1975)	140,117
4. Child Nutrition Programs[a]	Benefits: 1973	3,790
5. Railroad Retirement Benefits	1974 (eff. 1975)	5,296
6. Supplemental Security Income	1974 (eff. 1975)	7,438
7. Veterans' Pensions	1979	3,844
8. Food Stamp Program[b]	1971	10,954
9. All Other	varied	3,567
Total		210,739
QUASI-INDEXED ENTITLEMENT PROGRAMS		
1. Medicare (Parts A & B)	Pt A 1965 (eff. 1966) Pt B 1972 (eff. 1973)	40,275
2. Medicaid	1974	16,026
3. Other	varied	5,277
Total		61,578

Source: Congressional Budget Office, *Indexing with the Consumer Price Index: Problems and Alternatives* (Washington, D.C.: Government Printing Office, 1981), pp. 23–27.
[a]Includes the National School Lunch Program, the School Breakfast Program, the Summer Food Service, and Child Care Feeding programs.
[b]Although the CBO did not classify food stamps as an entitlement, the program functions in much the same way as other entitlements and is therefore included here.

changed. Entitlements were about one-quarter of the budget when the rush to index began but had risen to almost half when the trend had run its course. Indexation was initiated when low inflation meant low automatic adjustments and high economic growth meant that resources would be ample. Yet it was implemented under conditions in which inflation was high, growth low, and the budget faced big deficits.

Nonconventional Expenditures

The term *nonconventional expenditure* refers to benefits provided by means other than the grant of money. As used here, it refers to tax expenditures and direct or guaranteed loans.[49]

Tax expenditures are the revenue foregone by the government because of preferential provisions of the tax code that reduce taxes below what they would be in a "normal" tax system.[50] The term indicates that these provisions have financial effects similar to direct expenditures. Tax expenditures come in various forms, including exclusion of income from taxation, credits that lower tax liability, and preferential rates for certain activities. A $1,000 tax preference is equivalent to a $1,000 grant in two ways. First, the recipient is made better off by this amount, and, second, the government's deficit rises by this amount. There is one important difference between direct and tax expenditures, however. A direct expenditure is budgeted as an outlay, whereas a tax expenditure is not.

The government can also provide financial assistance by lending money or by guaranteeing private loans. Direct loans are similar to regular expenditures in that they entail a cost to the government and a benefit to the recipient. The cost and subsidy value of a loan depends on its terms, such as the interest rate and duration, and on the creditworthiness of the borrower. Two loans of equal amount will have different costs and benefits if the terms of the loan or the financial condition of the borrowers differ. This difference is not recognized in conventional budget accounts, which record the face amount of the loan as an outlay. This accounting rule overstates the cost of direct loans when they are made but ignores the cost to government of loans that are forgiven, forgotten, or defaulted. Because an outlay is recorded when the loan is made, the budget does not take account of the cost that ensues if the loan is not repaid.

When the government guarantees a loan, it pledges to repay the debt if the borrower defaults. There is no transfer of funds out of the treasury when the guarantee is issued. Nevertheless, guaranteed loans have the key characteristics of transfers. That is, borrowers obtain a benefit, and the government bears a cost, albeit a contingent one. The cost of the guarantee depends on the risk the government assumes. If default occurs, any ensuing payment is shown as a budget outlay.

Because they are not conventional expenditures, tax preferences and loans are often characterized as evasions of budget control.[51] It should be noted, however, that these types of transactions became increasingly prominent as federal spending shifted from the financing of agency operations to the financing of transfer payments. Much of the upsurge in tax expenditures and government-provided credit occurred during the growth years when direct expenditures were also rising and budget controls were weakened.[52] The government did not have a strong incentive to spend outside the budget, because it already had ample scope to spend within it. Apparently, the same expansionary conditions that prompted a rise in direct spending also spurred greater recourse to special financing schemes.

Tax expenditures and credit assistance are suitable substitutes for transfer payments but not for operational expenses. Governments do not normally pay for administrative operations by giving employees or suppliers tax relief or subsidized loans. But government can provide recipients of transfer payments the equivalent of direct benefits by reducing their tax liability or lending them money. The flow of benefits can be maintained by any means that assist recipients, whether or not the transaction is budgeted as an outlay. It is in this sense that credit and tax subsidies are genuine substitutes for direct spending. Not surprisingly, at the same time direct transfers were growing, so, too, were nonconventional expenditures.

Like many transfer payments, tax expenditures and credit assistance are entitlements. Normally, any eligible taxpayer or borrower can obtain those benefits on demand. Their total cost depends, therefore, on the behavior of taxpayers and borrowers, not on a preset budget limit.[53] Tax expenditures also are implicitly indexed. As tax liability and marginal rates change, so does the cost of these preferences.

CONCLUSION

In the quarter-century after World War II, growth became a good in itself—an economic good because it enhanced the wellbeing of Americans and assured high employment, a political good because it enabled government to provide more public benefits without lowering private consumption.

Growth became part of the national culture and the overriding expectation of executive and legislative policymakers. Claimants and guardians alike assumed that the next budget would be bigger than the current one, and they behaved in ways that produced this outcome. Spending departments sensed that program initiatives would be welcomed, and they actively searched for ideas and opportunities to claim additional funds. Expansionary cues streamed from agency plans, White House task forces, congressional hearings, party platforms, and interest-group agendas. The president's budget office adapted to the changed circumstance. It took on a broader portfolio of responsibilities, especially in developing legislation and new programs, and it let go of some controls that had been used to constrain spending. The budget office increasingly saw its role as improving, not blocking, program expansions, and as shaping them to the president's policies.

Expansion brought a steep rise in the transfer payments that distributed a substantial portion of the fiscal dividend. Entitlement gave recipients shares in future budgets, and indexation fixed these shares in real terms. Substitute forms of transfer became popular through preferences written into the tax code and access to government-provided or guaranteed credit.

The budget and the economy were intertwined, in their whole and in the parts. They were joined by a fiscal policy that stimulated expansion and a budget policy that spent the fruits of expansion. They also were joined by policies that made the distribution of private income increasingly dependent on the distribution of public expenditure.

The system worked. To keep it going required only that the economy cooperate by generating increments to pay the bills. In the exuberance of the 1960s, that seemed a manageable task. With the hindsight of later decades, we know it was not.

Notes

1. The transformation of budgeting from a control to a planning orientation is discussed in Allen Schick, "The Road to PPB: The Stages of Budget Reform," in *Public Administration Review* 26 (1966), pp. 243–58.

2. National income accounting was not yet fully developed before the 1930s; hence, GNP computations were not as accurate as they are today. For a discussion of sources and reliability of early estimates, see U.S. Bureau of the Census, *Historical Statistics of the United States: Colonial Times to 1970*, Part 1 (Washington, D.C.: Government Printing Office, 1975), pp. 215–16.

3. Among the elements of the New Deal that were discarded, central planning was probably the most prominent. See Herbert Stein, *Presidential Economics*, second revised edition (Washington, D.C.: American Enterprise Institute, 1988), pp. 34–37.

4. The *Congressional Quarterly*'s computation of conservative coalition scores was initiated in the late 1950s. There is strong reason to believe that the coalition was more powerful in the immediate postwar period, when party control of the Senate was almost evenly divided and Republicans had more House seats than they did after 1960. See Norman Ornstein and others, *Vital Statistics on Congress: 1987–1988* (Washington, D.C.: Congressional Quarterly, Inc., 1987), pp. 210–20.

5. Quoted in *Congressional Quarterly Almanac 1950* (Washington, D.C.: Congressional Quarterly, Inc., 1951), p. 166.

6. The measure passed the House by a 33-14 vote; the Senate approved it by a vote of 81-2.

7. The 1948 Republican platform declared that "government can and should encourage the building of better homes at less cost. We recommend federal aid to the states for local slum clearance and low-rental housing programs where there is a need that cannot be met either by private enterprise or by the states and localities." Quoted in Congressional Quarterly Almanac 1949 (Washington, D.C.: Congressional Quarterly, Inc., 1950), p. 276.

8. The displacement theory of government growth is associated with the work of Alan Peacock and Jack Wiseman. See their The Growth of Public Expenditure in the United Kingdom (London: Allen & Unwin, 1967).

9. The debt held by the public was $224 billion in 1947 and $237 billion in 1960. See U.S. Office of Management and Budget, Historical Tables, Budget of the United States Government, Fiscal Year 1989 (Washington, D.C.: Government Printing Office, 1988), table 7-1, p. 143.

10. Bureau of Economic Analysis, U.S. Department of Commerce, Long Term Economic Growth (Washington, D.C.: Government Printing Office, 1973). It is important to note that different sources may not be congruent on the amount of growth that occurred in a particular period. Moreover, the Bureau revises its computations from time to time, so that earlier published data may not be consistent with more recent ones.

11. The cycles were measured in terms of volume of industrial production. See ibid., p. 44.

12. Stein, op. cit., p. 115. Stein also notes the Keynesian view that failure to return the fiscal dividend to the private sector through additional spending or lower taxes would have resulted in a fiscal drag.

13. Wildavsky wrote that budgeting is incremental, not comprehensive. The beginning of wisdom about an agency budget is that it is almost never reviewed as a whole each year . . . . Instead it is based on last year's budget with special attention given to a narrow range of increases or decreases. Aaron Wildavsky, The Politics of the Budgetary Process (Boston: Little, Brown, 1964), p. 15.

14. For a discussion of incrementalism, see Allen Schick, "Incremental Budgeting in a Decremental Age," Policy Sciences 16 (1983), pp. 1–25.

15. Outlays rose from $98 billion in fiscal year 1961 to $119 billion in fiscal 1964. Approximately equal amounts of increase went to defense and human resource programs.

16. U.S. Council of Economic Advisors, Economic Report of the President, 1960 (Washington, D.C.: Government Printing Office, 1960), p. 6.

17. Quoted in Walter W. Heller, New Dimensions of Political Economy (Cambridge, Mass.: Harvard University Press, 1966), p. 31.

18. U.S. Council of Economic Advisors, Economic Report of the President, 1963 (Washington, D.C.: Government Printing Office, 1963), p. 74.

19. Heller, ibid., p. 9.

20. Economic Report of the President, 1963, p. 68.

21. Despite a heated economy and rising inflation, President Johnson refused to consider a tax increase until 1967, when the Vietnam War buildup was well under way. The surtax he proposed in early 1967 encountered strong opposition in Congress and was not enacted until the middle of 1968.

22. David C. Mowery and Mark S. Kamlet, "Games Presidents Do and Do Not Play: Presidential Circumvention of the Executive Branch Budget Process," in Policy Sciences 16 (1964), pp. 303–27.

23. The classical principles of budgeting were set forth in J. Wilner Sundelson, "Budgetary Principles," *Political Science Quarterly* (1935), pp. 236–63.

24. Data on the consolidation of appropriation accounts is provided in Joseph P. Harris, *Congressional Control of Administration* (Washington, D.C.: Brookings Institution, 1964).

25. According to Jesse Burkhead, "Except for apportionment, budget execution is regarded as a responsibility of departmental and agency management." (New York: Wiley, 1956), p. 354.

26. The last deficiency appropriation (P.L. 88-317) was enacted in 1964. Before then, the appropriations committees had separate subcommittees to deal with deficiencies. These subcommittees were abolished.

27. OMB Circular A-10 bars premature release of any budget information before publication of the president's budget, and the 1937 budget, for example, contains the following notice on the cover: "**CONFIDENTIAL**. To be held in STRICT CONFIDENCE and no portion, synopsis, or intimation to be published or given out until the READING of the President's Budget message has been begun . . . . Extreme care must therefore be exercised to avoid premature publication" (emphasis and capitalization in original).

28. Changes in the composition and behavior of the appropriations committees are described in Allen Schick, *Congress and Money: Budgeting, Spending, and Taxing* (Washington, D.C.: Urban Institute, 1980), chapter X.

29. Quoted in Larry Berman, *The Office of Management and Budget and the Presidency, 1921–1979* (Princeton, N.J.: Princeton University Press, 1979), p. 9.

30. President's Committee on *Administrative Management, Administrative Management in the Government of the United States* (Washington, D.C.: Government Printing Office, 1937), p. 20.

31. The evolution of the Bureau of the Budget into a presidential staff agency is discussed in Allen Schick, "The Budget Bureau That Was: Thoughts on the Rise, Decline, and Futures of a Presidential Agency," in *Law and Contemporary Problems* 35 (1970), pp. 519–39.

32. Quoted in Martha Derthick, *Uncontrollable Spending for Social Services Grants* (Washington, D.C.: Brookings Institution, 1975), p. 85.

33. See Norman M. Pearson, "The Budget Bureau: From Routine Business to General Staff," *Public Administration Review* 3 (1943), p. 139.

34. Richard Neustadt, "Presidency and Legislation: The Growth of Central Clearance," *American Political Science Review* 38 (1964), p. 660.

35. The objectives of PPB are explained in Charles L. Schultze, *The Politics and Economics of Public Spending* (Washington, D.C.: Brookings Institution, 1968).

36. Some effects of temporary authorizations are discussed in Louis Fisher, "Annual Authorizations: Durable Roadblocks to Biennial Budgeting," *Public Budgeting and Finance* 3 (1983), pp. 23–40.

37. The dispersion of congressional spending jurisdiction is analyzed in John F. Cogan, "The Evolution of Congressional Budget Decisionmaking and the Emergence of Federal Deficits" (unpublished manuscript, August 1988).

38. The changing pattern of federal grants is described in U.S. Office of Management and Budget, *Budget of the United States Government, Special Analyses*, Fiscal Year 1989, Special Analysis H.

39. See Charles G. Dawes, *The First Year of the Budget of The United States* (New York: Harper & Row, 1923).

40. The word "impoundment" was not used in Lucious Wilmerding, Jr., *The Spending Power* (New Haven, Conn.: Yale University Press, 1943). However, the word was already used in 1942, the period covered in J.D. Williams, *The Impounding of Funds by the Bureau of the Budget, The Interuniversity Case Program* (Tuscaloosa: University of Alabama Press, 1955).

41. U.S. Department of Justice, *Official Opinions of the Attorneys-General* (Washington, D.C.: Government Printing Office, 1898), p. 392.

42. William F. Willoughby, *The National Budget System with Suggestions for its Improvement* (Baltimore: Johns Hopkins University, 1927).

43. Section 1211 of the General Appropriations Act of 1950 authorized the reserving of funds from apportionment "to provide for contingencies, or to effect savings whenever savings are made possible by or through changes in requirements, greater efficiency of operations, or other developments subsequent to the date on which such appropriation was made available."

44. Title X of the Congressional Budget and Impoundment Control Act of 1974, PL 93-344.

45. The impoundment control process gives Congress an opportunity to change its mind and allow impoundments to continue. The extent to which Congress allows funds to be withheld depends on its budgetary relationship with the president. See chapter 4 for a discussion of recent experience under the Impoundment Control Act.

46. The growth of entitlements is discussed by R. Kent Weaver in "Controlling Entitlements," in *The New Direction in American Politics*, ed. John E. Chubb and Paul E. Peterson (Washington, D.C.: Brookings Institution, 1986), pp. 307–41.

47. Real spending (in 1982 dollars) rose $191 billion in the FY 1965–75 period. Payments for individuals accounted for more than 90 percent ($173 billion) of this rise.

48. Quoted in U.S. Senate, Committee on the Budget, *Indexation of Federal Programs*, Committee Print, May 1981, p. 144.

49. The concept of nonconventional expenditure and the manner in which it differs from offbudget transactions is discussed in Allen Schick, "Controlling Nonconventional Expenditure: Tax Expenditures and Loans," *Public Budgeting and Finance*, 6 (Spring 1986), pp. 3–19.

50. The definition and measurement of tax expenditures are discussed in Stanley S. Surrey and Paul R. McDaniel, *Tax Expenditures* (Cambridge, Mass.: Harvard University Press, 1985).

51. This view is taken by James T. Bennett and Thomas J. DiLorenzo, *Underground Government, The Off-Budget Public Sector* (Washington, D.C.: Cato Institute, 1983) and Dennis S. Ippolito, *Hidden Spending: The Politics of Federal Spending Programs* (Chapel Hill: University of North Carolina Press, 1984).

52. Most data series on tax expenditures were constructed after this term was defined in the Congressional Budget Act of 1974. Hence, one cannot readily measure the growth in these preferences before the mid-1970s. Direct loans quadrupled from $7 billion in 1965 to $28 billion in 1975, whereas guaranteed loans rose from $23 billion to $39 billion.

53. During the 1980s, various controls on credit were introduced, so that there now are annual limits on direct loan and guaranteed loan programs.

Chapter 3

THE ECONOMY VERSUS THE BUDGET: THE EMERGENCE OF FISCAL STRESS

The economy and the budget supported one another in the 1960s. Fiscal symbiosis was built on three related successes: (1) a widely accepted theory of how the economy works, (2) the effective application of this theory through a flexible budget and a responsive economy, and (3) a steady infusion of incremental resources from the economy into the budget. Keynesian consensus on the relation between aggregate revenue and expenditure on the one hand and growth, prices, and employment on the other provided a working model of a productive, stable economy. The model was implemented by the federal government through flexible budget policy and it could be adjusted at short notice to cyclical fluctuations. Normal growth of 4 percent or more a year assured that an expanding economy could support a growing government.

All three successes evaporated in the tumultuous years between the Vietnam War buildup and the OPEC oil shocks. Budget flexibility was the first casualty, a responsive economy the second. These props failed as stagflation took hold and the increments vanished or proved inadequate for the still-expanding budget. Finally, fiscal consensus was replaced by a babble of competing explanations of what had gone wrong and how the economy might be restored to health.

What emerged from the disarray was an economy at odds with the budget, the two drifting apart so that the performance of one was no longer reciprocated by predictable results of the other. This alienation was formally recognized in the Gramm-Rudman-Hollings targets, which purport to divorce the budget's condition from the economy's.[1]

This chapter's story begins with the breakdown of fiscal symbiosis in the Vietnam War era. In the 1970s, the estrangement of the economy and the budget was deepened by oversize deficits, a steady deterioration of the economy, and jarring policy reversals. The broken relationship of the economy and the budget spurred economists and others to challenge previously-accepted fiscal doctrine and to offer fresh prescriptions to remedy contemporary problems. The most prominent of these were the supply-side notions, which sever the link between macrobudgeting and economic behavior. With the economy and the budget on separate tracks in the 1980s—the former growing and the other still mired in deficits—policy shifted from flexible response to preset targets.

THE COLLAPSE OF FISCAL SYMBIOSIS: 1967–1973

"I do not believe recessions are inevitable," Lyndon Johnson proclaimed in his 1965 Economic Report. The president had good reason to be pleased with the performance of the economy and to express confidence that emerging problems could be corrected by timely intervention. Flexibility had been successfully tested a few years earlier when stimulative action spurred economic expansion. Johnson hedged his confidence with the recognition that "up to now, every past expansion has ended in recession or depression," but he insisted that "imbalance—not old age—is the threat to sustained advance."[2]

Within a year, the president faced imbalance, but not of the sort he had anticipated. Instead of a threat of a recession, the government had to deal with an overheating economy, as unemployment plummeted from 5 percent in February 1965 to 3.7 percent a year later while consumer prices advanced almost 3 percent. Johnson's economic advisors urged consideration of a tax increase, but the president, fearing that Congress would balk or cut into his Great Society initiatives, procrastinated for a full year. He asked for a 6 percent surtax in January 1967, upped the proposed increase to 10 percent in August, and waited almost another year for Congress to approve his recommendation.[3] When Congress finally acted, prices were 5.5 percent higher than they had been when the surcharge was first proposed. Inflation had become a serious concern.

The spending side of the budget also proved rigid. At first, Johnson refused to consider spending cuts. A strong economy could afford Great Society programs while paying for a war in Southeast Asia, he argued in the 1967 budget, submitted in January, 1966.

"Both of these commitments involve great costs. They are costs we can and will meet . . . . The struggle in Vietnam must be supported. The advance toward a Great Society at home must continue unabated."[4]

The next budget asked for a surtax, yet the president was still reluctant to trim his program objectives. Soon, however, economic and political conditions forced his hand. Even though it was operating at full potential, the economy could not accommodate spending demands; the fiscal 1968 deficit, initially projected to be $4 billion turned out to be $25 billion.[5] As the fiscal situation deteriorated, Congress held the surtax hostage to spending reductions. After protracted maneuvering, Johnson acceded to congressional demands and agreed to legislation that packaged a $6 billion cutback together with the surcharge.

This action made it clear that the government could not have it all, at least during wartime. Choices and trade-offs had to be made. As Johnson's final budget (for the 1969 fiscal year) conceded: "faced with a costly war abroad and urgent requirements at home, we have to set priorities. And 'priority' is but another word for choice. We cannot do everything we would wish to do. And so we must choose carefully among the many competing demands on our resources."[6]

The language of priorities had penetrated budgetary debate. Guns versus butter, tax increases versus spending cuts, discretionary needs versus mandatory requirements—these have been the stuff of budgetary conflict for the past twenty years.

It was widely assumed in the late 1960s that the fiscal squeeze would be temporary. The war would soon end, a peace dividend would be added to the fiscal dividend, and resources would again be plentiful.[7] Alas, neither the economy nor peace brought budget claims and resources into equilibrium. The surtax provided a one-year respite from deficit financing, and the winddown of Vietnam combat brought a cutback in real defense spending, but the explosive growth in transfer payments used up all of the slack and more. Between 1967 and 1973, these payments spiraled from 5 percent of GNP to 8 percent; in inflation-adjusted dollars, transfer outlays doubled during this brief span. Congress tried to rein in federal spending by limiting total outlays; it enacted five such limitations between 1967 and 1973. These generally exempted mandatory entitlements, which accounted for all or most of the runup in the expenditures.[8] A now-familiar pattern set in: discretionary spending was effectively controlled; mandatory payments were not. A strict limit on total outlays meant, therefore, that discretionary programs would be crowded out by the entitlements.[9]

Active fiscal policy had been tried and found wanting. Both revenues and expenditures were less pliant than had been expected. In theory, these fiscal aggregates could be moved up or down as con-

ditions warranted. When applied, however, discretionary intervention was chronically asymmetrical: it was politically easier to lower
taxes than to raise them, and easier to raise domestic spending than
to lower it. Intervention might be timely and effective when the
economy needed stimulus; it was sluggish and ineffective when restraint was called for. Fiscal policy, economists learned, could not
be conducted in a clean room that was sealed off from the influence
of politics and the realities of divided government (between the legislative and executive branches) and divided budgets (between discretionary and mandatory items).

Fiscal asymmetry was not the only disappointment. The responsiveness of the economy to adjustments in revenue or expenditure
also was weaker than had been expected. The Nixon team that took
over in 1969 targeted a lower inflation rate as its prime fiscal objective. Nixon's economists were willing to tolerate some lost output
and somewhat higher unemployment, but they did not expect the
task to be difficult or costly. Unemployment might, they thought,
edge a bit above 4 percent; inflation would recede from the 5 percent
peak; and the economy would be stabilized on a full-employment/
low-inflation course.[10] To manage this adjustment, they planned balanced budgets in 1970 and 1971. On a full-employment basis, the
swing would be quite substantial, from a $25 billion deficit in 1968
to virtual balance in 1969, and surpluses in each of the next two
years.[11]

As things turned out, the cost was higher than expected and the
benefits lower. The economy stumbled into a mild recession, and
unemployment, which stood at 3.4 percent in early 1969, soared to
6 percent by the end of 1970. Worse yet, the inflation rate did not
respond to the expected degree. Prices climbed 6 percent in 1969
and 5 percent the next year; after two years of efforts to moderate it,
inflation was about the same rate as when Nixon entered office. In
August 1971, with the presidential election only fifteen months away,
the White House abandoned its scripted policy and opted for across-
the-board wage and price controls.[12]

Whereas budget policy had been rigid in the late 1960s, the economy proved rigid in the early 1970s. It was easier to stir up inflation
than to get rid of it and easier to generate higher unemployment than
to achieve lower inflation. There was a plethora of explanations of
what had gone awry. Some focused on policy failures, others on the
economy. Fiscal restraint failed, according to one argument, because
it was not applied consistently or for a sufficient time. Key to this
argument was the transformation of planned balances into actual

deficits. Table 3.1 shows the discrepancy between plans and outturns in 1970 and 1971, the two fiscal years immediately preceding the wage-price freeze. Recession took a bite out of revenues and added to outlays, but it did not purge the economy of inflationary expectations. Perhaps moderation would have worked if the administration had stayed with it a bit longer, but political cycles usually are shorter than economic ones. Political impatience, economists learned, is a real constraint on any constrictive fiscal policy.

Another explanation of the high cost of moderation was the changing composition of the labor market. With more young workers and women in the market, it seemed to require a stronger dose of fiscal medicine to dampen inflationary pressures. The job could not be done at 4 percent unemployment. Because the costs could be much higher, the likelihood of success would be much lower.

The linkage of budgeting and the economy had been impaired, though it would take a few more years and additional disappointments for the full extent of the problem to be discerned. The nation moved from a situation in which the budget was expected to help the economy and the economy to help the budget to a situation in which each did damage to the other. The Nixon administration sought to stabilize the relationship by predicating budget policy on the full-employment concept. This concept measured budgetary balance in terms of the revenue and outlays that would ensue if the economy were operating at full employment. In extravagant language reminiscent of the optimism of the growth years, the 1972 budget characterized the full-employment budget as "a self-fulfilling prophesy: By operating as if it were at full employment, we will help to bring about that full employment."[13] Others saw use of this measure as a thin coverup of the actual deficit, but there was another reason for adopting the full-employment concept. It provided a practical rule for limiting the size of the deficit. Except "in emergency conditions," the 1972 budget declared, "expenditures must never be allowed to outrun the revenues that the tax system would produce at reasonably full employment."[14] This rule was to be the bridge from the fiscal abundance of the 1960s to the fiscal stress of the 1970s. It would enable the government to spend more than the fiscal increment, but not so much more as to unbalance the economy. But as conditions worsened, the full-employment concept was challenged and eventually dropped from the budget.

Whether measured conventionally or on a full-employment basis, deficits and fiscal stress were here to stay. What happened to the fiscal dividend?, a team of Brookings Institution budget experts asked

Table 3.1 ESTIMATED AND ACTUAL RECEIPTS, OUTLAYS, AND DEFICITS, 1966–81 (billions of dollars)

Fiscal year	Receipts			Outlays			Surplus or deficit (−)		
	Initial estimate	Actual	Difference	Initial estimate	Actual	Difference	Initial estimate	Actual	Increase or decrease (−) in the deficit
1966	123.5	134.5	11.0	127.4	137.8	10.4	−3.9	−3.3	−0.6
1967	145.5	149.6	4.1	145.0	158.4	13.4	0.5	−8.8	9.3
1968	168.1	153.7	−14.4	172.4	178.9	6.5	−4.3	−25.2	20.9
1969	178.1	187.8	9.7	186.1	184.6	−1.5	−8.0	3.2	−11.2
1970	198.7	193.7	−5.0	195.3	196.6	1.3	3.4	−2.8	6.2
1971	202.1	188.4	−13.7	200.8	211.4	10.6	1.3	−23.0	24.3
1972	217.6	208.6	−9.0	229.2	231.9	2.7	−11.6	−23.2	11.6
1973	220.8	232.2	11.4	246.3	246.5	0.2	−25.5	−14.3	−11.2
1974	256.0	264.9	8.9	268.7	268.4	−0.3	−12.7	−3.5	−9.2
1975	295.0	281.0	−14.0	304.4	324.6	20.2	−9.4	−43.6	34.2
1976	297.5	300.0	2.5	349.4	366.5	17.1	−51.9	−66.5	14.6
1977	351.3	356.9	5.6	394.2	401.9	7.7	−43.0	−45.0	2.0
1978[a]	401.6	402.0	0.4	459.4	451.0	−8.4	−57.7	−49.0	−8.7
1979	439.6	466.0	26.4	500.2	494.0	−6.2	−60.6	−28.0	−32.6
1980	503.0	520.0	17.0	532.0	579.6	47.6	−29.0	−59.6	30.6
1981	600.0	599.3	−0.7	616.0	657.2	41.2	−16.0	−57.9	41.9

Source: Budget of the United States Government.
Notes: The initial estimate is the estimate made in the budget for the particular fiscal year. The actual amount is the amount shown in the first budget after the fiscal year has concluded. The amounts shown here may vary from amounts published in historical series.
[a] Initial estimate for fiscal 1978 is taken from the revised budget submitted by President Carter.

in 1972. Their answer is worth quoting, because it shows how the optimism of one decade had been transformed into the pessimism of the next:

given the tax cuts of recent years and the large built-in growth of federal expenditures, the fiscal dividend in the near future is likely to be much smaller in relation to the size of the economy than historically has been the case in years of peacetime prosperity. At the same time, the growth in the demand for the public services furnished by the federal government is likely to be much greater. In the past, the problem in peacetime was how to deal with the resources channeled into the government by economic growth. For the immediate future at least, the problem appears to be one of trying to find enough resources to finance the growing demand for public services. Paradoxically, the growing absolute affluence of society is now accompanied by a relative squeeze on the resources of the federal government . . . . the problem of setting priorities in the public sector is becoming more, rather than less, acute despite the continuing rise in national income.[15]

To put the problem simply, the budget was programmed to grow faster than the economy. The government was spending more than the increment and was forecasted to do so even if economic growth remained strong. What was not foreseen at the time was how much more dire the budget situation would become when the economy stagnated.

THE PARALYSIS OF FISCAL POLICY: 1974–1981

Although their symbiosis had been disrupted, the economy and the budget still were interdependent. Weakness in the economy inevitably translated into lost revenue, somewhat higher spending, and a larger deficit. Applied Keynesians saw this as a stabilizing relationship. But in a period of high inflation and high unemployment, the linkage of the economy and the budget meant that adversity in one sector radiated to the other. Once the budget was supposed to stabilize the economy; during periods of stagflation, however, the economy destabilized the budget.

This turnaround occurred during the 1974–81 years, the period between the first OPEC oil shock and the election of Ronald Reagan. The oil embargo occurred during the tail end of the Nixon administration, a turbulent period in presidential-congressional relations, but one in which a determined effort was made to stabilize budget policy. Driven by its commitment to maintain a full-employment budget balance, the White House embraced what Herbert Stein has called "the old time religion."[16] Although unemployment was hovering around 5 percent, Nixon resisted legislative efforts to increase spending, and he impounded billions of dollars added by Congress. As table 3.1 indicated, in each of Nixon's last three budgets (the 1972–74 fiscal years), actual outlays varied by 1 percent or less from the total initially estimated eighteen months earlier.[17] In two of these fiscal years (1973 and 1974), the actual budget deficit was substantially below the initial estimate. This fiscal restraint did not do much to ease inflation, because prices were propelled upward by the expiration of wage-price controls, global food shortages, and the squeeze on oil supplies. Consumer prices were 18 percent higher when Nixon resigned in August 1974 than they had been when he was reelected in November 1972.

Inflation was accelerating when Gerald Ford took over. One of the first things he did as president was to propose a tax increase as the centerpiece of his campaign to "whip" inflation. Less than three months later, Ford proposed a big tax cut, and two months after that he signed an even bigger cut into law. This policy reversal was as sudden and startling as the runup in unemployment that occurred at the same time. In the few months between the tax increase proposal and the tax reduction law, 2.5 million workers were added to the jobless rolls; another million would be added in subsequent months, as the United States reeled under the steepest downturn since World War II.

The 1974–75 recession presented fiscal policymakers with a new, vexatious situation. As unemployment rose, so, too, did inflation. This confluence of economic ills violated accepted economic truths embedded in the Phillips curve, which showed a stable trade-off between wage inflation and unemployment. The predicament gave rise to a new term—*stagflation*—and to a new measure of economic stress—the *misery index*, which is the sum of the inflation and unemployment rates. This index was persistently high through the 1970s, and it exceeded 20 percent at the end of the decade (see figure 3.1). The index was well-named, for it reflected the distress experienced by a sizable portion of the population. The index also was a measure of policy failure, for despite the explanations offered at the time, the plain fact that both inflation and unemployment were high attested to the perceived incapacity of government to manage the economy.

One of the more convincing explanations of stagflation was that the steep spiral in oil prices cut into output (because consumers had

Figure 3.1   MISERY INDEX: 1967–87
(SUM OF INFLATION RATE AND UNEMPLOYMENT RATE)

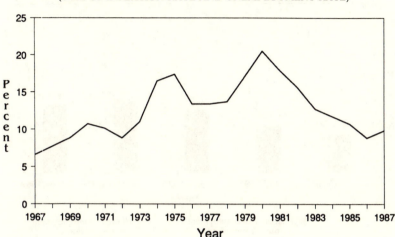

Inflation: Annual change in CPI, year to year.
Unemployment rate: Annual average.
Source: *Economic Report of the President.*

less purchasing power) and added to inflation (because the increased cost of energy radiated to other sectors of the economy). This explanation did not do much to show politicians how to get out of the mess. In fact, stagflation worsened throughout the 1970s; the economy did not return to pre-1974 employment rates. Figures 3.2 and 3.3 depict a progressive deterioration in performance throughout the decade. In each cycle during the 1970s, both the peak and trough in unemployment rates were higher than in the previous cycle. The highest unemployment rate marched steadily upward from 4.3 percent to 6.1 percent to 8.9 percent and, continuing into the 1980s, to 10.6 percent. The lowest rate showed a similar trend. Consumer prices also moved upward in a step progression through the early 1980s, but they tapered off afterward.

Regardless of its causes, stagflation destabilized fiscal policy and made it difficult for politicians to maintain a steady course. Budget actions taken to ease one problem would exacerbate the other, inducing politicians to retreat before their policies had a chance to work. The results were weak responses to the economic malaise, unstable fiscal policy, and budget outcomes that often varied sharply

Figure 3.2   UNEMPLOYMENT RATES: 1967–87, PEAKS AND TROUGHS

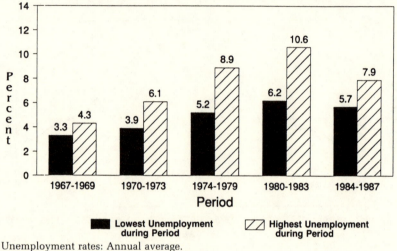

Period

■ **Lowest Unemployment during Period**   ▨ **Highest Unemployment during Period**

Unemployment rates: Annual average.
Source: *Economic Report of the President.*

from the planned levels. Each of these deficiencies in policies afflicted the two presidents of this period, Gerald Ford and Jimmy Carter.

Weak Fiscal Response

Both Ford and Carter had to avoid actions that would aggravate inflation or unemployment. "We sometimes discover," the 1975 Economic Report admitted, "when we seek to accomplish several objectives simultaneously that the goals are not always completely compatible. Action to achieve one goal sometimes works to the detriment of another."[18] Mindful of the high inflation rate, President Ford structured a stimulus package that would provide a quick boost to the economy while avoiding long-term imbalances. The tax cut was to be temporary, mostly in the form of a rebate on the previous year's taxes, and the line would be held on spending.

Congress, as might be expected, preferred to err more on the side of stimulus. It increased the size of the tax cut, added some anti-inflationary programs, and resisted the president's efforts (in late 1975) to link extension of the tax cuts to an equivalent reduction in federal spending.[19] Congress and the president continued to battle

Figure 3.3   INFLATION RATES: 1967–87, PEAKS AND TROUGHS

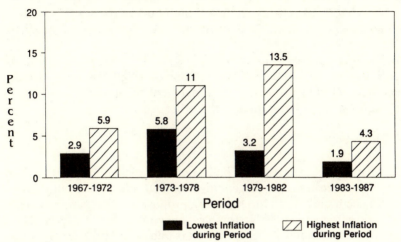

Period

■ Lowest Inflation during Period   ▨ Highest Inflation during Period

Inflation: Annual change in CPI, year to year.
Source: *Economic Report of the President.*

over budget policy throughout 1976, an election year during which more than 7 million workers lacked jobs. Congress passed expansionary legislation, Ford made frequent use of his veto power, and some additional funds became available. The overall response was mild, however, because the two branches were hobbled by the inflation-unemployment problem. The stimulus was less than it would have been if inflation had been low; the attack on inflation was weaker than it would have been if unemployment had been low.

With the election of a Democratic president in 1976, the White House and Congress cooperated on a stimulus package that combined tax cuts and spending increases to spur economic revival. Shortly after taking office, Jimmy Carter sent Congress a revised budget containing $30 billion (over a two-year period) in tax cuts and spending increases, but he did not expect this action to have a marked effect on economic conditions. His revised budget was forecast to raise output and reduce unemployment by only 0.2 percent in the first year and 0.3 percent in the second.[20] As much as they may have wanted to, Carter and Congress could not move too fast without risking a resurgence of inflation.

In fact, employment did better than Carter had expected, but inflation did worse. Real output rose 6 percent in 1976 and 5 percent the next year, but prices also trended upward, rising 6.8 percent in 1977 and 9 percent in 1978. The second oil shock, in 1979, brought still higher inflation and a return of high unemployment. The misery index reached a record 20 percent in 1980, the last year of the Carter presidency.

The relationship of inflation and unemployment paralyzed fiscal policy. Both moved up when the economy stagflated, but when the economy started to recover, improvement in one rate was accompanied by the deterioration of the other rate.

Unstable Policies

The fiscal response weak was both weak and vacillating. Nixon shifted from fiscal restraint to wage and price controls. Faced with a free-falling economy, Ford lurched from proposing a tax increase to calling for a reduction. This stop–go behavior continued with Carter who recommended an immediate tax rebate in 1977 but abruptly withdrew his proposal when Congress was about to act on it. This time, the reversal occurred because the economy appeared to be performing better than expected. Carter flip-flopped again in 1980, when he scrapped his budget two months after submitting it, and then negotiated a revised version with congressional leaders. This about-face was prompted by near panic in financial markets and extraordinarily high interest rates.

No less than in the previous decade, fiscal policymakers of the 1970s scoured each month's or quarter's economic news for clues about where the economy was heading. But there was a big difference between the fine-tuning of the 1960s and the stop–go budgeting of the 1970s. Fine-tuning was intended to stabilize the economy. Policy changes would be frequent, but they also would be small and manageable. The government would make many minor adjustments in order to avoid having to make major ones. The metaphor of fine-tuning suggested that someone was in charge and that budget adjustments would be made with confidence that they would keep the economy on an even keel. They would not be frantic reactions to onrushing developments beyond control or comprehension.

The policy switches of the 1970s were abrupt and large, as the government swung from contraction to stimulation and back. Budget officials did not quite understand what was happening or know what to expect, and they were unsure that their actions would have the intended effects. The latest news was so important to them because the budget was hostage to the economy. Monthly or quarterly surprises in the economic data could undo the government's revenue or spending plans.

Escalating and Unbudgeted Outlays

Sudden swings triggered the automatic stabilizers in the budget. The impact of stagflation on revenue was obfuscated by the contradictory pulls of a weak economy and rising prices. Whereas the former cut into revenue, the latter added to it, creating a situation in which federal receipts rose as economic activity declined. This unexpected pattern had consequences for revenue policy that are discussed in the next chapter. Spending, however, moved in only one direction—upward—as both stagnation and inflation spurred unbudgeted expenditure. Table 3.2 tallies the rise in "relatively uncontrollable outlays" from year to year and from the initial estimates in the president's budget through the close of the fiscal year.[21] Annual increases in "relatively uncontrollable" outlays were 10 percent or higher in each year form 1975 through 1981; at the end of this period, these outlays were more than double what they were only six years earlier. Some of this rise was due to demographic changes, such as increases in the number of elderly Americans. Much of it, however, was due to unfavorable economic conditions.

In some years, spending changes occurring within the budget year were greater than those made between years. The fiscal 1981 budget was an extreme example of instability in spending policy. Jimmy Carter's first budget for the fiscal year (submitted in January 1980)

Table 3.2 ESTIMATED AND ACTUAL RELATIVELY UNCONTROLLABLE
OUTLAYS, 1975–81
(billions of dollars)

Fiscal year	Original estimate	Actual outlays	Variance Increase or decrease (−)
1975	225.4	237.5	12.1
1976	262.8	267.7	4.9
1977	303.2	293.6	− 9.7
1978[a]	335.4	333.9	− 1.5
1979	375.3	366.1	− 9.2
1980	405.7	439.4	33.6
1981	453.5	485.0	31.6

Source: *Budget of the United States Government.*
[a]Estimates for this year are the revised estimates issued in February 1977.

recommended total outlays of $616 billion and a $16 billion deficit. Although the projected deficit was relatively small, it was too big for nervous markets. Two months later, after closed-door negotiations with congressional leaders, the president discarded his original budget and submitted a new one that promised to balance revenue and expenditure. Despite sizable increases in mandatory accounts, the new budget proposed to reduce overall spending by making deep cuts in some programs. But deteriorating economic conditions and spiraling transfer payments forced Carter to abandon any hope for a balanced budget. Carter's third budget for the fiscal year, presented as a midyear update in July 1980, projected $22 billion more spending than was indicated in his previous plan as well as a $30 billion deficit. By January 1981, the anticipated deficit had ballooned to $55 billion and total outlays to $662 billion. When the fiscal year ended, after Reagan had taken office, there was a slight drop in both outlays and the deficit below Carter's final estimate. Nevertheless, automatic increases in mandatory accounts had done more to change total outlays than had all the discretionary actions of the White House. The economy had become the destroyer of presidential dreams, compelling the chief executive to bow to developments beyond his control. *Force majeure* ruled public finance.

Fiscal chaos took a toll in budget procedure. Budgeting became a virtually continuous activity, as the budget appeared, disappeared, and reappeared in the course of the annual cycle. This disarray was not due simply to inconstancy in the White House—though there was plenty of that—but fiscal stress. The less slack a country has in its finances, the more budgets it is likely to go through during the fiscal year.[22] An affluent government can stay the course even if the budget is beset by adverse shocks; a constrained government will have to make midcourse adjustments. In extreme cases, the "real" budget—the one whose entries correspond to actual transactions—is known only after the fiscal year is over. When revenue and spending policy are known only after the fact, the budget cannot be a reliable instrument of fiscal policy.

The United States did not become a poor country in the 1970s, but it saw itself as poorer than it had been, and it lacked sufficient slack to withstand fiscal pressures. Per capita GNP and disposable income grew, but the increments supplied by the economy were not big enough to pay for spending growth. From a budgetary standpoint, stress cannot be measured simply in terms of growth in GNP or changes in other objective measures of performance. Rather, it represents a government's inability to satisfy all of the politically potent claims presented to it. If the federal government was less able to cope with its budgetary predicament, it was not because resources dwindled—they did not—but because demands on the budget soared more than resources did. Expenditures were programmed to grow, as noted in the previous chapter, and the rise in revenue was periodically adjusted downward to counter recession or to compensate for bracket creep as we will see in the next chapter.

The structural imbalance in the budget was masked by the impact of high inflation on projected revenue and on full-employment budget computations. Taxes were not yet indexed in the 1970s; hence, inflation had a positive short-term effect on federal receipts. High inflation also distorted the full-employment budget estimates and impaired their reliability as measures of the impact of the budget on the economy. With inflation pumping up potential revenue, the full-employment budget appeared more restrictive than it actually was, thereby biasing fiscal policy in a more expansionary direction than had been intended when the measure was introduced.

Table 3.3 shows that multiyear projections issued in the 1974–81 budgets consistently indicated a balanced budget several years ahead. These projections assumed that current revenue and spending policy would remain in effect and, with the exception of the projections issued in the fiscal 1978 budget, that they were on a full-employment budget basis. For eight consecutive years, the budget projected that the growth in revenue would be sufficiently greater than the growth in outlays so as to liquidate the deficit and provide a margin within a few years. The fiscal 1980 budget, for example, estimated that

Table 3.3 PROJECTED BUDGET MARGINS, 1974–81

Fiscal year	Final year for which margin was projected	Projected increase in outlays	Projected increase in receipts	Projected margin
1974	1978	59	94	35
1975	1979	153	185	37
1976	1980	206	252	61
1977	1981	145	260	99
1978[a]	1982	147	233	29
1979	1983	253	328	65
1980	1984	228	348	89
1981	1985	413	573	148

Source: The Budget of the United States, Fiscal Years 1974–1981.
[a]Projections in the 1978 budget were based on existing and expected employment rates. All others were made on a full- or high-employment budget basis.

within five years, full-employment revenue would rise $120 billion more than full-employment spending, providing an $89 billion cushion for program enhancements. Of course, the additional spending was to be paid for by inflated revenue, not by economic growth. When Congress adjusted tax rates downward, the margin never materialized, and the projected surplus turned into an actual deficit.

THE WITHERING AWAY OF FISCAL CONSENSUS

When the economy was functioning well, fiscal policy garnered much of the credit. "We are all Keynesians now," Milton Friedman admitted in 1965; "Now I am a Keynesian," Richard Nixon acknowledged in 1971. These statements did not mean that monetarists such as Friedman and fiscal conservatives such as Nixon had fully embraced the Keynesian prescriptions for managing the economy, but they did suggest mainstream consensus that the government can play a positive role.

When the economy faltered, so, too, did confidence in fiscal theory. The fiscal consensus could not withstand stagflation's blows to economic confidence. In addition to the confusion and paralysis caused by the combination of inflation and unemployment, there was concern over the creeping enlargement in the relative size of the federal sector, which, now that increments were inadequate, had to be financed by heavier debt and tax burdens. Even more troubling was the sudden slowdown and (for a time) halt, in productivity growth. After rising sharply in the postwar period (see table 2.2), productivity was flat in the late 1970s. Puzzled economists offered numerous explanations, but, lacking agreement on the causes of the problem, they could not coalesce on a solution.[23] There was still some recognition that the budget could have a beneficial impact on short-term performance, but a growing corps of economists saw government as responsible for long-term imbalances and inefficiency.

The erosion of consensus was evident in the wishy-washy Humphrey-Hawkins Act of 1978 and in the weak response to the second oil shock in 1979–80. The Full Employment (Humphrey-Hawkins) Act of 1978 was initially conceived of as a means of committing the government to a maximum 4 percent unemployment rate. Jobs would be guaranteed to workers who wanted them. What was enacted, however, was a toothless requirement that the president establish five-year objectives for reducing inflation and unemployment and for boosting output. Inflation, the law stipulated, should be driven down to 3 percent in five years and to zero percent within a decade, but Humphrey-Hawkins also decreed that this objective should be pursued in ways that do not impede progress toward low unemployment. Except for ritualistic reports, the law's objectives were discarded shortly after it was enacted.

The quick demise of Humphrey-Hawkins was reflected in government actions after the 1979 spiral in oil prices. With unemployment above 6 percent and rising sharply, Carter's fiscal 1981 budget, which was quite austere by conventional full-employment measures, was revised to be even more restrictive. As interest rates exploded above 20 percent, policymakers had to decide which economic ill to combat; they could not deal with all of them at once.

Economic disarray bred a slew of theories, some fundamentally at variance with the postwar orthodoxy, about what had gone awry and what should be done to correct the problem. There were bits and pieces of a consensus, but not enough to form a saleable fiscal policy. There was mainstream agreement that monetary and fiscal policy should be more closely coordinated, though there was persistent dispute as to whether growth in the money stocks should be put on automatic pilot corresponding to the long-term trend in output.[24] There also was agreement that more had to be done to purge inflation, but there was no consensus about what had generated the inflation in the first place. Many Keynesians held to the view that rude shocks to the economy, dating back to the Vietnam period and aggravated by severe energy shortages, had triggered inflationary expectations. Others attributed sustained inflation to government-made inefficiencies.

Economics thinking gravitated toward a longer-term perspective, in contrast to the Keynesian emphasis on short-term intervention. This shift was due to uncertainty over the efficacy of short-term adjustments, as well as to concern that the long-term potential of the economy had been damaged by efforts to fine-tune it. Attention to the short run had inevitably led to demand stimulation, which had a more immediate payoff than would efforts to enlarge future output. Not much could be done in the near term to boost the potential of the economy; its size was largely determined by past policies. But the extent to which available potential was utilized could be affected by current policy. Over time, critics of demand stimulation argued, this posture had led to inadequate savings and investment, low growth in potential output, and high inflation.

Shifting to a longer-term view loosened the policy linkage of today's budget and today's economy. But politicians still had a need for expedient means of doing good. To be successful, fiscal policy had to blend politics and economics; in seeking to improve the economy, it had to give politicians and governments credit for the well-being they produced or promised. The actual or anticipated improvement had to be concrete and immediate, not something that would accrue from decades of fiscal prudence and productive investment. Applied Keynesianism once was successful because it mixed economic success and political credit-taking; to forge a new fiscal consensus, a similar amalgam would have to be developed again.

Two fiscal theories emerged as possible successors to active demand management in the 1970s. One is a school of thought known as *rational expectations*. The other is the supply-side movement. The former has had limited influence on policy, but the latter played a big role in Ronald Reagan's economic program.

Rational expectations theory is rooted in the notion that government intervention is likely to be ineffective.[25] Beginning with the observation that fiscal stimulus has had progressively weaker impact, rational expectationists concluded that repeated intervention desensitizes economic actors to policy changes. Over time, therefore, a higher price has been paid in inflation to ameliorate unemployment, and vice versa. This deterioration, rational expectationists argued, has been caused by the fact that, having learned to anticipate the government's response to economic swings, rational actors have taken steps that discount the efforts in advance. For example, as the prospect of recession rise, entrepreneurs and others would expect the government to counter with stimulative actions, and they would incorporate the expected policy changes into their own behavior. Hence, if recession ensues and the government acts in the anticipated manner, its actions would not yield the predicted results. In extreme form, rational expectations means that regardless of what it does, the government could not produce dramatic change in the performance of the economy. Demand management would be neutral and, therefore, ineffective, with respect to real economic performance.[26] The unseen hand of the market would prevail over the seeing hand of government.

Rational expectations strengthened the emerging belief that the government should pursue a more stable budget course. But it could not be a full prescription for fiscal policy. If put into effect, it would leave the government culpable for economic failure but incapable of doing much about it. Despite the loss of confidence in Keynesian policy, the government could not walk away from political responsibility for the economy.

At least three factors dictate an active role for the federal government. One is that its very size precludes the government from remaining on the sidelines. With the government consuming or transferring more than 20 percent of the national income, its inaction can have as telling effect on the economy as its action. Second, inasmuch as politicians are likely to be blamed for poor performance, they are inclined to behave in ways that allow them to be identified with success. Third, to the extent that subpar performance is due to policy failures, government action is necessary to remove the impediments to allocative efficiency.

While rational expectations theory called for government to withdraw from active intervention, supply-side prescriptions called for it to intervene, if only to undo past policy errors. Indeed, it was perceived policy defects that gave rise to the supply-side movement. Supply-siders were convinced that an economy left to its own devices would perform quite well, but they regarded government action as necessary to remedy past policy mistakes. In particular, they attributed high inflation and unemployment to policies that depress productivity growth by discouraging savings and investment. Weak productivity adds to inflation by driving up unit costs and to unemployment by making the United States less competitive in world markets.

Supply-siders rejected the Keynesian insistence on a trade-off between inflation and unemployment.[27] Making government less burdensome, they were convinced, would relieve both problems. They also rejected the notion that fiscal policy influences economic behavior by affecting aggregate demand. As one of the leading supply-siders put it, "There is no payoff in focusing fiscal policy on the control of aggregate demand."[28] Instead, government affects behavior by altering the relative prices—that is, the costs and benefits—of different economic activities. The distribution of the tax burden and of government expenditure—not total revenue and expenditure, influences the actions of workers, employers, and others. Taxing interest income and allowing a deduction for interest payments make borrowing more advantageous than saving. High marginal tax rates and generous transfer payments change the relative benefit of work and leisure. High tax rates drive a "wedge" between the market value of production and the after-tax return to producers; what producers keep is less than the value of what they produce. The wider the wedge, the greater the distortion in relative prices and, hence, the greater the incentive to behave in ways that damage the long-term health of the economy.

With the election of Ronald Reagan in 1980, supply-side analysis became, for a while, the nation's fiscal policy, offering a vision of painless economic growth. Cutting taxes and making government regulation less intrusive would, the new president and supply-siders agreed, spur economic and productivity growth, stimulate savings and investment, and, when combined with monetary restraint, stabilize prices.

Unlike the theory of rational expectations, which told politicians what they could not do, supply-side prescriptions told them what they *could* do. As applied by President Reagan, supply-side was more than a theory of how the economy works. It also was the model of what the role of government should be. It thus joined together, Heclo and Penner explained,

the problem of a malfunctioning economy and the problem of a malfunctioning big government. It was an act of political theory to link the latter as the chief cause of the former. Under this overriding concept . . . all strands of the Reagan economy program were fully compatible and mutually reinforcing. All were means of hemming in government so as to release the inherent forces of the market economy and thus create sustained economic growth.[29]

Getting the government to adopt supply-side policies was a necessary step in establishing a new fiscal consensus. It was also necessary that the policy be perceived to have restored economic vigor and budgetary effectiveness. Consensus was still lacking, however, in 1989, when Reagan left office. Eight years after supply-side policies had been introduced, there was little agreement about what they had accomplished.

DEFICIT BUDGETING: 1981–1989

From the outset, Ronald Reagan staked the success of his presidency on the budget and the economy. The new president did not take the rational expectations view that the economy goes through self-correcting cycles and that therefore it would be appropriate for the government to remain on the sidelines. His ultimate aim undoubtedly was less government intervention, but in his first year, Reagan was an active and determined intervenor who spent much of his political capital on budget matters. He allowed the budget to dominate his political agenda, to pattern relations with Congress, and, through a series of prime-time telecasts, to shape his public image.

In sorting out what Reagan accomplished, one is struck by the sharp contrast between immediate success at the start and protracted stalemate in subsequent years. Few presidents so quickly molded the budget to their objectives; few left office so frustrated by budgetary friction and paralysis. In his first year, Reagan skillfully pressured Congress to revamp national priorities, downsize domestic government, and reduce tax burdens.[30] Reagan signed both a $750 billion tax reduction (over five years) and a $130 billion spending reduction (over three years) into law on August 13, 1981. Yet, from late 1981 until late 1987, when a summit agreement established a "cease fire," the president and Congress were locked in continuous budgetary warfare, with neither side able to dislodge the other from its basic positions. The 1987 budget summit committed the president to specific tax and spending policies for the remainder of his term. To honor the agreement, Reagan had to submit a budget at variance with his own preferences. "This budget does not fully reflect my priorities," Reagan declared in disowning his budget for the 1989 fiscal year.[31]

When he left office in January 1989, Reagan could point to a number of economic accomplishments. The economy was in the seventh consecutive year of growth, a peacetime record. Growth added more than 15 million jobs and cut the unemployment rate to slightly more than 5 percent, the lowest it had been since the early 1970s. The economic boom was accompanied by a sharp drop in both inflation and interest rates, and although both of these measures moved upward near the end of the Reagan presidency, they were still far below the peaks of the Carter years. The economic record was tarnished, however, by several failures. The gains were not evenly distributed. High-income groups benefited the most, whereas low-income persons fell further behind.[32] The marked decline in savings continued, and productivity growth was more sluggish than in previous expansions. Neither the cut in taxes nor other supply-side policies generated the expected improvement in savings and productivity.[33]

In terms of the relationship between the budget and the economy, the most alarming development was the upsurge in deficit spending. Before Reagan was elected, supply-siders were agreed that the budget deficit should not stand in the way of tax cuts. Some thought that the deficit, like other budget aggregates, was of little consequence for economic performance; some thought that the tax cuts would pay for themselves by spurring a rise in federal revenue; some believed that the added savings generated by the tax cuts would enable the government to finance the deficit.[34] Reagan, however, entered office with fairly conventional views on the evils of deficit spending, and he targeted a balanced budget as a key objective of his administration. Continuing a theme sounded throughout his successful campaign, Reagan attacked budget deficits in his first inaugural address:

For decades we have piled deficit upon deficit, mortgaging our future and our children's future for the temporary convenience of the present. To continue this long trend is to guarantee tremendous social, cultural, political, and economic upheavals. . . . . It is time to . . . get government back within its means, and to lighten our punitive tax burden. And these will be our first priorities, and on these principles, there will be no compromise.[35]

Two weeks later, in a national telecast, Reagan was even more specific in his commitment to end deficit budgeting. Pointing to a chart showing the gap between revenue and outlays, the president promised that the gap would narrow "as spending cuts continue over the next few years, until finally the two lines come together meaning a balanced budget."[36]

The two lines never converged. They started diverging at once, and the closest Reagan got to balance was the $128 billion deficit in his *first* budget. The difficulty of ending the deficit became apparent to the Reagan White House when it grappled with the details of the budget. Its first revised budget for the 1982 fiscal year (submitted in March 1981) projected a small surplus by the end of the president's first term, but this was predicated on achieving an additional $44 billion in unidentified savings.[37] As the administration became more familiar with the budget outlook, the estimated gap widened considerably. Barely a month after Reagan signed the spending and tax cuts into law, he launched a "September offensive" to obtain additional reductions. Congress balked this time, as it would each time Reagan demanded severe program cutbacks. Within another few months, the economy was moving into recession, budget receipts were plummeting below estimates, and the deficit was soaring. Table 3.4 reports that the actual deficit was $54 billion above projections in fiscal 1982 and $104 billion higher in the 1983 fiscal year. For the remainder of his presidency, Reagan had to decide whether to fight the oversized deficits or to take advantage of them. His political rhetoric continued to wage war on the deficit while his budget policies exploited the deficit to constrain domestic expenditures.[38]

Table 3.4 ESTIMATED AND ACTUAL RECEIPTS, OUTLAYS, AND DEFICITS, 1982–88 (billions of dollars)

Fiscal year	Receipts			Outlays			Deficit		
	Initial estimate	Actual	Difference	Initial estimate	Actual	Difference	Initial estimate	Actual	Difference
1982[a]	650.3	617.8	−32.5	695.3	728.4	33.1	45.0	110.6	65.6
1983	666.1	600.6	−65.5	757.6	796.0	38.4	91.5	195.4	103.9
1984	659.7	666.5	6.8	848.5	851.8	3.3	188.8	185.3	−3.5
1985	745.1	734.1	−11.0	925.5	946.3	20.8	180.4	212.3	31.9
1986	793.7	769.1	−24.6	973.7	989.8	16.1	180.0	220.7	40.7
1987	850.4	854.1	3.7	994.0	1,004.6	10.6	143.6	150.4	6.9
1988	916.6	909.0	−7.6	1,024.3	1,064.0	39.7	107.8	155.1	−47.3

Source: *Budget of the United States Government.*
Notes: The initial estimate is the estimate made in the budget for the particular fiscal year. The actual amount is the amount shown in the first budget submitted after the fiscal year has concluded. The amounts shown here may vary from amounts published in historical series.
[a]Initial estimate for fiscal 1982 is taken from the revised budget submitted by President Reagan.

Although budget deficits were standard operating procedure before Reagan, there was a startling difference between his deficits and those incurred in earlier periods. Previous deficits were relatively small; Reagan's were huge. A few statistics dramatize the difference. Budget deficits averaged $35 billion in the 1970s; they averaged more than $170 billion in the Reagan years. Reagan's deficits averaged more than 4 percent of GNP, compared with only 2 percent in the previous decade. By the time the books were closed on the Reagan era, the national debt (which grows faster than the deficit) had almost tripled, moving from $1 trillion to $2.8 trillion.

How did a president who campaigned on a platform to eradicate the deficit end up with the biggest imbalances in American history? Throughout his term, Reagan frequently castigated Congress for causing big deficits by refusing to enact proposed spending cutbacks. This claim is not borne out by the data set forth in table 3.5, which compares the actual budget results for fiscal 1986 with the forecast for that year when the president unveiled his economic program in 1981. The 1986 data are enlightening for two reasons. First, 1986 was the final year for which detailed projections were published by the Reagan administration when it unveiled its sweeping budget policy in 1981; and, second, the fiscal 1986 deficit was $221 billion, the highest yet recorded. In 1981, a $28 billion surplus was projected for fiscal 1986. Hence, the variance between the projection and the outturn was $249 billion. More than two-thirds of this gap was due to a shortfall in receipts. The remainder was due to increased interest payments. Congress did spend somewhat more than had been projected on transfer payments and domestic programs, but these increases were largely offset by a reduction in defense spending. Overall, congressional action or inaction was not a significant factor in the gargantuan deficits.[39] (Because inflation was much lower than had been projected in 1981, the table understates the increases in real domestic spending and overstates the cuts in defense.)

The economic factors underlying the entrenched deficit are a matter of dispute between supply-siders and their critics. The former attribute the deficit to Reagan's success in curbing inflation and to the Federal Reserve Board's error in sharply contracting the growth in the money supply, thereby causing the 1982 recession. The latter point to inconsistencies in Reagan's economic plan and to the imbalance between the tax and spending reductions. To these explanations may be added the character of economic growth in the 1980s.

Table 3.5 COMPARISON OF 1981 REAGAN PROJECTION AND 1986 REAGAN
BUDGET
(billions of dollars)

Item	1981 forecast of 1986 budget[a]	1986 actual	Contribution to variance between forecasted surplus and actual deficit	
			Amount	Percent[b]
Budget receipts	940.2	769.1	171.1	68.7
Defense outlays	342.7	291.1	51.6	− 20.7
Payments for individuals	445.7	449.4	3.7	1.5
Grants to state and local governments	45.1	59.5	14.4	5.8
Net interest	62.8	136.0	73.2	29.4
Other outlays	58.4	87.3	28.9	11.6
Offsetting receipts	− 42.3	− 33.0	9.3	3.7
Projected surplus	28.2	− 221.2	− 249.4	
				100

Sources: 1981 forecast taken from *Fiscal 1982 Budget Revisions* (March 1981), Tables 17 and 18; 1986 budget taken from *Historical Tables: Budget of the United States Government, Fiscal Year, 1989.*
Note: $17.6 billion in estimated military retirement outlays for fiscal year 1986 are shown in the defense rather than the payments-for-individuals category.
[a]Because of accounting and classification changes since 1981, the forecasted and fiscal 1986 budgets may not be strictly comparable.
[b]The percentages are each category's share of the $249 billion variance between the $28 billion surplus projected in 1981 and the $221 billion deficit actually incurred in 1986.

Supply-Side Explanations

According to this school, underestimation of the deficit was due largely to overestimation of inflation. Reagan initially forecast that the rise in consumer prices would moderate to 8.3 percent in 1982 and to 7.0 percent in 1983. In fact, consumer prices rose only 6.1 percent and 3.2 percent in these two years. With prices climbing much less than had been expected, the cut in taxes was much greater than had been planned and the reduction in real spending much less.[40] When individual income taxes were indexed in 1985 (after three phased-in cuts totaling 25 percent), they were pegged to much lower real marginal rates than had been intended. Reagan's 1981 economic plan was based on a gradual reduction in the growth of the money supply.[41] When the Federal Reserve Board tightened money much more quickly and severely than had been assumed, recession ensued, and nominal GNP was significantly below forecast. In 1986 alone, nominal GNP (which determines the amount of tax collections) was almost $700 billion below the level projected in 1981.

Critical Explanations

Big deficits were ordained from the start by the mismatch between the $750 billion (over five years) in tax cuts enacted in 1981 and the much smaller spending cuts enacted at the same time. Not only did the $44 billion in cuts fail to materialize but the administration won approval of significantly lower reductions than it requested. The 1981 blueprint called for $200 billion in program cuts over a three-year period. Congress, by its own count, cut only about $130 billion, and the actual value of the cuts was lower than that.[42]

Moreover, the 1981 economic plan was inconsistent. It could not achieve both the monetary targets and the forecast for nominal GNP. The administration came in with a high inflation forecast in order to pump up nominal GNP.[43] The drop in inflation and the tightening of the money supply exposed the contradictions in Reagan's policies.

The Inadequate Growth

The most remarkable characteristic of the deficit is that it persisted during the longest peacetime expansion. The United States did not grow out of the budget deficit in the 1980s. According to baseline projections issued by the Congressional Budget Office, it will not grow out of the deficit in the 1990s if current policies are continued.

Why were the 1980s the first peacetime period in American history that the deficit was bigger after protracted expansion than it was during the previous recession? The simple answer is that although economic growth was sustained, it was not sufficiently vigorous to keep pace with the rise in outlays. The inadequacy of growth is evident when the performance of the 1980s is compared with that of earlier decades. Real GNP grew 47 percent in the 1950s, 49 percent in the 1960s; 32 percent in the 1970s; and, with only one year to go in the decade, only about 25 percent thus far in the 1980s. Because the federal budget is programmed for growth, it takes more than a 2 to 3 percent annual expansion to avoid big deficits.

Not only were the causes of the big deficits in dispute, so, too, was the question of what, if anything, should be done to ameliorate them. Supply-siders generally preferred smaller deficits, but not if this was to be accomplished by raising taxes. Fiscal conservatives and Keynesians were concerned that the big deficits would consume the nation's meager savings and either crowd out private investment or compel the United States to borrow heavily from abroad.

Economists and others will argue over the efficacy of supply-side incentives for some time, but this approach has not restored fiscal consensus. Deficits of the magnitude incurred in the Reagan era may prove economically manageable, but they convey a powerful message of policy failure. "Our profession has never been more confused about the economic effects of the deficit," William Niskanen has said.[44] But even those who believe that the oversized deficit will not do lasting harm cannot claim that it was the intended outcome or that it was chosen on the basis of a fiscal norm. Rather, the deficit was the result of numerous executive and legislative actions and inactions, as well as of the surprises delivered by the economy.

INSULATING THE BUDGET FROM THE ECONOMY

More than any other factor, the big deficits fueled budgetary conflict in the 1980s. On one matter, however, politicians of all stripes were agreed: The deficit must be reduced. To do so required insulating budget policy from the performance of the economy. The key instrument for separating the budget and the economy was a set of deficit reduction targets that did not bend to changing circumstances. The Gramm-Rudman-Hollings (GRH) law of 1985 prescribed a series of annual reductions in the deficit, culminating with the promise of budgetary balance in the 1991 fiscal year. To enforce its targets, GRH established an automatic sequestration procedure by which a significant amount of budgetary resources would be canceled, reducing each year's projected deficit to the preset level.

Because they were established for a six-year period, the GRH targets had to disregard cyclical influences on the budget. Recourse to fixed fiscal norms, thus was consistent with diminished use of the budget for short-term adjustments. It also reflected a growing perception of the deficit as a structural problem that would not be remedied by economic growth. When big deficits arrived in the early 1980s, the conventional practice was to dissect them into cyclical and structural components, the former resulting from economic weakness, the latter from a chronic imbalance of receipts and outlays. By mid-decade, however, there was a pervasive realization that this classification contributed to the persistence of huge deficits as cyclical shortfalls augmented future structural imbalances by adding to the debt burden and interest charges. With interest payments accounting for more than half of the annual deficit, it became apparent that today's cyclical problem would become tomorrow's structural deficiency.

To stabilize the debt and interest burden, budget objectives became more limited and insular. Balancing the budget, or at least narrowing the deficit, regained primacy over balancing the economy. There was widespread support for the view that the budget cannot do much fiscal good unless its own structural problems are eased through deficit reduction. In light of the vacillations of the 1970s and the deficits of the 1980s, a more stable budget policy was seen as a good in itself.

The establishment of fiscal targets was preceded by a similar development in monetary policy, with the Federal Reserve Board announcing a target range for each year's growth in the monetary aggregates. Monetary targets, which also were adopted in other industrialized democracies, were prompted by uncertainty about economic conditions, lack of confidence in cyclical policies, and lengthy lags between policy adjustments and economic impacts.[45]

There have been proposals to institutionalize the fiscal norm of a balanced budget in the U.S. Constitution. This would take fixed targets a large step beyond the GRH process and, except in time of crisis, wall off the budget from the economy. A constitutional amendment requiring a balanced budget was approved by the Senate in 1982, but it failed to obtain the necessary two-thirds majority in the House. A constitutional target would be inherently more rigid than a statutory one. Whereas the former can be altered only through the time-consuming amendment process, the latter can be altered by legislation.

The GRH target is not so much a budgetary objective as a budget influencer. Its primary role is to sway current budget decisions, not to lock the government into a course of action that would ensure fulfillment of the objective by a predetermined time. As a political statement, the GRH target must be simple. It cannot become enmeshed in the complications of the economy or the details of the budget. Its strength comes from ease of understanding, not from analytic sophistication. By setting an overall target before spending claims are presented, the government counters pressure for additional funds with restrictive norms that have widespread support.[46]

The notion implicit in GRH—that budget policy should look in-

ward to correcting its own imbalances rather than the economy's—
is not fully implementable. Complete insulation from the economy
is not feasible because the sensitivity of revenue and, to a lesser
extent, outlays to economic conditions would force the budget to
veer from the GRH path if a recession occurs. Congress recognizes
this linkage in the GRH law by allowing itself the option to suspend
the deficit targets in case of weak growth or a projected recession.
Moreover, GRH requires only planned—not actual—adherence to
the target. No corrective action has to be taken after the final projections have been made if the economy or any other factor blocks
attainment of the target. In fact, the target has not been met in any
of the fiscal years for which the GRH process has been completed
thus far (1986–89).

Even if the economy cooperates, Congress can modify the targets
whenever it deems them too onerous. It made one such modification
in 1987, scheduling smaller deficit reductions in the years immediately ahead and postponing the fiscal year in which balance is to
be achieved until 1993.[47] Further modifications are likely to be made
from time to time.

Because GRH has not operated under recessionary conditions, its
fiscal viability has not really been tested yet. It remains to be seen
whether the federal government can be indifferent to the impact of
the economy on the budget or of the budget on economic conditions
for an extended period. The wall of separation may not be able to
withstand shocks of the magnitude that beset the economy in the
1970s, or the brief but sharp downturn that occurred in 1982.

CONCLUSION

The period reviewed in this chapter began with the budget and the
economy sustaining one another and ended with policies that divorced the condition of the budget from the performance of the economy. The period began with consensus on fiscal policy and ended
in dissension over the appropriate course of action. It began with
small deficits and ended with truly gargantuan ones.

Whether a cause or effect of turmoil, the deficit was the dominating
budget story of this period, and especially of the Reagan years. Recent
budget history would have been a lot different if the deficit had been
a lot smaller. The process would have operated in a calmer, more
orderly fashion, Congress would have been in more substantial com-

pliance with established procedures, the President's budget would have retained its commanding influence, and few questions would have been asked about the government's capacity to budget.

The deficit is a measure of the imbalance between the claims on the budget and the capacity of the government to finance those claims. One of the lessons of this period is that ordinary economic growth does not suffice to redress the imbalance. If the economy had been as expansive in the 1970s and 1980s as it was in the two preceding decades, the deficit would have been moderate, and it would not have incapacitated federal budgeting.

Given its economic performance, the federal government had only two major options for restoring balance. One was to generate additional revenue to cover escalating claims, and the other was to trim the claims to fit available resources. The persistence of deficits indicates that the government did not take enough of either of these steps. The next chapter discusses the difficulties of cutting expenditures. The chapter after that looks at its record with respect to taxation.

Notes

1. There is one major exception to this statement. Although the Gramm-Rudman-Hollings targets are preset, they can be suspended if a recession is anticipated or a "growth recession"—less than 1 percent real growth in two consecutive quarters—has occurred.

2. U.S. Government, *Economic Report of the President*, January 1965, (Washington, D.C.: Government Printing Office, 1965), p. 10.

3. The battle over the surcharge is recounted in Lawrence C. Pierce, *The Politics of Fiscal Policy Formation* (Pacific Palisades, Calif.: Goodyear Publishing Company, 1971), especially chapter 7.

4. *The Budget of the United States Government, Fiscal Year 1967*, p. 35.

5. Because unemployment was below 4 percent, the full-employment budget deficit also was $25 billion.

6. *The Budget of the United States Government, Fiscal Year 1969*, p. 8.

7. President Johnson's 1968 Economic Report sounded an optimistic note: "But one day peace will return. . . . We will have that 3 percent of output [the percentage of national output diverted to the war effort] to add—over a year or two—to our normal 4 percent a year of economic growth." *Economic Report of the President*, February 1968, p. 28.

8. Experience with the spending limitations is recounted in Allen Schick, *Congress and Money: Budgeting, Spending, and Taxing* (Washington, D.C.: Urban Institute, 1980), pp. 32–43.

9. To the extent crowding out has occurred, it is reflected in constant-dollar expenditures. That is, nominal spending rises, but not sufficiently to adjust for inflation. For example, between 1968 and 1973, discretionary domestic spending rose from $40 billion to $53 billion. But, adjusted for inflation, these expenditures were lower in 1973 than they had been in 1968.

10. Herbert Stein (who was a member of the Council of Economic Advisors at that time) described the administration's expectations as follows: "The Administration had an ideal picture of the way in which the situation might develop. Unemployment would rise to a little over 4 percent, which was thought to be the rate of unemployment at which inflation would be stable. With a slight excess of unemployment above the 4 percent level, the inflation would decline. . . . When the inflation had declined sufficiently, and the expectation of price stability had become sufficiently strong, the economy would return to full employment (4 percent unemployment)." Herbert Stein, *Presidential Economics*, 2d rev. ed. (Washington, D.C.: American Enterprise Institute, 1988), p. 150.

11. See *The Budget of the United States Government*, Fiscal Year 1972, p. 9.

12. The controls had two phases: Phase I was an absolute freeze on wages and prices for 90 days; Phase II allowed increases of up to 5.5 percent.

13. *The Budget of the United States Government*, Fiscal Year 1972, p. 7.

14. *Ibid.*, p. 9.

15. Charles L. Schultze and others, *Setting National Priorities: The 1973 Budget* (Washington, D.C.: The Brookings Institution, 1972), p. 409.

16. See Herbert Stein, *op. cit.*, p. 187ff.

17. In each of these (and some subsequent) years, actual outlays were below the revised estimates issued when the fiscal year was about half over. This pattern suggests a tendency to overestimate outlays in the revised estimates, so as to make the next year's budget requests appear to be more favorable by comparison. Another possible explanation of this pattern is that agencies are unwilling to admit that not all of the money planned to be spent during the fiscal year in progress will be spent.

18. U.S. Government, *Economic Report of the President*, February 1975, p. 7.

19. Congress did include an antispending pledge in the tax cut extension (PL 94-164), but this statement had no binding effect and was ignored the next year. See *Congressional Quarterly Almanac*, 1975 (Washington, D.C.: Congressional Quarterly, 1976), p. 134.

20. U.S. Office of Management and Budget, *Fiscal Year 1978 Budget Revisions* (Washington, D.C.: Government Printing Office, 1977), p. 10.

21. Publication of these data is prescribed by section 601 of the Congressional Budget Act of 1974; hence, 1975 was the first fiscal year for which OMB reported on the variance between estimated and actual relatively uncontrollable outlays.

22. The theme of continuous budgeting and of repetitive, disappearing budgets was developed by Naomi Caiden and Aaron Wildavsky in *Planning and Budgeting in Poor Countries* (New York: Wiley, 1974).

23. Many of the reasons are discussed in Edward F. Denison, *Accounting for Slower Economic Growth: The United States in the 1970s* (Washington, D.C.: Brookings Institution, 1979); see also Rudolph G. Penner, "Economic Growth," in *Challenge to Leadership*, ed. Isabel Sawhill (Washington, D.C.: Urban Institute Press, 1988), pp. 67–100.

24. The argument for a stable monetary policy is associated with Milton Friedman; see his *A Program for Monetary Stability* (New York: Fordham University Press, 1959).

25. For discussions of rational expectations theory, see David G. Tuerck, "Rational

Expectations and Supply Side Economics: Match or Mismatch?" in *Essays in Supply Side Economics*, ed. David G. Raboy (Washington, D.C.: Institute for Research on the Economics of Taxation, 1982), pp. 65–92.

26. Taken to its logical extreme, rational expectations means "that whatever is wrong with the economy could not have been caused by government. Government neither helps nor hurts." Lester C. Thurow, *Dangerous Currents: The State of Economics* (New York: Random House, 1983), p. 144.

27. Senator Lloyd Bentsen, at the time chairman of the Joint Economic Committee, introduced the Committee's 1980 annual report with a ringing endorsement of supply-side principles. "America does not have to fight inflation during the 1980s by periodically pulling up the drawbridge with recessions that doom millions of Americans to unemployment. The Committee's 1980 report says that steady economic growth, created by productivity gains and accompanied by a stable fiscal policy and a gradual reduction in the growth of the money supply over a period of years, can reduce inflation significantly during the 1980s without increasing unemployment." U.S. Congress, Joint Economic Committee, *Joint Economic Report, 1980*, S. Rept. 96-618, p. 1.

28. Norman B. Ture, "Supply Side Analysis and Public Policy," in Raboy, *op. cit.*, p. 25. Ture continues: ". . . the size of the deficit should not be perceived as a relevant variable for policy manipulation in the interests of attaining designated levels—or rates of growth in— employment, output, income, etc."

29. Hugh Heclo and Rudolph G. Penner, "Fiscal and Political Strategy in the Reagan Administration", in *The Reagan Presidency: An Early Assessment*, ed. Fred I. Greenstein (Baltimore: Johns Hopkins University Press, 1983), p. 28.

30. Reagan's early budget successes are analyzed in Allen Schick, "How the Budget Was Won and Lost", in *President and Congress: Assessing Reagan's First Year*, ed. Norman J. Ornstein (Washington, D.C.: American Enterprise Institute, 1982), pp. 14–43.

31. See "The Budget Message of the President", *The Budget of the United States Government, Fiscal Year 1989*, pp. 1–6

32. See Joseph J. Minarik, "Family Incomes" and Isabel V. Sawhill, "Poverty and the Underclass," in Sawhill, *op. cit.*

33. Supply-siders had an explanation for the low savings rate in the 1980s as well as for other policy failures. They pointed out that because of the postwar baby boom, there were a large number of young adults who typically save little while they purchase homes and establish families. See Paul Craig Roberts, "Supply-Side Economics—Theory and Results," *The Public Interest*, 93 (Fall 1988), p. 35.

34. See Don Fullerton, "On the Possibility of an Inverse Relationship Between Tax Rates and Government Revenues," National Bureau of Economic Research, Working Paper no. 467 (April 1980).

35. The inaugural address is reprinted in *Congressional Quarterly Almanac 1981* (Washington, D.C.: Congressional Quarterly, Inc., 1982), pp. 11–12E.

36. This speech, delivered on February 5, 1981, is reprinted in *Ibid.*, pp. 13–15E.

37. Reagan's Budget Director, David Stockman, described the political use of unidentified savings—known as the "magic asterisk"—as follows: "If we couldn't find the savings in time—and we couldn't—we would issue an IOU. We would call it 'future savings to be identified.' It was marvelously creative. A magic asterisk item would cost *negative* $30 billion . . . . $40 billion . . . . Whatever it took to get to a balanced budget in 1984 after we toted up the individual budget cuts we'd actually approved." See David A. Stockman, *The Triumph of Politics: Why the Reagan Revolution Failed* (New York: Harper and Row, 1986), p. 124.

38. Reagan's budgetary confrontations with Congress and his tactical use of the deficit

to constrain federal spending are chronicled in Joseph White and Aaron Wildavsky, *The Battle of the Budget* (University of California Press, forthcoming).

39. The same conclusion is reached in John C. Weicher, "Accounting for the Deficit," in *Contemporary Economic Problems: The Economy in Deficit*, ed. Philip Cagan (Washington, D.C.: American Enterprise Institute, 1985), p. 5.

40. Roberts, *op. cit.*, p. 30, argues that "The forecast failed to predict the deficit not because of its optimism about economic growth, but because of its pessimism about inflation . . . . When the Fed brought inflation down rapidly, far below the Administration's forecast, the budget plan collapsed. The spending 'cuts' in nominal dollars that were achieved in 1981 were converted into increases in real outlays, and revenues projected on a more gradual reduction in inflation failed to materialize."

41. See *A Program For Economic Recovery*, February 18, 1981, pp. 22–23.

42. The problems of calculating the actual spending cuts made in 1981 are discussed in John W. Ellwood, *Reductions in U.S. Domestic Spending* (New Brunswick: Transaction Books, 1982).

43. See Stein, *op. cit.*, p. 269–71.

44. William Niskanen, "The Political Economy of Gramm-Rudman and Other Policy 'Accidents'," Paper presented at the 1987 Annual Meeting of the American Economic Association, p. 9.

45. See Organization for Economic Cooperation and Development, *Monetary Targets and Inflation Control* (Paris: 1979).

46. A British Government paper on public expenditure issued in 1984 argued for preset targets: "There will be some who will argue that it makes little sense to consider, still less to decide upon, public spending totals without a clear idea of the implications for individual programmes. The government believes that such thinking has been largely responsible for the upward drift of public expenditure over many years. It is necessary to turn the argument round the other way, to decide first what can and should be afforded, then to set expenditure plans for individual programmes consistently with that decision." *The Next Ten Years: Public Expenditure and Taxation Into the 1990s*, Cmnd. 9189, March 1984, p. 13.

47. The following table shows the maximum deficit levels prescribed in the 1985 GRH law and the revised levels set in the 1987 modifications (in billions of dollars):

Fiscal Year	1985 Law	1987 Law
1986	$171.9	—
1987	144	—
1988	108	144
1989	72	136
1990	36	100
1991	0	64
1992	—	28
1993	—	0

Chapter 4

CUTTING BACK AND SPENDING MORE

Budgeting is an adaptive process that is molded to the needs and opportunities of the times. Adaptation to changing conditions is essential if budgeting is to remain an effective policy and management process of government. Budgeting cannot be practiced the same way and produce the same results when resources are scarce as when they are plentiful. In chapter 2, we saw how budgeting was adapted to postwar economic and program expansion. The arrival of more austere circumstances in the 1970s and efforts to cut back federal spending in the 1980s have impelled budgeting to adjust again, this time from an incremental process that encourages expansionary claims to a process that constrains the growth in spending. To cut, expectations have to be changed, and the capacity to ration resources has to be bolstered.

The adjustment has been difficult, not only because it is generally easier to expand than to contract but because changes made during the growth era entrenched strong claims on the budget and weakened the control of expenditure. The key developments were the growth of mandatory expenditure, especially indexed entitlements, and Reagan's determination to increase defense spending steeply. This chapter concentrates on the adjustments made to slow the growth of spending during the Reagan years. It confronts a problem that is reflected in the title of the chapter: At the same time that programs have been cut, spending has continued to rise. The problem is attributable to the political difficulty of cutting back, characteristics of contemporary budgeting that drive expenditures upward even when programs have been retrenched, and the manner in which the cuts have been made and measured.

THE CUTTING TOOLS

Over decades of experience, budget makers in the legislative and executive branches developed the capacity to fine-tune federal spending to produce each year's desired outcomes. By focusing on the amount by which spending should be varied from the previous year's level, executive and legislative controllers could engineer relatively sizable increases when expansion was the order of the day, and smaller increases (or reductions) when finances were tight or the demand for economy in government strong. This capacity to adjust each year's spending to the circumstances at hand enabled the government to keep the budget at or close to balance despite cyclical swings in economic conditions.

The tools for cutting expenditure were simple but adequate. Budget makers would estimate available resources and would scour the lists of items requested by agencies to determine where savings could be obtained. They had a few operating rules that helped them obtain the desired results: disapprove requested increases, slow down purchases and other expenses, and abolish vacant positions. Funds could be saved by giving agencies less than a full adjustment for inflation, and in a particularly tight budget, resources could be taken away from them.

Nowadays, however, the government cannot exercise sufficient restraint simply by restoring the controls and procedures that enabled it to hold down spending in the past. The old controls were designed for discretionary expenditure (principally, the expenses of agency operations, defense spending, and some grant programs), which accounted for almost all federal spending in the pregrowth era. These controls were centered around the annual review, by both executive and legislative budgeters, of departmental estimates, and their efficacy depended on the discretion of the president and Congress to provide more or less than had been appropriated the year before. Today, however, the bulk of the budget is spent on mandatory charges, such as indexed entitlements and interest payments. These mandatory expenditures cannot be effectively controlled by presidential and appropriations review. No matter what the president recommends or the appropriators decide, the amounts spent will be determined by existing laws, not by new budget actions. To hold down the rise in mandated costs, it has been necessary to devise new cutting tools that can reach to the laws establishing entitlements and payment formulas. This section first examines the tools for cutting discretionary spending; it then turns to the means of curtailing mandatory expenditure, including loans made or guaranteed by the government.

Cutting Discretionary Expenditure

When Ronald Reagan sought to downsize domestic government in 1981, there was no impediment to requesting cuts in federal programs. Getting the proposed cuts approved by Congress was a difficult task, but relationships had stabilized into a fairly predictable division of labor between the two branches. The president typically would ask for more than had been provided the previous year, and the appropriations committees, which closely monitored the size of the increment, would withhold part of the requested increase. This pattern of behavior allowed the appropriations committees both to cut back and to spend more, and thereby to satisfy conflicting pressures facing congressmen—that is, to expand programs and to cut the budget.[1]

By recommending discretionary domestic spending well below the previous level, Ronald Reagan disrupted the comfortable routine of the appropriations committees and made it difficult for them to claim that they were both cutting expenditures and enriching programs. But simply asking for less was not sufficient to enable the president to prevail in Congress. There was a high probability that the appropriations committees, when forced to choose between the two courses, would continue to behave as incrementalists. In the short run, the president's popularity and political skills might suffice to carry the day. But there was a real possibility that even if domestic appropriations were cut, they would resume an upward course once relations with Congress returned to a more normal pattern. To obtain durable cutbacks, the president needed new tools to deal with discretionary appropriations. In 1981, he turned to reconciliation, a process generally associated with mandatory expenditure. We will consider this device in discussing mandatory spending later in this section.

Reagan inherited another weapon that could be used to trim discretionary items—the power to impound appropriated funds. We noted in chapter 2 that although the withholding of funds was an old practice, the emergence of the term *impoundment* after the New Deal reflected a change in the concept of appropriations from a "lid on spending" to a "mandate to spend." Impoundment led to periodic confrontations between the president and Congress and to the Impoundment Control Act of 1974, which set forth ground rules for resolving disputes between the two branches. The Act, by enabling the president to propose impoundments and Congress to overturn them, had the potential to augment or to constrain presidential power. Whether it did one or the other depended on the vigor of the president and Congress in exercising their respective impoundment powers.

Under the rules specified in 1974, the president could either defer or propose the rescission of appropriated funds. Deferrals, which delay the use of funds, would continue in effect unless disapproved by either the House or Senate; rescissions, which cancel prior appropriations, would take effect only if they were enacted into law within forty-five days after being proposed.[2] Both Gerald Ford and Jimmy Carter—the first presidents equipped with this power—had some success (as shown later in this chapter, in table 4.4) in rescinding and deferring appropriated funds. But Ronald Reagan made much greater use of the impoundment process at the start of his presidency than his predecessors had. Reagan recommended the rescission of $15 billion in 1981, more than the total proposed by Ford and Carter in the previous six years. Congress approved $12 billion of this amount and it also accepted, by inaction, the deferral of some $11 billion that year and the next. Reagan's early impoundment successes gave him a fast start in curtailing discretionary programs, and demonstrated how a process designed to regulate conflicts between the president and Congress could become a powerful cutting tool.

Budgeting for Discretionary and Mandatory Expenditure

As mandated costs grew in budgetary prominence, the government needed new tools for dealing with them. The almost two-thirds of the budget spent on entitlements and interest cannot be cut through either impoundment or appropriation.[3] To avoid a double standard in which discretionary programs are effectively controlled, whereas mandatory ones escape scrutiny, Congress united the two types of spending in a comprehensive budget process.[4] The 1974 Budget Act was instigated by a variety of concerns, but it probably would not have been enacted if virtually all spending had continued to be for discretionary items controlled by the appropriations committees.[5]

The Budget Act combined discretionary and mandatory spending into two annual budget resolutions, one scheduled for adoption early in the session before Congress acted on appropriations and other budget-related legislation, the other late in the session after work on these measures had been completed.[6] When the Budget Act was being developed, there was considerable sentiment in Congress to impose strong controls on spending, but the enacted version was essentially a neutral instrument that could augment or curtail expenditure as Congress saw fit. In the 1975–80 period, the new budget process probably exerted modest upward influence on spending; in Reagan's first year, 1981, it was used boldly to obtain sizable cuts in both discretionary and mandatory programs.[7] Key votes on the budget resolution shortly after Reagan took office paved the way for enactment of many of the cutbacks proposed by the president.

By itself, the budget resolution has limited utility as a cutting tool. It can make the first incision, but it cannot actually cut programs out of the budget. There are two reasons for this incapacity. First, the resolution is a concurrent resolution, not a statute; hence, it cannot make or change laws. Second, the resolution sets forth spending totals and broad priorities; it does not identify specific programs. The policies enunciated or assumed in a budget resolution are effective only to the extent that they are implemented in appropriation bills and other budget measures.

Its limited scope gives the resolution potential advantage as a cutting tool. Members vote on total spending and on the size of the deficit before they consider funding levels for specific programs. Therefore, they can vote to cut back without knowing precisely where the cuts will fall. Of course, this advantage can turn into a drawback if Congress fails to implement the cuts anticipated in the budget resolution. In 1981, some swing members, who supplied Reagan's margin of victory, were persuaded to support reductions in the resolution by assurances that they could later vote for somewhat higher appropriations.[8] In subsequent years, it was not uncommon for members to "do the right thing" in the budget resolution by voting to cut federal spending, and then turn around and "do the right thing" in appropriation bills by voting to spend more on popular programs.[9]

Cutting through Reconciliation

Failure to carry through on the policies adopted in the budget resolution is especially serious in the case of mandated programs because the budgeted cuts do not materialize unless Congress passes legislation taking back benefits obligated in existing law. The president's role is potentially weak because Congress can ignore his proposals to trim entitlements, as it usually did when Ford and Carter recommended cuts. In the 1970s, the adopted budget resolution repeatedly assumed that "legislative savings" would be achieved by curtailing entitlements. But to realize the assumed savings, the same committees that had devised the benefit programs in the first instance had to initiate legislation undoing their own accomplishments. Not surprisingly, they were rarely willing to do so, with the result that legislative inaction triumphed over budget policy, and the promised savings vanished.

The solution to this problem came a year before Reagan took office, when Congress made initial use of the reconciliation process established in the 1974 Budget Act. The original purpose of reconciliation was to align the spending and revenue decisions made after adoption of the first budget resolution with the policies finalized in the second resolution. For example, if Congress had appropriated more than the amount allowed in the second resolution, it could use reconciliation to reduce spending to the budgeted level. Reconciliation was to be activated shortly before the fiscal year was to start, when spending plans were already firm. As things turned out, reconciliation could not be used in this manner because it was unrealistic for Congress to take back in September the funds it had provided only one or two months earlier.

In 1980, Congress shifted reconciliation from the second resolution to the first, and it targeted the process on old entitlements rather than on new appropriations.[10] Reconciliation's strength comes from instructions adopted in the budget resolution directing certain committees to report changes in expenditures under their jurisdiction. The instructions tell each designated committee the amount of savings it has to produce, and they usually set a deadline by which implementing legislation is to be reported. Although the instructions do not specify which programs are to be cut, the affected committees generally have a good idea of where the ax will fall. Assumptions about the cuts to be made are sometimes published in the reports accompanying the budget resolution, but committees are not bound by these expectations, and they can meet the savings target by making cuts elsewhere. Affected committees submit their recommendations to the budget committees, which package the proposals without substantive change in an omnibus reconciliation bill.[11] Congress then considers the entire bill under expedited procedures in the Senate and under special rules restricting the floor amendments that can be offered in the House.[12]

The initial use of reconciliation in 1980 was quite limited. Outlay savings were limited to a single fiscal year and totaled only about $4 billion. Some committees met their target by recommending temporary savings, which automatically expired the following year, or

by manipulating the date for making certain payments. In 1981, reconciliation was stretched to three years in the expectation that its
longer reach would spur committees to produce permanent savings.
That year's reconciliation was the vehicle for the enactment of the
bulk of the cuts sought by President Reagan. According to estimates
made at the time, Congress pruned about $160 billion in budget
authority and $130 billion in outlays over a three-year period, far in
excess of the savings generated in any other year.[13] Although a few
committees trimmed a bit less than they were instructed to do, most
met their savings target, and some exceeded it.

These outsized savings were due to the breadth of that year's reconciliation exercise. The instructions covered both mandatory entitlements and discretionary expenditure funded in annual
appropriation bills. In fact, about 60 percent of the cutbacks were in
discretionary accounts. The extension of reconciliation to discretionary programs was critical to the achievement of Reagan's budget
objectives. Without it, the president had no assurance that the cuts
would be lasting. Even if they provided less in 1981, the appropriations committees could revert to incremental behavior in subsequent years.

Applying reconciliation to appropriations was a complicated procedure that drew authorizing committees into the process. To cut
future appropriations, it was necessary to lower future authorizations
below enacted or projected levels.[14] If the rules were followed, the
lower authorizations would constrain the amounts that Congress
appropriated in subsequent years.

Controlling Loans and Guarantees

By the early 1980s, loans and guarantees were big business. The
volume of direct loans was almost $40 billion in 1981, up from $19
billion in 1974, when the Budget Act was enacted. During the same
period, the annual volume of guaranteed loans ballooned from $30
billion to $83 billion.

OMB and the budget committees moved in the early 1980s to
install a credit budget that would parallel the regular budget process
and would be subject to similar controls. As credit budgeting evolved,
loans and guarantees were controlled by three sets of legislative
decisions—authorizations, appropriations, and budget resolution—
the same types of congressional action that govern direct spending.
Authorizing legislation establishes each credit program and, in most
cases, limits the amount of loans or guarantees that may be outstand-

ing at any time. This control predates the credit budget system.[15] Appropriation bills impose annual limits on the amount of loans or guarantees that may be issued for each account that has credit activity. At present, appropriation limits are set for approximately one-third of the direct loans and three-quarters of the guaranteed loans made each year. Each budget resolution limits total direct loan obligations and guaranteed loan commitments and allocates these amounts among the functions in the budget. The limitations are a ceiling for the year immediately ahead and a target for the two years beyond that.

Near the end of the Reagan presidency, OMB proposed fuller integration of the credit budget and direct expenditure. It recommended that the federal budget record the subsidy value of new loans as current expenditure. In the case of direct loans, the difference between the face value of the loan and the amount it brought in when resold would be budgeted as the subsidized cost; in the case of guaranteed loans, the subsidy would be the cost of reinsurance purchased by the government. This plan has not been approved by Congress.[16]

How Much Was Cut?

How vigorously were the cutting tools wielded during the Reagan presidency? The tools discussed in this section differ in the extent to which cutbacks can be clearly linked to their use. The most certain cuts were those made in 1981 and 1982 through the rescission procedures of the Impoundment Control Act. The rescissions, which require the active concurrence of Congress, canceled previous appropriations. Although not every dollar rescinded was a dollar saved—some of the rescinded funds probably would have lapsed—billions of dollars were pared from federal spending. The deferrals made at the same time are more difficult to assess. Some lowered future spending levels, but many merely shifted the use of funds into the next year.

It is also difficult to measure the impact of the credit controls on loan activity. There is some evidence that many appropriation limitations have been set well above anticipated credit levels, and they have not effectively constrained the volume of loans or guarantees.[17] Nevertheless, there has been a steep downturn in recent direct lending. After rising to $53 billion in 1985 (before the new credit controls were in place), direct loan obligations declined to $27 billion in 1988. (This is a gross amount; hence, it does not include loan repayments or asset sales.) This has been a steeper decline than in any other area of the budget. There also has been some moderation in loan guarantees, which receded to $100 billion in 1988 from the $159 billion peak reached two years earlier.[18] Part of the drop-off was probably caused by the credit controls, but part was undoubtedly due to other factors that reduced demand for federally assisted credit, such as the sharp drop in interest rates and changes in agriculture and housing, two credit-hungry sectors. One should not rule out the possibility that some credit activity has been shifted off-budget—beyond the reach of new controls—to federally sponsored enterprises.[19] The volume of loans issued by these enterprises soared from $119 billion in 1981 to $425 billion in 1988, a far greater increase than ensued in direct or guaranteed lending by federal agencies.[20]

Measuring the reductions achieved through the reconciliation process poses a number of problems. The most important of these pertains to the "baseline" estimates, an important measuring rod that is examined in the next section. Another problem is that after the first wave of cuts in 1981, Congress restored some benefits or raised authorization/appropriation levels. "Each year," David Stockman complained, "they chip away, adding partial benefit restorations to whatever hostage legislation comes along. Such provisions were added to the deficit reduction bill in 1984 and the farm bill in 1985."[21] Medicaid is another program in which benefits were expanded in the late 1980s after having been cut earlier in the decade. Because of these policy reversals and the temporary status of many cutbacks, one would greatly exaggerate the savings made through reconciliation by adding up the reductions claimed each year the process was used.

Those who have looked closely at the numbers generally agree that sizable reductions were made in federal spending, but much less than was claimed in 1981. David Stockman has estimated that fiscal 1986 outlays were $52 billion below what they would have been if pre-Reagan policies had been continued.[22] The Congressional Budget Office has published a slightly higher estimate, a $56 billion reduction in fiscal 1985 outlays compared to the pre-Reagan baseline.[23] According to CBO, the cuts were almost equally divided between mandatory programs and discretionary domestic expenditure. But because the latter takes a much smaller share of the budget, it has has borne disproportionately higher cutbacks.

Although the cuts have forced discretionary spending down, they generally have merely slowed or stabilized the growth in mandatory expenditure. Payments for individuals (almost all of them entitlements) slipped from 10.8 percent of GNP in 1981 to 10.4 percent in 1988; nondefense discretionary spending dropped much more steeply, from 5.2 percent of GNP to 3.3 percent.[24] Mandatory spending has grown faster than inflation; nondefense discretionary spending has increased much slower. After adjustment for inflation, payments for individuals rose more than 15 percent during the Reagan years, whereas real discretionary spending dropped more than 35 percent. The reported decline in nondefense discretionary spending surely has been overstated by budget gimmicks such as asset sales. Yet, it is highly probable that through freezes and some cutbacks, this area of the budget lost real resources.[25]

The fate of discretionary programs suggests that some of the old cutting tools may have been more effective than the newer ones. Reconciliation, the process best suited for curtailing mandatory expenditure, appears to have had a weaker influence than the appropriations process. The budget deficit and the threat of presidential veto probably have been a bigger drag on spending than has the opportunity to instruct committees to trim mandatory programs. One reason for this is that in contrast to most mandated spending, which continues to rise unless Congress acts to reduce benefits, virtually all discretionary programs require new appropriations each year. Another is that after succumbing to Reagan's demands at the start, Congress blunted some of the tools used to cut the budget.

DULLING THE TOOLS

White House efforts to retrench domestic spending persisted throughout the Reagan presidency, but, after 1981, they were generally unsuccessful. Here and there, Congress terminated a few programs. The broader picture, however, was of Congress holding on to programs despite the constrained budget environment by giving agencies only a partial adjustment for inflation. The programs saved by Congress one year were targeted for elimination by Reagan the next year. This pattern continued until the close of the Reagan era. Reagan's last budget, submitted in January 1989, called for saving more than $30 billion by ending or curtailing some 80 programs. Virtually all of the terminations proposed in that budget had been requested in previous Reagan budgets and had been denied by Congress.

The period from 1982 until 1989 was one of protracted budgetary conflict and stalemate. Reagan repeatedly demanded spending cuts, and Congress refused to go along with most of them. Not every year was a replay of the previous one, however. Both the president and Congress contoured their behavior to the political calendar. As elections approached, Reagan moderated his demands for cuts and was more willing to reach accommodations with Congress. Deficit reductions were enacted in three consecutive election years—1982, 1984, and 1986—and the 1987 budget summit agreement was negotiated with an eye on the next year's elections.

It was characteristic of these deficit reductions to be portrayed as "down payments," modest inroads into the deficit made through a combination of relatively minor revenue and spending adjustments. In each year, Congress gave Reagan much less by way of cutbacks than he had asked for, and it openly used baseline projections to trumpet its budget-cutting accomplishments.

Congress did more than "just say no" to the president. In the course of rebuffing the White House, Congress significantly weakened the capacity of the government to cut the budget. The White House also contributed to attenuation of the government's budget-cutting capabilities by demanding unrealistic cutbacks, using inflated budget figures to claim bigger cuts than were being made, and competing with Congress to devise bookkeeping gimmicks. As a result, George Bush entered office in 1989 with less effective cutting tools at his disposal than Reagan had eight years earlier. Budgeting has not been reprogrammed for growth, but neither has it the capacity to slice big chunks from federal spending. The development of baselines has created a facade of budget slashes that obscures the fact that several of the instruments used to cut spending in Reagan's first year have been dulled both by Congress and by the executive branch.

The Alchemy of Baselines

To explain how Congress has attenuated the government's cutback tools, it is necessary to begin with a technical matter that has broad policy implications—the baseline used to define and measure cutbacks. The baseline is a legitimate concept that has been put to questionable use. In the hands of skilled manipulators, it has become the alchemy of federal budgeting, capable of transforming an increase into a reduction.

For many decades—possibly from the very start of federal budgeting—a cut was defined as a reduction below the previous spending level or below the amount requested by the president. Now, however, a cut usually refers to a level of spending below the baseline. Almost all references to cutbacks or deficit reduction take the baseline as their reference point. Thus, it is impossible to measure the amount being cut without first computing the baseline.

The baseline assumes that existing programs will continue without policy change. It adjusts projected expenditures for estimated inflation and mandated workload changes.[26] A simple example will show how a baseline is constructed and used. A program spending $100 million a year and projected to have an annual 5 percent increase in participants and a 5 percent inflation rate would have approximately a $110 million baseline for the next year, a $121 million baseline for the second year, and a $133 million baseline for the third year. These hypothetical extrapolations are highly sensitive to the assumptions underlying them. Any action projected to reduce spending below these hypothetical levels would be scored as a cutback, even if spending would still be above the previous year's.

The government has two main instruments for reducing spending below the baseline. One is to appropriate less for discretionary programs; the other is to modify eligibility rules or payment rates for entitlement programs. Suppose that a discretionary program with the spending profile outlined above receives a $105 million appropriation for the next year. Using their "old math," the appropriations committees would record this as a $5 million increase. This traditional way of keeping score has one big advantage. It does not require any assumptions about future behavior or conditions but is based solely on past action. There is no place in it for supposition about what might happen in the future, no need to speculate about what next year's inflation rate might be. When the baseline is used, the same $105 million appropriation is scored as a cutback, even though it is above the previous level. The political advantage of transforming an increase into a reduction is enormous because it enables the appropriations committees to continue their historic role of cutting the budget and financing programs.

The baseline computations are a bit more complicated for entitlements. In these programs, past spending may not be a reliable guide to future demands on the budget. If Congress does nothing, future spending almost certainly will differ from past levels because of changes in the number of eligible recipients and payment rates. Each year, for example, Social Security costs automatically rise because of an increase in the elderly population and the mandatory adjustment of payments for inflation. To hold Social Security spending constant would require a cutback in eligibility or payments. If Congress changes Social Security or other entitlements, it can only estimate the effects on future spending. In computing cuts in entitlements, the baseline's scorekeepers must make assumptions about the behavioral changes that might ensue from legislative action. Estimates must be made of future spending if current policies are continued and of the impact of changes on those projected spending levels. The difference between the two sets of figures is the increase or decrease from the baseline. To avoid the chaos, ill-feelings, and misunderstanding that might result from midsession changes in the underlying estimates, the assumptions used when the reconciliation instructions are formulated are generally retained through the budget cycle. They are not usually revised to take into account later economic or program data. Any variance between assumed and actual conditions will result in higher or lower savings than were expected when the reconciliation instructions were issued.

In baseline budgeting, therefore, all reported cutbacks are assumed. The assumed savings are realized only to the extent that the economic or programmatic assumptions materialize. Any deviation between the actual and assumed behavior will result in an overestimation or underestimation of the reported cuts. It is often impossible to determine the true size of the cuts because the detailed assumptions embedded in the baseline are not published, and the assumptions are not adjusted as later data become available. Just about the only thing that can be said confidently about the baseline is that the official data are likely to be wrong.

Baseline calculations are not academic exercises; they are the metric of federal budgeting. As former OMB official Timothy Muris has written, they determine "the fate of program proposals. CBO estimates are the starting point for program analysis and the ending point to determine whether proposals exceed the allocations of the congressional budget resolution."[27] How did the baseline garner this decisive role in budgeting? Interest in the baseline was spurred initially by section 605 of the Congressional Budget Act, which requires the president to prepare an estimate of the "budget outlays and proposed budget authority that would be included in the budget for the following fiscal year if programs and activities of the United States government were carried on during the year at the same level as the current fiscal year without a change in policy."

The "current policy baseline," as the concept was then called, was devised by the Senate Budget committee in the mid-1970s, shortly after the congressional budget process was launched.[28] The committee wanted a neutral measure that would not be influenced by the president's budget and that would enable Congress to distinguish between changes in spending resulting from new actions and those resulting from past decisions, economic conditions, and other non-legislative factors. The baseline enabled the committee to measure Congress's impact on the budget. Presumably, any variance between the baseline and the congressional budget would be due to policy changes.

The baseline also enabled the Senate Budget Committee to claim that it was cutting the budget even though its allocations exceeded the president's recommendation. This was a much-welcomed quality, for the committee struggled in its early years to demonstrate that it was controlling expenditures while accommodating program demands. But after several years of use, the current policy baseline was strongly attacked by Senate Republicans and some Democrats, who argued that it had an expansionary bias and distorted the public's perception of what Congress was doing to the budget.[29] In response, the committee switched to a narrower "current law" baseline, which, unlike the current policy version, does not inflate discretionary appropriations. The current law baseline is significantly below the current policy projection, and, because of the compounding effect of inflation on the outyears, the gap between the two widens for each year that the projection is extended into the future. In 1979, for example, CBO estimated that baseline outlays under current policy assumptions would be 2.5 percent above current law projections in the first year, 5.5 percent in the second year, and 8.3 percent in the third year.[30]

When he became OMB director in 1981, David Stockman brought Congress's baseline concepts with him. But rather than use the current law baseline, he applied the broader current policy measure instead. This enabled him to claim substantially higher savings in discretionary programs and to claim the same inflated savings in entitlements. At the time that he was publicly trumpeting the cutbacks, Stockman was confiding to journalist William Greider that they were greatly overstated. "There was less there than met the eye . . . . What this was was a cut from an artificial CBO base. That's why it looked so big. But it wasn't . . . . The numbers are just out of this world. The government would never have been up at those levels in the CBO base."[31] Budget expert John Ellwood has estimated that the budget authority savings from the reconciliation act would have been 37 percent lower and the outlay savings 72 percent lower if the current law baseline had been used instead of the current policy measure.[32] The estimated fiscal 1982 outlay savings from reconciliation were \$35 billion on a current policy basis but only \$10 billion on a current law basis.

Why did Republicans, who only a few years earlier lambasted the current policy concept as biased and expansionary, embrace it in 1981, and why did congressional Democrats go along with this method of measuring the cutbacks? The simple but sufficient answer is that the Republicans wanted to magnify the reported savings, and the Democrats wanted the actual cuts to be less than they appeared to be. The current policy baseline allowed the Republicans to claim more savings and the Democrats to save more programs, a happy combination for politicians facing difficult choices.

As the budget predicament tightened in the 1980s, all budget makers climbed aboard the current policy bandwagon. The House Budget Committee computed its budget resolution, and most authorizing committees reported their recommendations in terms of the baseline. (The "current policy" label has been dropped, but this is the measurement almost always used in baseline projections.)[33] Although they still compare their actions to the previous appropriation and the president's request, the appropriations committees also have found it convenient to hide behind the baseline. The baseline was used by presidential and congressional negotiators to hammer out summit agreements on the budget in 1987 and 1989. When these agreements were reached, only changes to the baseline were published. The baseline numbers were not disclosed, nor was the previous spending level.

The baseline has become a dense barrier separating budget insiders, who know what the numbers mean, from outsiders, including seasoned budget observers, who cannot figure out what is being done to the budget unless they uncover the assumptions behind the numbers. If they manage to do so, outsiders will find that the baseline has discouraged budget cuts in a number of ways. First, as already noted, it permits budget makers to label an increase above the previous spending level as a reduction. This transformation has been especially useful in the 1980s because Reagan's penchant for requesting less than the previous level for many domestic programs hindered Congress's ability to claim that it was controlling the budget and adequately financing authorized programs. The baseline now substitutes for the president's budget in enabling Congress to take credit for cutbacks.

Second, by blowing up the baseline to unrealistically high levels—well above the amounts likely to be spent—the president and Congress have exaggerated the claimed deficit reduction. Defense spending, federal pay, and medicare have been three favorite areas for using this ploy. In 1984, Congress adopted a budget resolution based largely on an agreement with the White House that assumed $149 billion in deficit reduction over a three-year period. More than one-third of the claimed savings ($58 billion) were to be achieved by holding future increases in defense spending below the baseline. These savings were claimed at a time when the defense buildup was beginning to moderate and when there was no prospect that appropriations would even come near baseline levels. A similar accounting trick was used in 1986 to claim $22 billion in defense savings despite an appropriation that was $8 billion above the previous year's level.

Federal pay has been a fertile area for manipulation of the baseline. Each baseline assumes an annual increase for federal pay. Any increase below the assumed rate is logged as a deficit reduction, even if Congress does not actually reduce appropriations by an amount equivalent to the assumed savings in pay. Medicare has also invited manipulation because the baseline assumes bigger-than-likely increases in reimbursement rates to hospitals and physicians. All it takes to claim savings is to raise reimbursements by an amount less than has been assumed in the baseline. During the 1980s, Congress reportedly has lopped some $50 billion from it, but Medicare spending has tripled.

Third, the rules used in constructing the baseline have enabled inventive budget makers to fabricate cutbacks by making temporary adjustments in expenditure. Congress takes full credit for temporary savings that reduce spending in the year(s) immediately ahead but have no impact on long-term expenditures. In computing the dollar value of cuts, the baseline's scorekeepers do not distinguish between nonrecurring adjustments and more durable program modifications. In 1981 and 1982, for example, Congress claimed substantial reconciliation savings by temporarily reducing Medicaid payments to the states, Medicare reimbursements to hospitals, cost-of-living adjustments in military and civil service pensions, and food stamp allotments.[34] Temporary savings are the best kind because—unlike permanent ones, which can be claimed only once—they can be counted again and again.[35] For example, billions of dollars have been claimed as savings by repeatedly deferring the annual federal pay increase from October to January. Because the postponement is supposed to be temporary, the next year's baseline assumes that the pay increase will revert to October. When it is delayed again, additional savings materialize.

The baseline's rules invite other manipulations of the fiscal calendar, such as the deferral of program enhancements into the out-years. If Congress were to increase a program's spending at once, the added cost would show up in that or the next year's baseline. If, however, the increase is scheduled to take effect two to three years later, it will not appear in either the current or future baselines as a spending increase. By the time the increase is phased in, it will be safely tucked into the baseline as old spending, not as an increase.

Although it has been misused and has generated a great deal of misunderstanding, the baseline is a necessary and proper tool of modern budgeting. The government cannot intelligently budget for entitlements without making baseline-type assumptions. Moreover, the baseline provides a uniform measure for comparing legislative and executive actions, takes into account the inexorable impact of inflation on public expenditure, and provides a simple means of measuring the dollar effects of policy changes on the budget. In the 1980s, however, the baseline acquired another, less reputable, use—that of stifling the government's capacity to cut expenditure.

Appropriating Less and More

The 1980s have been a stressful period for congressional appropriators. For decades, their role has been to cut the budget and to increase spending. Past presidents have cooperated by asking for relatively big increases, which were trimmed back by Congress when it appropriated the money. But, when Reagan called for widespread cuts in domestic programs, the appropriations committees were not able to continue their old role. With the budget precut by the president, the appropriations committees were precluded from behaving as they had in the past. Cutting still more would force spending well below the level preferred by Congress and would breach the objective of increasing program resources.

By doing the cutting for them, Reagan induced the appropriations committees to become program advocates. This was not an easy transformation, however, because many members of these committees still had an image of appropriations as a process for cutting federal spending. Here is where the baseline came to the rescue. It enabled the appropriations committees to define cuts in terms of the inflated baseline rather than the president's lower request. Appropriations actions were linked to the baseline via the annual congressional budget resolution. Although they were wary of the congressional budget process and resented its intrusion into their areas of responsibility, the appropriations committees used the budget resolution to defend themselves against presidential complaints that they were "busting" the budget. As long as the resolution was within the baseline and appropriations were within the resolution, these committees could argue that they were behaving in a responsible manner. Moreover, the committees took advantage of the huge defense increases requested by the president to shift funds to other sectors while remaining within budget.

The behavior of the appropriations committees is evident in the data displayed in tables 4.1 through 4.3,which are derived from unpublished files of the Congressional Budget Office. The tables are limited to the 1986–89 fiscal years because comparable data are lacking for earlier years. The tables cover only discretionary appropriations, the portion of the budget under jurisdiction of the appropriations committees. Three caveats must be noted in using the data presented in these tables. First, the CBO computations differ from those of OMB, especially regarding the budgetary impacts of congressional actions. Second, CBO sometimes has reclassified some amounts from discretionary to mandatory accounts. Hence, the data should not be used to compare budgetary levels in different fiscal years. Finally, some entries are distorted by technical factors or bookkeeping gimmicks.

Table 4.1 reveals that the budget resolution's total budget authority for discretionary appropriations was below the baseline in each of the four years but above the president's request in two of the years. By being consistently below the baseline, the resolution sheltered Congress and the appropriations committees against presidential complaints and enabled them to claim that they were cutting expenditures. Note, however, that virtually all the cutting was confined to defense and international programs. Over the four years, the budget resolution was about $75 billion below the baseline for discretionary appropriated accounts, but more than $60 billion of this was attributable to cuts in the national defense and international affairs functions. In the two years (1987 and 1988) that Congress budgeted less for appropriations than the president had requested, the entire shortfall resulted from extraordinarily deep cuts in defense. Excluding defense, Congress appropriated about $20 billion more than Reagan wanted in each of those years. The budget resolution paved the way for the appropriations committees to transfer funds from defense to domestic accounts while staying within the congressionally approved budget.

Table 4.2 sheds light on how the appropriations committees balanced the conflicting demands to finance programs and cut the bud-

Table 4.1 BUDGET AUTHORITY FOR DISCRETIONARY APPROPRIATIONS SET FORTH OR ASSUMED IN THE BUDGET RESOLUTION, BASELINE, AND THE PRESIDENT'S BUDGET, FISCAL YEARS 1986–89 (billions of dollars)

	1986			1987		
	Baseline	President's budget	Budget resolution	Baseline	President's budget	Budget resolution
Domestic functions	135.7	118.2	122.7	127.5	107.7	126.3
Defense and international programs	349.1	316.5	322.7	321.6	344.3	310.0
TOTAL	484.8	434.7	445.4	449.1	452.0	436.3

	1988			1989		
	Baseline	President's budget	Budget resolution	Baseline	President's budget	Budget resolution
Domestic functions	140.2	122.3	141.8	143.7	140.0	142.0
Defense and international programs	322.2	333.4	307.2	326.9	318.4	318.4
TOTAL	462.4	455.7	449.0	470.6	458.4	460.4

Source: Unpublished Congressional Budget Office printout.
Notes: See accompanying text for warnings concerning interpretation of these data. Domestic Functions include all budget functions except national defense and international affairs.
Table includes only appropriations; it does not include other actions of Congress affecting spending levels.
Computations are based on the President's budget as reestimated by CBO.

Table 4.2 ANALYSIS OF APPROPRIATION ACTIONS: SELECTED BUDGET FUNCTIONS, FISCAL YEARS 1986–1989

	NUMBER OF TIMES APPROPRIATION WAS					
Function	above president's budget and baseline	above president's budget, below baseline	below president's budget, above baseline	below president's budget, below baseline	equal to president's budget, above baseline	equal to president's budget, below baseline
Administration of justice	66	21	31	66	1	3
Agriculture	2	30	17	50	0	3
Commerce and housing credit	23	24	18	56	4	3
Community and regional development	37	41	6	34	5	2
Education, training, employment, and social services	87	39	27	77	2	12
Energy	15	18	5	31	9	10
General science, space & technology	21	2	19	17	2	2
Health	79	39	17	88	3	3
Income security	42	28	1	13	1	1
International affairs	57	25	21	88	9	22
Natural resources and environment	105	78	20	93	19	15
Transportation	76	48	32	51	0	1
Veterans benefits and services	15	10	1	21	6	1
TOTAL	625	403	215	685	61	78
(Percentage of all actions)	(30.2)	(19.5)	(10.4)	(33.4)	(3.0)	(3.8)

Source: Unpublished Congressional Budget Office printout.
Notes: Table includes only appropriations; it does not include other actions of Congress affecting spending levels.
Computations are based on the president's budget as reestimated by CBO.
Table does not include 5 cases in which the appropriation was greater than the president's budget and equal to the baseline and 14 cases in which the appropriation equaled both the president's budget and the baseline.

Table 4.3A COMPARISON OF DISCRETIONARY APPROPRIATIONS TO THE
BUDGET RESOLUTION, THE BASELINE AND THE PRESIDENT'S
BUDGET APPROPRIATION ACCOUNTS, FISCAL YEAR 1986
(billions of dollars)

Function	Appropriations	Appropriations compared with		
		President's budget	Baseline	Budget resolution
DOMESTIC FUNCTIONS				
General science, space & technology	$ 9.3	$ 0.2	$ 0.4	$ 0.5
Energy	5.9	− 2.1	− 2.9	− 0.5
Natural resources & environment	13.6	− 0.9	− 1.8	− 1.5
Agriculture	2.1	− 0.1	− 0.2	0.8
Commerce and housing credit	2.6	− 0.7	− 0.8	− 0.3
Transportation	10.3	− 1.7	− 2.1	− 0.2
Community and regional development	5.7	− 0.6	− 1.3	− 0.3
Education, training, employment & social services	21.3	− 0.5	− 1.8	− 1.1
Health	10.3	0.1	− 0.4	− 0.1
Income security	15.8	10.6	− 2.2	− 0.2
Veterans' benefits	10.8	− 0.1	− 0.3	− 0.4
Administration of justice	6.7	0.3	0.1	a
General government	7.5	1.1	0.2	0.4
General purpose fiscal assistance	0.6	0.1	0.6	0.6
Allowances	0.0	− 1.5	− 0.9	2.1
SUBTOTAL DOMESTIC	122.5	4.2	− 13.4	− 0.2
NONDOMESTIC FUNCTIONS				
National defense	288.3	− 4.9	− 37.1	− 14.9
International affairs	18.7	− 4.5	− 4.9	− 0.7
SUBTOTAL NONDOMESTIC	307.0	− 9.4	− 42.0	− 15.6
GRAND TOTAL	429.5	− 5.2	− 55.3	− 15.8

Source: Unpublished Congressional Budget Office printout.
Notes: See text for warnings concerning interpretation of these data.
[a]Amount is less than $50 million.
Table includes only appropriations; it does not include other actions of Congress affecting spending levels.
Computations are based on the president's budget as reestimated by CBO.
Totals may not add due to rounding.
These notes apply to Tables 4.3A through 4.3D.

Table 4.3B COMPARISON OF DISCRETIONARY APPROPRIATIONS TO THE
BUDGET RESOLUTION, THE BASELINE AND THE PRESIDENT'S
BUDGET APPROPRIATION ACCOUNTS, FISCAL YEAR 1987
(billions of dollars)

| Function | Appropriations | Appropriations compared with | | |
		President's budget	Baseline	Budget resolution
DOMESTIC FUNCTIONS				
General science, space & technology	12.5	3.1	3.2	3.4
Energy	4.4	− 0.1	− 1.2	− 1.0
Natural resources & environment	16.7	3.2	1.7	2.2
Agriculture	2.3	0.6	0.1	0.2
Commerce and housing credit	2.8	− 1.5	− 0.3	0.1
Transportation	24.4	17.1	13.6	13.5
Community and regional development	5.7	1.3	− 0.5	− 0.3
Education, training, employment & social services	24.1	5.4	1.6	0.1
Health	12.1	2.3	1.4	1.2
Income security	13.5	5.1	− 2.7	− 1.1
Veterans' benefits	11.4	0.8	0.2	0.3
Administration of justice	8.4	1.5	1.7	1.4
General government	8.4	0.5	1.4	1.2
General purpose fiscal assistance	0.6	0.6	0.6	0.6
Allowances	0.0	− 0.4	− 1.0	− 1.0
SUBTOTAL DOMESTIC	147.3	39.5	19.8	20.8
NONDOMESTIC FUNCTIONS				
National defense	286.3	− 34.7	− 15.4	− 6.7
International affairs	17.7	− 5.6	− 2.2	0.7
SUBTOTAL NONDOMESTIC	304.0	− 40.3	− 17.6	− 6.0
GRAND TOTAL	451.2	− 0.8	− 2.1	14.9

Table 4.3C COMPARISON OF DISCRETIONARY APPROPRIATIONS TO THE
BUDGET RESOLUTION, THE BASELINE AND THE PRESIDENT'S
BUDGET APPROPRIATION ACCOUNTS, FISCAL YEAR 1988
(billions of dollars)

Function	Appropriations	Appropriations Compared with		
		President's budget	Baseline	Budget resolution
DOMESTIC FUNCTIONS				
General science, space & technology	10.7	− 0.7	0.2	− 0.6
Energy	5.7	0.4	− 1.0	− 0.3
Natural resources & environment	16.4	1.8	− 0.5	a
Agriculture	2.3	0.5	a	0.2
Commerce and housing credit	2.9	0.9	− 0.4	− 0.2
Transportation	10.9	2.4	− 0.5	− 1.1
Community and regional development	6.3	1.2	− 0.5	− 0.3
Education, training, employment & social services	25.2	4.5	0.4	− 1.6
Health	13.0	− 0.9	0.4	− 0.2
Income security	13.7	3.9	− 0.9	− 1.5
Veterans' benefits	11.8	0.1	− 0.2	− 0.2
Administration of justice	8.7	0.2	− 0.2	− 0.4
General government	8.7	− 0.1	0.3	a
Allowances	0.0	0.0	− 0.9	0.7
SUBTOTAL DOMESTIC	136.3	14.2	− 3.8	− 5.5
NONDOMESTIC FUNCTIONS				
National defense	292.1	− 20.5	− 11.4	2.3
International affairs	17.8	− 3.0	− 0.9	0.4
SUBTOTAL NONDOMESTIC	309.9	− 23.5	− 12.3	2.7
GRAND TOTAL	446.3	− 9.4	− 16.1	− 2.7

Table 4.3D COMPARISON OF DISCRETIONARY APPROPRIATIONS TO THE
BUDGET RESOLUTION, THE BASELINE AND THE PRESIDENT'S
BUDGET APPROPRIATION ACCOUNTS, FISCAL YEAR 1989
(billions of dollars)

| | | Appropriations compared with | | |
| | | President's | | Budget |
Function	Appropriations	budget	Baseline	resolution
DOMESTIC FUNCTIONS				
General science, space & technology	12.7	−1.2	1.5	−0.3
Energy	6.1	−0.7	−0.3	0.5
Natural resources & environment	16.9	1.7	−0.3	0.9
Agriculture	2.3	0.2	−0.1	0.1
Commerce and housing credit	2.8	0.5	−0.2	a
Transportation	11.6	2.3	0.5	0.5
Community and regional development	6.5	0.7	−0.7	0.7
Education, training, employment & social services	26.3	−0.1	a	−1.0
Health	14.3	0.7	0.8	0.8
Income security	13.8	0.3	−0.9	−0.9
Veterans' benefits	12.2	0.2	−0.2	0.1
Administration of justice	9.6	−0.2	0.5	0.2
General government	9.0	−0.2	−0.3	0.2
Allowances	0.0	0.1	0.0	0.0
SUBTOTAL DOMESTIC	144.1	4.3	0.3	1.8
NONDOMESTIC FUNCTIONS				
National defense	300.0	−0.3	−8.3	−0.3
International affairs	18.2	0.1	−0.4	0.1
SUBTOTAL NONDOMESTIC	318.2	−0.2	−8.7	−0.2
GRAND TOTAL	462.3	3.9	−8.3	1.9

get. It reports on more than 2,000 appropriation decisions during the four years. (Each appropriation account represents one decision for each year.) The table covers all discretionary domestic functions except revenue sharing, which has been phased out, general government, which is small and shows only minor variance between the requested and appropriated amounts; and Medicare and Social Security, which are entitlements. The entries in table 4.2 indicate that Congress has frequently appropriated more funds than were requested by the president. Approximately half of the discretionary appropriation decisions, as measured by the total for each account, were above the president's budget, and a slightly higher portion were below the baseline. The data suggest that the appropriations committees have not blanketed the budget with a single decision rule. Sometimes they have come out above the president's budget but below the baseline, and sometimes below the budget and the baseline, and sometimes above both. In a constrained budget environment, there has been a great deal of shifting among accounts as Congress has substituted its priorities for those of the president.

Some of the shifts have occurred among domestic functions, as the appropriations committees have exercised considerable independence from the functional allocations set forth in the budget resolution.[36] The most significant shifts, as previously mentioned, have been from defense to domestic functions. The process of transferring funds in this direction starts with the budget resolution and continues when Congress makes appropriations. Table 4.3 compares the total discretionary appropriation for each function with the president's request, the baseline, and the amount assumed in the budget. The most revealing entries are the subtotals for the domestic and the defense/international categories. In each of the years, the total appropriated for the defense/international functions was below both the president's request and the baseline; in all of the years, the discretionary domestic appropriations exceeded the amount requested by the president. In three of the years, the defense/international cutbacks sufficed to fully offset the domestic increases, so that total discretionary appropriations were below the president's request.

The fiscal 1989 appropriations were an exception to this pattern. This was one of the few years in modern history during which Congress appropriated more than the president requested. This anomaly occurred solely because the defense cutbacks were shallower than in previous years, not because Congress exceeded the president's domestic request by an unusual margin. Reagan's fiscal 1989 request for defense conformed to the terms of the 1987 budget summit. Hence,

Congress could not make significant cuts in it.[37] In the absence of large reductions in defense, even modest add-ons in domestic programs caused total discretionary appropriations to exceed the president's request.

During the Reagan years, the big increases requested by the president for defense made room for enlarged domestic appropriations and allowed the appropriations committees to continue their traditional role of cutting the budget and increasing program resources. When, pursuant to the summit agreement, Reagan moderated his request for defense funds, there no longer was sufficient room in the budget for Congress to play this role. Forced to choose between cutting the budget and enhancing domestic programs, Congress opted for the latter.

OMB officials reportedly told Reagan that by asking so much more for defense, he was opening the door to higher appropriations for domestic programs. The president did not buy the argument because he was committed to the defense buildup and believed that the less he asked for defense, the less it would get. If Reagan was right, then his actions may have led to both higher defense and domestic appropriations than would have ensued if the president had asked for a smaller defense budget.

In shifting funds from defense to nondefense appropriations, Congress had to neutralize the president's veto power. It did so by packaging all or most of the regular appropriation bills into an omnibus continuing resolution that was presented to the president on a take it or leave it basis. Seven of the thirteen regular appropriations bills for the 1986 fiscal year were enacted in a single measure. All of the fiscal 1987 and 1988 appropriations were provided in omnibus continuing resolutions.

The continuing resolutions compelled the president to accept higher domestic spending than would have been the case had the appropriation bills been presented to him individually. Reagan could have vetoed these omnibus measures, but if he did, the result might have been a messy budget conflict, a shutdown of government agencies, and possibly lower defense appropriations than were offered in the continuing resolution. Moreover, Congress cleverly packaged things the president wanted, such as assistance to the Contras in Nicaragua, into the continuing resolutions. Congress skillfully held presidential demands hostage to Reagan's acceptance of the omnibus measures.

The fiscal 1989 appropriations were enacted in individual bills, not in a continuing resolution. The budget summit accomplished for fiscal 1989 what the continuing resolution had done in previous years. It forged a veto-proof agreement between the presidency and congressional leaders covering all appropriations, domestic and defense. These agreements protected the salient interests of both branches. Congress got more for domestic programs and the president got more for defense than he might have if the bills had been acted on individually. The president cut spending in his budget, Congress cut spending in its budget resolution, but appropriations continued to rise, albeit at a rate only slightly higher than inflation and less than the growth rate of GNP.

The Disappearing Impoundment Power

Appropriation is not a president's final opportunity to control discretionary spending. The president can use the 1974 Impoundment Control Act (ICA) to propose the rescission or deferral of funds. Impoundment is a barometer of the budgetary relationship of the president and Congress. When the president dominates the relationship, Congress tends to accept the impoundments; when Congress is dominant, it often rejects them. It should come as no surprise, therefore, that each president who has operated under the ICA rules has had a different success rate. Table 4.4 indicates that Gerald Ford, who faced a Congress controlled by the opposition, won cancellation of only 7 percent of the funds proposed by him for rescission. By refusing to act, Congress compelled the release of more than 90 percent of the withheld funds. Jimmy Carter benefited from Democratic control of Congress, but he still obtained approval of less than 40 percent of his proposed rescissions.

Over the eight years of his presidency, Ronald Reagan's success rate for rescissions was almost the same as his predecessor's. But there was an astounding difference between Reagan's first two years and the next six. In 1981 and 1982, Reagan prevailed on Congress to cancel $16 billion in appropriations. But in 1983–88, Reagan won only $400 million in rescissions. Reagan's success rate thus dropped from 69 percent in 1981–82 to a niggardly 2 percent in 1983–88. Congressional rejection became so predictable that Reagan did not even bother to propose rescissions in 1988.

The record of deferrals has followed a similar course, but to track it, a distinction must be made between routine actions and those seeking to change policy. The routine deferrals are authorized by the Antideficiency Act, which permits the withholding of funds when program objectives can be accomplished without spending the full amount provided for them. Inasmuch as routine deferrals do not

Table 4.4 RESCISSIONS AND DEFERRALS, 1975–88
(dollars in millions)

	Proposed	Accepted[a]	Percentage accepted
Rescissions			
Ford (1975–77)	$7,405	$530	7.2
Carter (1977–81)	6,946	2,580	37.1
Reagan (1981–82)	23,269	16,080	69.1
Reagan (1983–88)	20,011	400	2.0
Total Rescissions	57,631	19,589	34.0
Policy Deferrals[b]			
Ford	23,904	14,145	59.2
Carter	12,905	7,314	56.7
Reagan (1981–82)	6,788	6,174	91.0
Reagan (1983–88)	22,333	7,736	34.6
Routine Deferrals[b]			
Ford	16,623	16,610	99.9
Carter	17,943	17,928	99.9
Reagan (1981–88)	66,817	66,284	99.2
Total Routine Deferrals	101,383	100,820	99.4

Source: U.S. Office of Management and Budget.
[a]For rescissions, accepted means that Congress passed legislation rescinding the funds; for deferrals, accepted means that Congress did not disapprove the deferral.
[b]Routine deferrals are those authorized under the Antideficiency Act; all others are classified as policy deferrals.

alter policy, Congress has acceded to 99 percent of them. But it has subjected policy deferrals—those designed to reduce program or spending levels—to much tougher review. Over the years, Congress has gone along with only slightly more than half of the policy deferrals. Here, too, Reagan was much more successful in his first two years than in the next six. More than 90 percent of the policy deferrals submitted by him in 1981–82 were permitted to continue, compared with only 35 percent in the remainder of his presidency.

In 1981 and 1982, Reagan used the impoundment power to control spending. Since then, Congress has used the impoundment power to control the president. In the case of rescissions, this reversal has required nothing more than a change in attitude. Rather than acting on the president's proposals, as it did in the early years of ICA, Congress has prevailed by inaction. Deferrals are a different matter, however, because if Congress does nothing, the president gets his way. Converting the deferral process into an instrument of congressional control has been accomplished by changing the rules of the game. The first step in this development was the 1983 Supreme Court decision in *Chadha v. INS*, which held that all legislative vetoes (including the method by which Congress could overturn the deferral of funds) violate the U.S. Constitution. At the time, *Chadha* was seen as a blow to congressional power because it took away the legislature's ability to nullify certain executive actions. Pursuant to *Chadha*, it appeared that Congress no longer had effective recourse when the president deferred funds. Within a few years, it became clear that lacking the power to overturn deferrals, Congress would restrict the president's power to initiate deferrals. The issue was joined in 1986 when Reagan deferred some $10 billion that he did not want spent. Congress's response was to insert a provision in that year's supplemental appropriation bill nullifying most of the policy deferrals.[38] It took more forceful action in 1987, when, in the course of amending the Gramm- Rudman-Hollings law, it terminated the president's power to make policy deferrals.[39] Ronald Reagan was the first president in American history expressly barred from deferring funds to slow down federal spending or to reduce the deficit. His impotence was reflected in the fact that Reagan did not file a single policy deferral in 1988, the first year since enactment of ICA that this type of impoundment was not used.

Reagan saw the weakening of his impoundment power as a major constraint in the government's ability to control spending. One of his last Saturday radio addresses as president was devoted to this topic. "The verdict is in," Reagan declared:

> The current system does not work. Can you imagine if a head of a household or a business were forced to spend every dime that was budgeted, even if savings were available? Well, that's the situation the President is now in . . . . Since 1982, I have requested Congress to take back unneeded funds more than 460 times, and 83 percent of the time they refused. Most of the time they didn't even bring it up for a vote; they simply said, "No, spend it all."[40]

The verdict is not as simple as Reagan painted it. Impoundment is a limited power. It can be directed only at appropriations not at entitlements. Congress sees impoundment as a "second swing of the bat," an opportunity for the president to get through rescission or deferral what he failed to obtain when the appropriation was made. Impoundment is as much a fight over power as it is over money. Loss of impoundment has undoubtedly added to federal spending. More importantly, it has subtracted from presidential power.

Blunting the Reconciliation Process

Reconciliation was the difference in 1981. Without it, even a president as popular and persuasive as Reagan might not have carried the day. He certainly would not have won enactment of many of the cuts voted by Congress. After 1981, reconciliation was a recurring feature in congressional budgeting, but its effectiveness diminished. There is an extraordinary disparity between the enormous savings achieved in 1981 and the puny ones approved in later years. In fact, the 1981 savings greatly exceeded the combined outlay reduction claimed in all of the other years in which reconciliation has been activated. Although, as noted, the savings estimates are open to serious challenge, there is no doubt that reconciliation's potency as a cutback tool has been crippled. Telling evidence of this debilitation comes from the reconciliation measure enacted in 1987 to implement the budget agreement negotiated by the president and Congress. That measure reportedly trimmed less than $4 billion from fiscal 1988 spending and only about $6 billion from the next year's. Even these relatively small amounts were inflated by baseline tricks and other gimmicks. A true accounting would show that the 1987 savings, spurred by that year's stock market crash, were negligible.

The blunting of this cutting tool did not just happen. It was engineered by congressional leaders and committees that did not want to equip the president and the budget committees with effective cutback powers. It was not hard to cripple reconciliation because it is not an inherently potent process. At all stages, reconciliation depends on the willingness of key congressional participants to make it work. Reconciliation is a vulnerable process because it has serious built-in weaknesses. Although the Budget Act directs committees to respond to reconciliation instructions, it provides no effective sanctions if they fail to do so. The instructions do not dictate which programs are to be cut or how the savings are to be measured. If committees concoct false or unrealistic savings, the budget committees cannot unilaterally substitute more appropriate cutbacks. They can ask the House or Senate to approve alternative savings, but the floor is not always a hospitable place for sorting out conflicts among committees or for making hard choices. Even when legitimate savings have been recommended, there is no assurance that they will materialize. The Budget Act does not require that Congress enact the reconciliation bill. It only provides that Congress, when instructed by a budget resolution, prepare and consider such a measure.[41]

Given the limitations of the process and the diversity of participants who have to cooperate, it is a marvel that reconciliation works at all. It worked in 1981 because of Reagan's extraordinary influence. It worked in subsequent years only because Congress shaped reconciliation into a somewhat different process each time it was applied. After the first shocks of the new process wore off, committees acquired the acumen to turn reconciliation into something quite different from what it was originally designed to be. They made reconciliation serve their own ends and interests rather than those of deficit reduction. The reconciliation story of the 1980s is that it has been transformed from a process that compelled committees to do things against their will into a vehicle for advancing their own legislative objectives. Committees that resented reconciliation when it was first applied learned, over the course of a decade, how to exploit it. Once it was the budget committee that pushed for reconciliation. Now it is the legislative committees that clamor for the opportunities it brings.

This transformation is illustrated by the reduced scope of the reconciliation process. In 1981, reconciliation was applied to both mandatory and discretionary expenditure. Since then, however, discretionary authorizations, whose spending is determined in annual appropriations, have been off limits. The overwhelming sentiment in Congress has been to cut discretionary programs only through the normal authorizations-appropriations route.[42] Reconciliation was narrowed for one reason—to reduce antagonism toward the process. The broader the reach of reconciliation, the more committees have to be cajoled to produce savings and, consequently, the more resentment is built up. At reconciliation's peak in 1981, about thirty House and Senate committees, almost all the committees with legislative jurisdiction, were drawn into the process. Many authorizing committees resented having to produce savings in programs over which they lacked financial control. The appropriations committees were angered by the trespass on their jurisdiction, and both sets of committees blamed the budget committees for grabbing too much power.[43] With reconciliation narrowed, hostility abated, but so did the opportunity to cut expenditures.

Some committees gamed the process by recommending smaller savings than were called for in the instructions and by resorting to accounting ploys and other gimmicks that overstate the real savings. The budget committees generally have not challenged modest displays of independence by other committees, and they often have been willing to settle for eighty or ninety cents on the reconciliation dollar. The budget committees have to be quite selective in the fights they pick. In line with Sam Rayburn's fabled advice, they "got along" in the 1982–88 years by "going along," even when the cutbacks fell short of the instructions.

This accommodating posture also characterized their response to budgetary legerdemain. The budget committees turned the other cheek when the 1986 reconciliation bill shifted a $680 million revenue payment from the 1987 fiscal year to the previous year and counted this amount as a spending cut. The same law took credit for cutbacks enacted in previous legislation, and it had so many other false savings that it was openly referred to on Capitol Hill as "blue smoke and mirrors."[44]

Medicare has been an especially fertile area for inventive budgeting. Payment schedules have been advanced, delayed, or stretched out; hospital and physical reimbursement rates have been frozen and refrozen; temporary provisions have been extended to claim the savings a second or third time.[45] The special rules of the baseline have been plumbed to raise payments and to report the increase as a cutback. As the savings attributed to reconciliation have plummeted, the gimmickry has escalated. The 1987 reconciliation bill had several provisions that purported to cut Medicare spending without paring services. One provision extended an expiring requirement that Part B premiums recoup 25 percent of program costs, another continued a temporary reduction in payments to hospitals for capital expenses, and a third slowed the processing of Medicare claims.[46] If such tricks were removed from the count, the savings enacted in 1987 would be seen as puny.

Some committees have deftly exploited the reconciliation process to expand programs. Several reconciliation bills have increased Medicaid benefits for pregnant women and low-income children.[47] These "sweeteners" have induced some committees to endorse Medicare cutbacks, since the savings in this program offset the Medicaid enhancements. The way the baseline works, committees have been able to hide the true impact of program expansions on the deficit by taking credit for the short-term savings while phasing in the sweeteners over a number of years.

Some committees have undermined reconciliation by turning it into a vehicle for the enactment of extraneous legislation (including entire authorizations) that have nothing to do with the budget or with deficit reduction. The Senate has adopted the Byrd rule—a bar against the insertion of nongermane provisions into reconciliation bills—which has reduced but not eliminated extraneous provisions. By taking advantage of reconciliation's special procedures—a closed or limited rule in the House, a time limit and restrictions on floor amendments in the Senate—committees have advanced legislation that otherwise might have been challenged on the floor or might have lacked sufficient momentum to get enacted on its own. One of the reconciliation bills enacted in 1986 shows how the process has become a magnet for nongermane legislation. Although it hardly reduced the deficit, that bill had provisions that assisted workers displaced by foreign competition, reauthorized the Small Business Administration, established a tobacco support program, reauthorized the Corporation for Public Broadcasting, made dozens of changes in Medicare and Medicaid, and distributed billions of dollars in escrowed offshore oil receipts. A fair reading of its legislative history suggests that this measure was enacted principally because of its other baggage, not to reduce the deficit.

One of the ironies of reconciliation is that as its impact on the deficit has diminished, it has been increasingly labeled as *the* deficit reduction bill. Deficit reduction has not vanished, but it has become more symbol than reality. In a difficult political world, in which Congress is cross-pressured to cut the budget and spend more, it is a wonderful thing that congressmen can get credit for doing something about the deficit without having to do very much.

THE TRIUMPH OF POLITICS

The behavior of Congress in using and then blunting its cutback tools might appear to be nothing more than legislative gamesmanship.[48] Congress gave and then crippled the power to impound funds; it sliced billions from the budget by means of reconciliation procedures and then turned the process into a means of thwarting substantial cutbacks; it manipulated baseline assumptions and appropriation decisions to spend more while claiming that it was cutting back. But there was much more than jockeying for political advantage in Congress's refusal to ratify many of Reagan's cuts. Congress was responding to the strong influences playing on it. What happened inside was driven by what was happening outside.

Budgeting has become increasingly politicized. Signs of increased political activity come from the prerelease leaks of budget details, the opening up of appropriations markups, and increases in the number of floor amendments on money bills. There is more media attention to budget issues than in the past, more interest-group

monitoring of developments, more conflict over finances, more in-
stant analyses of budget options, more alternatives offered to the
government's proposals. Legislative debate has been increasingly fis-
calized, and substantive issues have often been narrowed to their
financial implications. In some sessions during the 1980s, more than
50 percent of the roll call votes in the House or Senate have been
related to the budget.[49] Other perspectives often have been crowded
out.

Heightened political activity has not been confined to the budget,
but it inevitably has added to pressure on budget makers. Statistics
show a sharp rise in congressional mail during this decade, an increase both in the number of political action committees and in the
financial resources at their command, and an increase in the number
of journalists and "Washington representatives" stationed in the nation's capital.[50] The influence of political activists on budget outcomes is uncertain, but it is clear that Reagan's efforts to shrink
domestic government have not induced claimants to withdraw from
the federal budgetary arena. There is some evidence of increased
attention to state and local governments, but this additional activity
has not led to abatement in pressure on the budget.[51]

In 1981, the spenders were caught off guard. They were over-
whelmed by Reagan's immense popularity and by the sweeping
changes he proposed, and they were unfamiliar with the new roles
of budget cutting. Afterward, they quickly learned how to subvert
the rules, and they successfully campaigned against repeated efforts
to trim federal spending.

Reagan's budget revolution, as David Stockman acknowledged in
The Triumph of Politics, succumbed to political opposition. To
Stockman, it was mostly the politics of greed, of farmers fattening
up on federal handouts, businesses protecting their subsidized loans,
cities asking for aid to the poor but using the money for tennis courts
and shopping centers. It was the politics of the pork barrel and of
the vote trade. Government, Stockman came to believe, had grown
so big and generous that feeding at the trough had become a national
pasttime joined in by Americans of every social class and economic
condition.[52]

Members of Congress saw the clamor for public benefits as the
politics of democracy. They were highly sensitive to shifts in public
opinion and to the preferences of back-home voters. Reagan won in
1981 because public opinion was on his side. He lost in subsequent
years because most Americans did not favor his budget policies.

Table 4.5, drawn from two *Washington Post*/ABC News polls conducted six years apart, offers convincing evidence of this shift.[53] In 1981, Medicare was the only domestic program a majority of respondents wanted increased. By 1987, day care, Social Security, and Medicaid had joined the list. Even more telling was the drop in the percentage of those polled who wanted spending reductions. Except for Medicare, every program reported in table 4.5 showed a declining

Table 4.5 CHANGING ATTITUDES TOWARD SELECTED DOMESTIC PROGRAMS

"Do you feel spending for the following federal government programs should be increased, decreased, or left about the same?

	1981	1987
Loans and grants to college students		
Increase	22%	46%
Decrease	29	14
The same	48	39
Day care programs		
Increase	38	57
Decrease	15	8
The same	46	34
Medicaid (health care for the poor)		
Increase	44	61
Decrease	13	6
The same	41	32
Medicare (health care for the elderly)		
Increase	57	74
Decrease	3	3
The same	39	22
Food stamps		
Increase	15	27
Decrease	49	26
The same	33	45
Social Security		
Increase	49	63
Decrease	8	5
The same	40	31
Unemployment insurance		
Increase	23	33
Decrease	25	12
The same	49	52
Aid to music and the arts		
Increase	13	16
Decrease	43	24
The same	41	59

Source: *The Washington Post*/ABC News Polls.

percentage of respondents favoring cutbacks over the six years. In 1987, food stamps was the only nondefense program covered in this survey that more than one-quarter of respondents wanted curtailed.

When the public changed its mind, Congress changed its behavior. It could not go along with Reagan by disregarding public opinion. And it could not rebuff Reagan merely by turning down his demands. It also had to disable the cutting tools that had been wielded a few years earlier.

The shift in public opinion and in congressional behavior reflect much more than pure greed. The shift is a recognition of the extraordinary linkage between the federal government's finances and the well-being of Americans. To explain this development, let us recall a theme sounded in chapter 2. The growth of government and the changing composition of public expenditure have made budgeting a more transparent process and Congress a more permeable institution. Entitlements are a fact of budgetary life and a political state of mind. Those who receive the transfer payments that total more than half of the trillion dollars spent each year have a stake in the budget no less than that of the federal agencies that submit formal requests. But they are outsiders to the budget process and—along with other outsiders such as contractors, state and local governments, and hospitals—they must use political means rather than administrative channels to influence outcomes. Although increased lobbying and attention to the budget are part of a larger change in national politics, this charge also has been spurred by the growing prominence of transfer payments.

Table 4.6 reveals an extraordinary increase over the past three decades in the number of persons receiving direct financial support from the government. The numbers are staggering. Almost 40 million American receive monthly Social Security checks. More than 20 million rely on federal assistance in paying for medical care. About 20 million use vouchers to purchase food. Some 14 million live in subsidized housing, about 10 million are on the welfare rolls. Some of the increases in the beneficiary population have been driven by demographic trends, such as the growing ranks of elderly Americans. Some have been propelled by economic circumstances, such as the persistence of poverty in the United States. Regardless of the cause, the evidence is overwhelming that Reagan's cutbacks have not dented the major transfer programs.

Government transfer programs are not just entries in the budget. They are the principal income support for millions of Americans. In 1970, transfers, including those from nonfederal sources, accounted

Table 4.6 BENEFICIARIES OF MAJOR GOVERNMENT TRANSFER PROGRAMS
(number in millions)

Program	1960	1970	1980	1990
Social Security	14.3	25.8	35.4	39.5
Medicare	0	19.9	27.5	33.2
Medicaid	0	14.5	21.6	25.8
School Lunch	13.6	22.4	26.6	25.0
Food Stamps[a]	4.3	8.5	19.3	18.1
Assisted Housing	1.6	3.5	10.6	14.0
Aid to Families with Dependent Children	3.0	7.4	10.6	10.9
Supplemental Security Income[a]	2.8	2.9	3.7	4.2
WIC[a]	0	0.1	2.0	3.8
Veterans' Payments	4.0	4.7	4.7	3.6
Unemployment Insurance[b]	2.1	2.1	3.8	2.4[c]

Source: *Budget of the United States Government, 1990, Major Policy Initiatives*, p. 36.
Unemployment insurance data from *Ecnomic Report of the President, 1989*, Table B-42.
Note: Because of duplication—some persons received benefits from two or more programs—the number of beneficiaries cannot be added up to determine the total number of persons receiving transfer payments.
[a]Predecessor programs included.
[b]Weekly average insured unemployment.
[c]1987 data.

for about 10 percent of total personal income in the United States; in the 1980s, they have consistently supplied about 15 percent of all personal income. As reported in table 4.7, more than 40 percent of all households (families and unrelated individuals) which have income receive government transfer payments. More than one of every five households receives Social Security payments, and substantial numbers receive other forms of assistance, such as unemployment compensation or public assistance.

Government transfers are especially important in assisting low-income persons. A detailed examination of transfers by the Census Bureau (summarized in table 4.8) found that for millions of Americans they spell the difference between living in poverty and having incomes above the poverty level. Without transfers, more than 50 million persons would have been impoverished in 1986. Some 23 million persons were lifted above the poverty level by transfer payments. Ironically, much of the alleviation of poverty has come from non-means-tested programs, particularly Social Security and Medicare, that go to all age-eligible persons, regardless of their income.

With the living standards of millions of its citizens directly dependent on one or another form of public assistance, the government

Table 4.7 TRANSFER PAYMENTS AS A SOURCE OF INCOME FOR FAMILIES
AND UNRELATED INDIVIDUALS
(numbers in thousands)

	1980		1986	
	Number of all households with this income source	Percentage of all households with this income source	Number of all households with this income source	Percentage of all households with this income source
Total number of families and unrelated individuals with income	60,178	100.0%	64,328	100.0%
SOURCE OF INCOME				
Social Security[a]	13,879	23.1	14,754	22.9
Supplemental Security Income	1,649	2.7	1,773	2.8
Public Assistance or Welfare	3,570	5.9	3,653	5.7
Veterans' Payment Income	2,352	3.9	1,678	2.6
Unemployment Compensation	5,984	9.9	5,143	8.0
Worker's Compensation	1,364	2.3	1,703	2.6
Government Transfer Payments	26,355	43.8	26,447	41.1

Source: U.S. Bureau of the Census, Current Population Reports, Series P-60. *Money Income of Households, Families, and Persons in the United States: 1969–1986.*
Note: Because some households receive payments from two or more programs, the number of households should not be added up to determine the total receiving transfer payments.
[a]Includes Railroad Retirement recipients.

cannot substantially retrench transfer programs without risking severe political and economic repercussions—not necessarily from the poor but from more affluent beneficiaries. Reductions in transfer payments would have the same financial impact on beneficiaries as would reductions in the wages paid workers. In both cases, there would be an immediate and visible loss in disposable income. As entitlement programs have matured, an implicit social contract has been forged between the government and its citizens. This is widely seen as a moral obligation that can be broken only in truly extraordinary circumstances. The spread of entitlements has nurtured expectations among Americans that the government will provide for them in old age and assist them during illness or unemployment. These deeply rooted expectations cannot be brushed aside when

Table 4.8 NUMBER OF PERSONS IN POVERTY, 1986
(numbers in millions)

Category	before government transfers added to income		after government transfers added to income		reduction in poverty population	
	Number	Percentage	Number	Percentage	Number	Percentage
Older persons (65 years +)	13.3	47.5	2.5	9.0	10.8	81.1
Persons 18 to 64 years	22.1	15.0	14.3	9.7	7.8	35.3
Younger persons (under 18)	15.1	24.0	10.8	17.1	4.3	28.8
Whites/any age	37.3	18.4	19.1	9.4	18.2	48.8
Blacks/any age	11.7	40.4	7.5	26.0	4.2	35.9
Hispanics/any age	6.4	34.0	4.4	23.4	2.0	31.3
All persons/any age any race	50.6	21.2	27.6	11.6	23.0	45.4

Source: U.S. Bureau of the Census, Current Population reports, Series P-60, no. 164-RD-1, *Measuring the Effect of Benefits and Taxes on Incomes and Poverty: 1986.*
Notes: See source for definitions and methodology.
Government transfers include Social Security and other means and non-means-tested transfers, the fungible value of Medicare and Medicaid, and the value of food and housing benefits.

financial conditions or a change in presidential command generate pressures for adjustments in spending policy. Workers who have planned for retirement by looking ahead to promised Social Security benefits cannot quickly change course when they have reached or are nearing retirement. Persons dependent on government assistance may not be able to shift for themselves if their social safety net is removed.

As the budget has become more politically vital, it has become more difficult to adjust expenditure by stealth, behind the closed doors of the budget process. When it contemplates cutbacks, the government has to reckon with the probability of embarrassing leaks, a bad press, defections from within, and intense pressure from affected interests. Even when the government has had the will to cut, the way has been politically difficult.

STICKY EXPENDITURE

The political constraints on cutting back and the dulling of the tools available to Congress have resulted in "sticky expenditures," claims on the budget that respond only weakly, if at all, to contraction policies.[55] Sticky expenditures tend to rise even when the government attempts to retrench. These expenditures come in a variety of forms: treaties and other international commitments, bonds obligating the payment of principal and interest, contractual obligations to providers of services, entitlements mandating payments to eligible persons, and other commitments.

Most sticky expenditures are controllable, but not through appropriations action alone. To avert the expenditure, the law giving rise to the obligation has to be repealed. This is why narrowing reconciliation, the principal tool for controlling sticky expenditure, has been so damaging to cutback efforts.

Sticky expenditures tend to drift upward. Drift is a condition in which spending continues to rise, even in the absence of new commitments, as a result of the weight of past decisions on future budgets. Because of drift, federal expenditure has been relatively insensitive to changes in budgetary conditions. Evidence of spending drift can be found in recent federal budgets. In the late 1980s, for example, a substantial part of the continuing rise in defense outlays was due to the military buildup approved earlier in the decade. Billions of dollars were added to annual outlays as the weapons ordered years earlier were delivered. In 1980, only $36 billion in defense outlays were derived from prior-year contracts. In 1988, prior commitments accounted for $115 billion in such outlays.

Expenditure updrift is most pronounced in transfer payments that have experienced a steady rise in the number of participants (see table 4.6). When Ronald Reagan was president, the Social Security and Medicare rolls added approximately half a million participants each year. Outlays in these and some other entitlement programs were driven upward by cost-of- living adjustments in pensions, food stamp payments, and veterans' benefits as well as by inflationary pressures in the medical sector.

This updrift accounted for most of the year-to-year rise in federal spending during the 1980s. Table 4.9 shows the percentage of each year's outlay growth that was attributable to the rise in Social Security payments, medical care costs, interest charges, prior-year contracts, and other commitments. Although the data are not nearly as precise as the table indicates, they present an unmistakable pattern.[56] In each year, the bulk of the spending rise resulted from sticky, updrifting expenditure. In two of the years, 1986 and 1987, more than 100 percent of the rise was attributable to these expenditures. This means that there may have been cuts in the remaining, unsticky

Table 4.9 ANNUAL INCREASE IN STICKY OUTLAYS AS A PERCENTAGE OF
INCREASE IN TOTAL OUTLAYS, FISCAL YEARS 1981–88

Fiscal year	Social Security	Net interest	Medical care	Other mandated costs	Prior-year contracts	Percent of total increase resulting from sticky outlays
1981	26	20	12	9	7	74
1982	22	23	12	14	18	89
1983	21	7	12	26	11	76
1984	17	49	15	−49	38	70
1985	11	19	12	9	18	69
1986	23	15	15	32	44	129
1987	65	19	61	−2	30	174[a]
1988	19	22	16	3	2	63

Source: For 1981–84, Summary Table 18 in *Budget of the United States Government, Fiscal Year 1986*; for 1985–88, *Historical Tables, Fiscal 1990 Budget*, Table 8.1.
Notes: OMB periodically revises its computation and classification of these data; hence, data taken from one year's budget might not be strictly comparable with data from another year's budget.
The data are not adjusted for "undistributed employee share, employee retirement."
[a]These percentages may be misleading and overstated because of accounting gimmicks that held down total outlay increase.

portion of the budget. In the other years, updrift consumed two-thirds or more of the increase.

Consider what this phenomenon has meant for Washington's budget makers. They have not reaped much credit for the escalation in spending, because all or most of it has been due to past decisions. Nor have they had new benefits to distribute, because most or all of the increment has been spent before they have made a single decision. Their misfortune has been to be blamed for both the spending cuts that the budget's dire finances force them to make and for the updrift in total spending that past commitments mandate. For them, budgeting in the 1980s was a frustrating and unpleasant chore.

The fact that much sticky expenditure is in the form of entitlements has greatly complicated the task of adjusting spending patterns to financial conditions. Politically, changing a law can be harder to achieve than merely cutting the budget; it is likely to be more difficult to take away a right vested in law than to oppose a claim for spending increases. In the "entitlement state," budget guardians cannot thwart claims by inaction alone. Claimants, in contrast, can get their way by letting the law speak for them. Indexation and other causes of expenditure drift also work to the disadvantage of conservers. They cannot constrain spending simply by holding the line on current levels. Even when they are only trying to curtail spending increases, they must behave as budget cutters seeking to take away benefits promised to recipients.

CONCLUSION

In the Reagan years, budgeting became a continuous struggle. Budget makers would seek to cut back, only to find spending drift upward again. Congress finally gave up trying. Why take the onus for retrenching programs when the next batch of budget news might show spending—or the deficit—as high as before? Seen in this perspective, impairing the budget's cutback capacity was a rational response to updrifting expenditures.

Yet politicians could not ignore the massive deficit. If they could not do the cutting themselves, they had to devise other means of doing the job. In 1985, they invented a new cutting tool—the sequestration process. This creature of the Gramm-Rudman-Hollings Act had one big advantage: The cutting would be done automatically, without leaving political fingerprints. The path that took Congress to Gramm-Rudman-Hollings was one in which conflict over budget policy disrupted established procedures and turned budgeting into an annual scramble to complete difficult and divisive chores. Budgeting, as we will see in chapter 6, became an improvised process, with each year's procedures tailored to the opportunities of the moment.

Notes

1. The fullest and most insightful account of the "old" appropriations process remains Richard F. Fenno, *The Power of the Purse: Appropriations Politics in Congress* (Boston: Little, Brown, 1966).

2. Deferral and rescissions are mutually exclusive categories. Every impoundment is classified as one or the other. The Impoundment Control Act prescribes rules to prevent use of the deferral procedure to cancel funds. Deferrals cannot be proposed beyond a single fiscal year or for a period of time that would preclude use of the funds. In the case of rescissions, the forty-five days are of "continuous session." Periods during which Congress is not in session do not count toward the forty-five days.

3. Generally, trust-funded entitlements have permanent appropriations, whereas those

funded by general revenue receive annual appropriation. The appropriations committees have some limited jurisdiction under the Congressional Budget Act to review new entitlements and to propose cutbacks, but they have not exercised this power to a significant degree.

4. Six years before the Congressional Budget Act, the executive budget was unified by combining trust funds and federal funds. The unified budget enabled the president to make decisions on budget totals.

5. The Joint Study Committee on Budget Control, which was established by Congress in 1972 to recommend changes in legislative budgeting, emphasized the weak jurisdiction of the appropriations committees. See its report of April 18, 1973.

6. Congress dropped the second budget resolution in the early 1980s. This change was formally incorporated into the rules in the 1985 legislation establishing the Gramm-Rudman-Hollings process. The single resolution is supposed to be adopted by April 15 each year.

7. Some critics of the congressional budget process assert that it has a prospending bias. They point to the fact that, unlike appropriations, where members vote on discrete items, in the budget resolution they decide on broad functional priorities. This has the effect, they argue, of increasing the size of the logroll or the payoff to obtain support. Rather than obtaining support by adding modest amounts for projects in a Member's district or state, Congress now trades in hundreds of millions of dollars, or more, for major programs. In this writer's view, the events of 1981 clearly attest to the use of the budget process to cut deeply into federal spending.

8. The 1981 developments were discussed in Allen Schick, "How the Budget Was Won and Lost," in *President and Congress: Assessing Reagan's First Year*, ed. Norman J. Ornstein (Washington, D.C.: American Enterprise Institute, 1982), pp. 14–43.

9. To discourage this behavior, Rep. David Obey has proposed enactment each year of an omnibus measure that would include both the budget resolution and all regular appropriation bills. The Obey scheme is discussed in Allen Schick, *The Whole and the Parts: Piecemeal and Integrated Approaches to Congressional Budgeting*, U.S. Congress, House Committee on the Budget, February 1987.

10. This shift and the early use of reconciliation in 1980 and 1981 are discussed in Allen Schick, *Reconciliation and the Congressional Budget Process* (Washington, D.C.: American Enterprise Institute, 1980). The use of reconciliation to alter revenue legislation is discussed in the next chapter.

11. In some years, the House has acted on committee recommendations separately and then packaged the legislation into an omnibus measure when it went to conference with the Senate.

12. The Budget Act sets a time limit on consideration of the reconciliation bill in the Senate. As a result, the measure cannot be filibustered. Although there is no comparable limitation in the House, the House usually adopts a special rule that sets restrictive terms for considering the reconciliation bill.

13. These estimates were made by the House Budget Committee when the reconciliation bill was being considered and are published in the House Committee on the Budget, *A Review of the Reconciliation Process*, Committee Print, October 1984, p. 32. Slightly different estimates were made by the Congressional Budget Office shortly after the bill was enacted.

14. House Rule XXI bars unauthorized appropriations, which is interpreted to cover appropriations in excess of the authorized amounts. Senate Rule XVI has similar but significantly weaker restrictions. Both chambers have procedures that enable them to bypass the rules and appropriate in excess of authorized levels.

15. The growing prominence of the credit budget is reflected in the devotion of an

entire section to it in the fiscal 1990 budget. The section explains the concepts and applications of credit budgeting. See Office of Management and Budget, *Budget of the United States Government, Fiscal Year 1990*, Part 6.

16. The reforms are explained in *ibid.*, pp. 6–22ff.

17. Data on the appropriation limitations are provided in Office of Management and Budget, *Budget of the United States Government, Fiscal Year 1990, Special Analyses, Special Analysis F*.

18. See *Budget of the United States Government Fiscal Year 1990, Historical Tables*, Section 14.

19. The federally sponsored enterprises (FSEs) are private organizations established by the federal government. The fiscal 1990 budget identifies nine such enterprises. Because the FSEs are private, their transactions are not included in the budget. However, financial statements of the FSEs are annexed to the budget *Appendix*.

20. See Allen Schick, "Federally Sponsored Enterprises: The Next Budget Crisis?" in Tax Foundation, *Tax Features* (January/February 1989).

21. David A. Stockman, *The Triumph of Politics: Why the Reagan Revolution Failed* (New York: Harper & Row, 1986), pp. 405–06.

22. *Ibid.*, p. 401.

23. See Congressional Budget Office, *Baseline Budget Projections for Fiscal Years 1985–1989* (February 1984), Appendix D.

24. The data on payments for individuals are taken from OMB's *Historical Tables*. OMB does not classify expenditures into mandatory and discretionary categories. CBO reports that mandatory spending was 10.7 percent of GNP in 1981 and 10.5 percent in 1988, whereas nondefense discretionary spending was 5.7 percent of GNP in 1981 and 3.7 percent in 1988. See Congressional Budget Office, *The Economic and Budget Outlook: Fiscal Years 1990–1994* (February 1989), table F-6.

25. OMB, *Historical Tables*, table 11.1.

26. Mandated workload changes are those required by law, such as an increase in the number of Social Security or food stamps participants. These changes do not include workload increases in discretionary programs, such as a rise in the number of patents processed by the Patent Office.

27. Timothy J. Muris, "The Uses and Abuses of Budget Baselines," unpublished paper, January, 1989, p. 32. This informed paper provides numerous examples of how the baseline has been manipulated to distort the size of cutbacks.

28. Parts of this paragraph and of a few other paragraphs in this subsection are adapted from Allen Schick, In Ornstein, *op. cit.*, pp. 30–32.

29. During markup of the first budget resolution for the 1978 fiscal year, Senate Budget Committee Chairman Edmund Muskie acknowledged that "there is a growing impression around this table that the current policy number represents an inflated figure that . . . contains some water." Quoted in Allen Schick, *Congress and Money: Budgeting, Spending and Taxing* (Washington, D.C.: Urban Institute, 1980), p. 263.

30. The two types of baselines are compared in *Reductions in U.S. Domestic Spending*, ed. John W. Ellwood (New Brunswick: Transaction Books, 1982), pp. 34–39.

31. Quoted in William Greider, "The Education of David Stockman," *The Atlantic Monthly* (December 1981), p. 51.

32. Ellwood, *op. cit.*, p. 45.

33. Current practices and issues in the use of baselines are discussed in *Budget of the United States Government, Fiscal Year 1990, Special Analysis A*.

34. The budget impact of these expediences is discussed in Congressional Budget Office, *Baseline Budget Projections for Fiscal Years 1985–1989* (February 1984), p. 78.

35. Muris, *op. cit.*, p. 49, estimates that $7 billion of the Medicare savings claimed in the 1980s have been due to extensions of temporary provisions.

36. The appropriations committees do not have to conform to the functional allocations set forth in the budget resolution. When it allocates amounts to the House Appropriations Committee pursuant to section 302(a) of the Congressional Budget Act, the House Budget Committee specifies an amount for each function. The Senate Budget Committee allocates a lump sum to the appropriations committee; it does not identify specific budget functions.

37. Congress's ability to shift funds to domestic programs was also impaired by an agreement at the budget summit on the amounts to be provided for international programs.

38. See *Congressional Quarterly Almanac*, 1986, pp. 576–78.

39. PL 100-119; section 1013(b) of the Impoundment Control Act, as amended.

40. *Weekly Compilation of Presidential Documents*, vol. 24, no. 51 (December 26, 1988), p. 1643.

41. The Budget Act has some weak, ineffectual sanctions to spur action on reconciliation bills. Section 310 (f) of the act, as amended, provides for Congress to complete action on any required reconciliation bill by June 15. It also provides for a point of order in the House (during the month of July) against a resolution of adjournment.

42. "Quasi-entitlements" that cannot be controlled effectively through discretionary appropriations are still subject to reconciliation directives. The House Budget Committee has defined quasi-entitlements as "programs that function as though the spending is mandatory, but are legally discretionary programs . . . spending in such programs technically could be controlled by the Appropriations Committee, but such an approach is usually unrealistic." House Committee on the Budget, *A Review of the Reconciliation Process* (October 1984), p. 49. Food stamps are an example of a quasi-entitlement.

43. In 1981, the reconciliation instructions prepared by the House Budget Committee were broadened by floor amendments to cover more committees and produce deeper cuts. Despite the fact that it favored a more restrained use of the reconciliation process, the Budget Committee was blamed for excessive use of the reconciliation process, the Budget Committee was blamed for excessive use of power.

44. The legislative history and provisions of this law are reviewed in James Saturno, *Omnibus Budget Reconciliation Act of 1987: A Summary of Congressional Action on P.L. 100-203*, Congressional Research Service, Report N. 88-296 (April 12, 1988).

45. See Allen Schick, "Controlling the 'Uncontrollables': Budgeting for Health Care in an Age of Megadeficits," in *Charting the Future of Health Care*, ed. Jack A. Meyer and Marion Ein Lewin (Washington, D.C.: American Enterprise Institute, 1987), pp. 13–34.

46. This and other features of Medicare legislation in the 1980s are reviewed in chapter 6.

47. Muris, *op. cit.*, p. 48, estimates that the 1987 reconciliation law added $3.6 billion to spending over a five-year period, but because most of the additional amount will be incurred in 1991 and 1992, it was not factored into the baseline when the measure was enacted.

48. This section heading is taken from the title of David Stockman's book, which chronicles the early budget struggles during the Reagan presidency.

49. Data on budget-related roll calls are compiled in Allen Schick, *Crisis in the Budget*

Process: Exercising Political Choice (Washington: American Enterprise Institute, 1986), p. 42–43; also see Norman Ornstein et al., Vital Statistics on Congress, 1987–1988 (Washington, D.C.: Congressional Quarterly, 1987), tables 7-9 and 7-10.

50. Ornstein, ibid., contains a rich vein on trend data on congressional mail, campaign financing, and other measures of political activity.

51. See Harold Wolman and Fred Teitelbaum "Interest Groups and the Reagan Presidency," in The Reagan Presidency and the Governing of America, ed. Lester M. Salamon and Michael S. Lund (Washington, D.C.: Urban Institute, 1984), pp. 297–333.

52. There are points in The Triumph of Politics at which Stockman demonstrates a keen understanding of democratic politics. Here are some excerpts from the epilogue to his book. "The politics of American democracy made a shambles of my anti-welfare state theory . . . . Whatever its substantive merit, it rested on the illusion that the will of the people was at drastic variance with the actions of the politicians.

But the political history of the past five years mostly invalidates that proposition. We have had a tumultuous national referendum on everything in our half-trillion dollar welfare state budget. . . . Congressmen and Senators ultimately deliver what their constituencies demand . . . the spending politics of Washington do reflect the heterogeneous and parochial demands that arise from the diverse, activated fragments of the electorate scattered across the land. What you see done in the halls of the politicians may not be wise, but it is the only real and viable definition of what the electorate wants" pp. 376–77.

53. The broad support for increased or stable spending was found in numerous surveys conducted during the last few years of the Reagan presidency. For example, a 1987 poll for Time magazine found the following majorities of those polled favoring increases: health programs for the elderly—78 percent; environmental programs—73 percent; aid to the homeless—71 percent; health services for the poor—71 percent; nutrition programs for mothers and infants—55 percent; low- and moderate-income housing—54 percent; loans and grants to college students—52 percent. Time, March 30, 1987, p. 37.

54. The following table, taken from the 1988 Statistical Abstract (table 678), shows the trend in sources of income since 1970:

Sources of Personal Income (percentage)

Item	1970	1975	1980	1983	1986
Wage and salary disbursements	66.3	63.7	60.7	59.1	59.1
Transfer payments	10.3	14.2	14.4	15.6	14.7
Other[a]	23.3	22.1	24.8	25.3	26.3
Personal Income	100.0	100.0	100.0	100.0	100.0

[a]Other: other labor income, proprietor's income, rental income for persons, personal dividend income, personal interest income, and the outlays for personal contributions for social insurance.

55. The concept of "stickiness" has been borrowed from economics, where it is used to explain why prices are sometimes slow in adjusting to changing market conditions. "Sticky" is preferred rather than "inflexible" or "rigid" expenditure because the latter adjectives suggest that expenditures do not adjust at all. The evidence is that adjust-

ment does take place, but not as responsively as might occur if expenditure were less "sticky."

56. The data in table 4.9 are affected by periodic reclassifications of relatively controllable and relatively uncontrollable spending by OMB. Because of these reclassifications, OMB's historical series go back only to 1985. Therefore, the data in table 4.9 are drawn from several different sources that might not be compatible with one another. Another complication is that the breakdown of different types of expenditure is affected by accounting tricks, offsetting collections, and other changes. Nevertheless, the table provides useful, albeit imprecise, data on budget trends.

Chapter 5

THE POWER NOT TO TAX ENOUGH

The capacity to budget cannot be assessed solely in terms of the government's control of expenditures. Effective budgeting also requires an ability to link revenues and outlays, to decide how much should be raised in light of the claims on public funds. When a government has chronic deficits, one must assess its revenue actions to determine the extent to which the shortfall is due to an inadequate linkage of the two sides of the budget.

The linkage of revenues and outlays is inherently looser in the federal government than in American states and localities. Lacking a strict balanced budget requirement and having extraordinary access to capital, the federal government can budget for expenditures without explicitly considering whether an increase in spending would compel an upward adjustment in taxes or other sources of revenue. Unlike localities, which typically review tax policy each year, the federal government can take the estimated tax yield as a given and then decide whether outlays should be permitted to exceed receipts and by how much.

The linkage of revenue and expenditure was loosened by postwar growth and by compensatory fiscal policy. Protracted growth bred confidence in the capacity of the economy to generate sufficient resources to finance program expansions; compensatory fiscal actions legitimized shortfalls in revenue due to cyclical conditions. As discussed in chapter 2, by orienting the budget to the potential of the economy, applied Keynesianism allowed the government to pay less attention to actual or projected revenue. Moreover, if actual receipts fell short of planned levels, no corrective action would have to be taken during the fiscal year. The revenue shortfall was seen as an aid to economic recovery.

Deteriorating budget conditions in the late 1960s and early 1970s incited concern over the relationship of receipts and outlays. Congress held President Johnson's proposed surtax hostage to spending cuts in 1967, and it refused to act on tax legislation until agreement was reached with the White House on expenditures. This arrangement was ad hoc, however. It did not provide for integration of revenue and spending decisions on a recurring basis.

Congress sought to institutionalize the linkage of revenue and expenditure in the budget process it established in 1974. It decreed that each budget resolution was to set forth the recommended level of federal revenues and the amount, if any, by which the aggregate level of federal revenues should be increased or decreased.[1] To ensure that revenue policies would be formulated in a manner consistent with congressional budget decisions, the 1974 act barred consideration of tax legislation until the Spring budget resolution had been adopted.[2] Through the Budget Act's reconciliation procedure, Congress could direct the House Ways and Means Committee and the Senate Finance Committee to report changes in tax laws. The reconciliation process enabled Congress, for the first time, to combine revenue and spending legislation in a single measure.[3] To enforce budget decisions and guard against tax reduction that would add to the approved deficit, the Budget Act ruled out legislation that would cause total revenue to fall below the level set in the final budget resolution.

The Budget Act clearly recognized that deficits can result from either revenue or spending policies, and it designed a process that would treat both sides of the budget in a symmetrical manner.[4] The act generally relies on procedural rules to ensure that Congress legislates within the framework of its approved budget.[5]

Despite these rules, major revenue decisions have sometimes been made independently of the budget process. The leading instance was the Tax Reform Act of 1986 (TRA), the most far-reaching tax legislation since World War II. TRA was structured to be revenue neutral over a five-year period. That is, the new tax system was estimated to yield the same revenue over this period as the one it replaced. Inasmuch as the budget deficit peaked at $221 billion in 1986—the year that TRA was enacted—it might seem surprising that Congress would go through the trouble of overhauling the tax code without generating additional revenue. The commitment to revenue neutrality effectively cordoned off tax legislation from that year's budgetary actions. Revenue neutrality excluded the budget committees and others concerned about the deficit from influencing tax policy. In March 1986, just about the time the Senate Finance Committee began serious work on the measure, a bipartisan group of fifty Senators wrote to President Reagan urging that TRA be delayed:

While we consider tax reform an important effort, we do not believe it should move ahead prior to further action to reduce the deficit. We continue to believe the deficit is the most pressing problem confronting our nation. . . . Therefore, until a firm, definite agreement has been reached between Congress and the White House, we do not believe tax reform should be considered or debated by the United States Senate.[6]

The Finance Committee (with White House encouragement) ignored this plea and produced a bill that won overwhelming approval in the Senate and strongly influenced the legislation finally enacted into law. The divorcement of tax reform from the budget was so thorough that when it was discovered that TRA would produce an $11 billion gain in its first year but revenue losses in some later years, the Senate approved a soon-forgotten amendment declaring that these fluctuations should not be counted in determining compliance with the Gramm-Rudman-Hollings deficit target.[7]

Because it is exceedingly rare for Congress to enact revenue-neutral legislation, TRA was not representative of the many other tax measures approved in the 1970s and 1980s. But TRA does demonstrate that the close congressional coordination of tax and budget policy sought in the 1974 Act has not always materialized. Some revenue measures have been effectively linked to the budget, whereas others have been more influenced by economic policy or other factors. The 1980 reconciliation act, the 1982 Tax Equity and Fiscal Responsibility Act (TEFRA), the 1984 Deficit Reduction Act (DEFRA), and the 1987 reconciliation act drove or were driven by budget decisions. Each of these measures sought to reduce the deficit by increasing federal revenue. But another batch of revenue measures moved through Congress with much weaker ties to the budget. These include the tax reductions enacted in 1975, 1976, and 1977. These laws were passed during a period of economic stress and rising tax burdens. Hence, they were less influenced by the condition of the budget than by the desire to alleviate tax pressures. The 1981 law was a special case. It was not procedurally linked to the congressional budget process, but as a key part of Reagan's economic program, it was closely coordinated with that year's budget decisions. Table 5.1 sets forth the revenue effects of these and other laws estimated at the time they were enacted. A clear pattern emerges from a comparison of the two sets of measures. The legislation loosely linked to the budget subtracted much more revenue than was added by the laws formally integrated with budget policy.

Budget-related revenue measures have the financing of government as their principal objective. The tax laws acted on—relatively

Table 5.1 ESTIMATED REVENUE EFFECTS OF MAJOR TAX ACTS, 1975–87
(billions of dollars)

Tax Act/Year	Estimated Revenue Effects				
	1st year	2nd year	3rd year	4th year	5th year
Tax Reduction Act of 1975	− 22.8	not projected			
Tax Reform Act of 1976	− 15.7	− 12.8	− 6.8	− 7.4	− 6.2
Tax Reduction and Simplification Act of 1977	− 2.6	− 17.8	− 13.8	not projected	
Revenue Act of 1978	− 19.3	− 37.5	− 44.2	− 52.1	− 58.0
Omnibus Reconciliation Act of 1980	3.6	2.5	4.2	7.0	11.1
Crude Oil Windfall Profit Tax Act of 1980	6.1	12.2	16.3	19.2	20.0
Economic Recovery Tax Act of 1981	− 37.7	− 92.7	− 150.0	− 199.2	− 267.7
Tax Equity & Fiscal Responsibility Act of 1982[a]	18.0	37.7	42.7	51.8	63.9
Deficit Reduction Act of 1984	1.1	10.6	16.5	22.5	25.2
Consolidated Omnibus Budget Reconciliation Act of 1985	0.8	2.5	2.8	2.9	3.1
Tax Reform Act of 1986	11.5	− 16.7	− 15.1	8.0	12.0
Omnibus Reconciliation Act of 1987	9.1	14.1	15.1	not projected	

Source: Joint Committee on Taxation.
Note: The table covers general revenue; it does not include legislation earmarking revenue to the social security trust fund or other programs. These estimates were made by the Joint Committee on Taxation at the time the particular legislation was enacted. The estimates may vary from the actual effects of the tax measures.
[a]Includes the revenue impact of compliance provisions.

independently of the budget—have other objectives in mind. These include controlling government expenditures, stabilizing and redistributing the tax burden, providing subsidies and other benefits through the tax system, and earmarking funds to designated programs. In view of the fact that the revenue impact of these measures has been greater than is the impact of the budget-related measures, it is fair to conclude that the production of revenue is often subordinated to other legislative objectives.

This chapter reviews the various objectives of tax policy as they have been pursued through revenue legislation enacted since the 1974 Budget Act. After completing this review, the chapter concludes with an assessment of the linkage of revenue and budget policy.

CONTROLLING GOVERNMENT EXPENDITURES

In contrast to the notion that the government writes tax legislation to finance expenditures, recent actions suggest that it often legislates for the opposite purpose—to curtail expenditures. The use of tax legislation to control spending is predicated on the expectation that spending will rise to consume all available revenue. According to this view, the more it has, the more government spends. Hence, curtailing resources, or slowing their rise, effectively reduces spending below a level it would otherwise reach.

Denying revenue is likely to be a more effective control in states and localities, which are required to balance their operating budgets, than in the federal government, which can avoid a reduction in expenditures by incurring larger deficits. From the vantage point of the late 1980s, it seems evident that the massive tax cuts enacted in 1981 and the ensuing deficits constrained the growth in federal spending. "We believe," Milton Friedman wrote in 1988, "the deficit has been the only effective restraint on congressional spending. . . . Relying on the deficit to check spending is admittedly a second-best solution—but it is better than nothing."[8]

Was spending control by means of forced deficits the principal objective of the 1981 Economic Recovery Tax Act (ERTA), which chopped an estimated $748 billion off federal revenue over a five-year period? In assessing the extent to which the federal government has behaved in this manner, one must distinguish between the motives and the after-effects of that tax legislation. Table 5.1 shows ERTA's disproportionate revenue impact compared with all the other laws (other than those affecting Social Security and other earmarked taxes that are not included in the table) enacted since 1975. With the federal government deprived of so much revenue, it is understandable that the resulting deficit has been seen by some as the real aim of ERTA, not just as the end product of a serious policy mishap. This view was vigorously argued by Senator Daniel Moynihan. In a 1983 article, Moynihan contended that "the deficits were purposeful. . . . Any massive reduction in something as fundamental as the income tax was going to bring about a massive loss of revenue. And this was intended."[9]

Motive is important in this case because it goes to the heart of the question of whether contemporary deficits are due to failings in political will or to flaws in the machinery of budgeting. Some support for Moynihan's argument comes from a televised address by Reagan shortly before the key House vote on the 1981 tax measure:

If the tax cut goes to you, the American people . . . that money returned to you won't be available to the Congress to spend, and that, in my view, is what this whole controversy comes down to. Are you entitled to the fruits of your own labor or does government have some presumptive right to spend and spend and spend?[10]

Although there is no doubt that Reagan wanted to constrain spending, this does not prove that he engineered the deficit to accomplish the same objective. The 1981 telecast asking for public support of his tax legislation also promised a balanced budget in a few years.[11] Moreover, near the end of his long presidency, Reagan himself regarded the deficit as his most conspicuous failure.[12]

A fair reading of the record is that Reagan wanted both less spending and smaller deficits. But once the deficit became entrenched, the president was not inclined to do much about it. He was convinced that tax increases enacted to reduce the deficit would generate additional expenditures instead, and he preferred to have a smaller government with a bigger deficit than a bigger government with a smaller deficit.

More could have been done in 1981 to link tax legislation and the deficit problem. The tax cut was stretched out a bit to ease the short-term deficit problem. The size of the cuts was enlarged in the out-years, however. Over a five-year period, Congress reduced taxes by a projected $750 billion, approximately $30 billion more than Reagan requested. But the first-year reduction was only about two-thirds of the amount that Reagan originally requested. Shifting the bulk of the cuts to the outyears reflected the sentiment that the future would take care of itself. In view of Reagan's landslide victory, taxpayer attitudes, and competition between Republicans and Democrats to produce the winning measure, it is understandable that taxes were reduced without adequate attention to the long-term budgetary impact.

STABILIZING THE TAX BURDEN

Before the mid-1970s, tax policy was often made by nondecision and inertia. Major tax legislation was infrequent, as evidenced by the long intervals between the 1949, 1954, and 1969 revisions of the internal revenue code. Congress frequently tinkered with the tax laws and passed a number of minor tax bills each year, but these had only a slight impact on the budget.

The increments provided by an expanding economy obviated the need for legislation to generate additional revenue. In fact, because of the progressive individual income tax, federal revenue grew faster than the economy. Left to its own devices, a progressive income tax would push taxpayers into higher marginal tax brackets. To counter this tendency, Congress adjusted the brackets from time to time. A more serious spur to legislative action was stagflation in the late 1970s and early 1980s. The combination of high inflation and low growth imposed rising tax burdens on millions of Americans at a time when real disposable incomes were declining. In inflation-adjusted dollars, the median after-federal-tax (including Social Security taxes) income of one-earner families dropped from $7,743 in 1972 to $6,523 in 1981.[13] This decline in real disposable income was accompanied by escalating tax burdens. Table 5.2, adapted from computations made by Joseph Minarik, displays the change in average and marginal tax rates at five-year intervals from 1965 through 1980. Taxpayers earning one-half the median family income saw their average tax rate jump from 2.5 percent in 1965 to 5.4 percent in 1980. Families earning the median income experienced a steep

Table 5.2 AVERAGE AND MARGINAL TAX RATES FOR 4-PERSON FAMILIES AT MULTIPLES OF THE MEDIAN FAMILY INCOME, SELECTED YEARS (percentage)

	1965	1970	1975	1980	1984
One-half median income					
Average rates	2.5	6.0	2.7	5.4	6.0
Marginal rates	14.0	16.8	26.0	16.0	14.0
Median income					
Average rates	7.9	10.0	9.6	11.6	10.3
Marginal rates	17.0	19.5	22.0	24.0	22.0
Twice median income					
Average rates	12.0	14.7	15.2	18.3	16.0
Marginal rates	22.0	25.6	32.0	43.0	33.0
Five times median income					
Average rates	20.4	25.0	28.1	32.4	26.1
Marginal rates	39.0	49.2	53.0	59.0	49.0
Ten times median income					
Average rates	30.9	33.9	37.8	41.4	33.3
Marginal rates	53.0	59.5	62.0	68.0	50.0

Source: Joseph J. Minarik, *Making Tax Choices* (Washington, D.C.: Urban Institute, 1985), tables 4 and 5.

rise in average tax rates from 7.9 percent in 1965 to 9.6 percent in 1975 and 11.6 percent in 1980. The trend in marginal rates also was sharply upward, especially for those at or above the median income.[14]

The spiral in tax rates hiked individual tax receipts from 9.8 percent of total personal income in 1975 to 11.6 percent in 1981.[15] During these years, individual income tax receipts climbed from 8.0 percent of the gross national product to a record high of 9.6 percent.[16]

Congress responded to soaring tax burdens by reducing taxes in four consecutive years: 1975, 1976, 1977, and 1978. The reductions were relatively modest, however, and they did not fully compensate for bracket creep. Congress was evidently constrained in the amount of relief it was willing to provide by budget deficits then averaging about $60 billion a year. Trapped between pressure to reduce both the deficit and taxes, Congress tried to provide a little of each, but it failed to accomplish much of either.

Ronald Reagan escaped from this quandary by making tax relief and deficit reduction compatible rather than antagonistic objectives. By advocating tax cuts to stimulate the economy and reduce tax burdens, Reagan gained tax reductions in 1981 (as table 5.1 showed) greatly exceeding those enacted in the previous decade. These cuts had the intended impact on tax rates. By 1984, families at or above the median income generally had lower average and marginal tax burdens than they had at the start of the decade, as table 5.2 reveals. Note, however, that these burdens still remained high compared with the rates prevailing in the 1960s and the 1970s.

This upward creep in the tax burden fed discontent with the tax system, made it even more difficult for politicians to support tax increases, and led to the emphasis on lower marginal rates in the 1986 tax reform. Strong evidence of taxpayer discontent came from the annual public opinion survey sponsored by the Advisory Commission on Intergovernmental Relations (ACIR). As shown in the first part of table 5.5, when this poll was first conducted in 1972, only 19 percent of interviewees rated the federal income tax as the worst tax.[17] By 1980, 36 percent saw it as the worst tax. Obviously, tax reduction in the 1970s did not suffice to ease discontent over the federal tax burden. It was not until tax rates were substantially lowered in 1986 that disgruntlement abated.

As long as inflation was modest, there was political gain in legislating periodic adjustments in tax burdens. Politicians could take credit for reducing taxes while still supplying government with a rising flow of revenue. But when inflation soared, politicians were blamed for not doing enough to protect taxpayers against bracket creep and escalating taxes. To avoid blame, Congress indexed the income tax brackets in 1981 (effective in 1985) to changes in consumer prices.[18] By making automatic adjustments, indexation took away most of the government's "inflation dividend." Henceforth, there could be a substantial rise in real revenue only through economic growth or explicit tax increases.

DISTRIBUTING BENEFITS

In addition to stabilizing the tax burden, Congress has reduced taxes in order to furnish benefits to particular groups of taxpayers. Viewed from this perspective, revenue legislation has been a political substitute for spending legislation. Rather than imposing taxes to pay the bills, Congress writes tax legislation to distribute benefits to some portion of the population.

The power to provide benefits is inherent in tax legislation. Congress provides two main types of benefits. First, in the course of reducing the tax liability of a broad class of taxpayers, it redistributes the tax burden so that some groups end up paying a smaller share than before. Second, when changing the tax laws, it makes special preferences available to certain taxpayers. Congress has used both approaches in recent years.

Redistributing the Tax Burden

When Congress reduces taxes, it often redistributes the tax burden. All taxpayers may have their payments reduced, but not all to the same extent. Redistributive outcomes are unavoidable in a progressive tax structure. If all taxpayers were given the same dollar reduction, higher income persons would be made to bear a larger share of the tax burden. If, however, all taxpayers were given the same percentage cut, the dollar value of the reductions would be far greater for wealthy persons than for poorer ones.

The deficits, which constrained the amount of tax reduction voted in the 1970s, sharpened competition for redistributive benefits. Within a fixed budget for tax reduction, more for one group of taxpayers left less for others. Table 5.3 shows that lower income taxpayers garnered most of the benefits in the 1975 and 1976 legislation, whereas higher income taxpayers benefited the most from the 1978 and 1981 mea-

Table 5.3 ESTIMATED REDUCTION IN INDIVIDUAL INCOME TAXES BY INCOME CLASS, SELECTED LEGISLATION, 1975–1981 (for married couples with two dependents)[a]

Income class	Tax Reduction Act of 1975			Tax Reform Act of 1976			Revenue Act of 1978			Economic Recovery Tax Act of 1981		
	Prior law	Reduction	Percent reduction	Prior law[b]	Reduction	Percent reduction	Prior law	Reduction	Percent reduction	Prior law	Reduction[c]	Percent reduction
$ 5,000	$ 98	$296	—[d]	$ 98	$398	—	$ –300	$ 200	—	$ –500	$ 0	—
10,000	867	252	29.1	867	216	24.9	446	72	16.1	374	83	22.2
15,000	1,699	170	10.0	1,699	180	10.6	1,330	97	7.3	1,233	281	22.8
20,000	2,660	200	7.5	2,660	180	6.8	2,180	167	7.7	2,013	464	23.1
30,000	4,988	100	2.0	4,988	180	3.6	4,232	315	7.4	3,917	914	23.3
40,000	7,958	100	1.3	7,958	180	2.3	6,848	536	7.8	6,312	1,438	22.8
50,000	n.a.			n.a.			9,950	627	6.3	9,323	2,158	23.1
60,000	n.a.			n.a.			13,496	862	6.4	12,634	2,928	23.2
100,000	n.a.			n.a.			28,880	1,002	3.5	27,878	5,822	20.9

Source: Joint Committee on Taxation.

Notes: "n.a." = data are not available.

Negative figures indicate that some persons received refundable earned income credits in excess of their tax liability. These estimates were made at the time of enactment by the Joint Committee on Taxation using its assumptions concerning standard deductions and/or deductible personal expenses.

[a]Data provided for 1981 Economic Recovery Tax Act pertains to one-earner families with two dependents. For remaining Acts, number of earners is not specified.

[b]Since the 1975 tax cuts were temporary, the comparison drawn for the Tax Reform Act of 1976 is with the 1974 tax laws.

[c]The amounts shown in this column are the reductions estimated for 1984, the first year that the tax reductions enacted in 1981 were fully implemented.

[d]Percent reductions cannot be computed because persons in this income class received earned income credit in excess of tax liability.

sures. In both dollar and percentage terms, persons earning less than $10,000 received bigger reductions in 1975 and 1976 than did those who had twice as much or more income. This tilt was accomplished by providing most of the reduction through adjustments in the standard deduction, a rebate of past taxes, and a uniform tax credit. In addition, Congress established an earned income credit that entitles certain low-income persons to payments from the government in excess of their tax liability.

By the late 1970s, however, Congress was faced with strong demands to stimulate investment and capital formation. It responded by giving most of the benefits of the 1978 tax reduction to high-income persons and business. The 1978 law gave taxpayers in the $60,000 bracket five times the dollar reduction accorded those making $20,000. It also lowered the capital gains tax and the minimum tax on persons claiming high deductions and exclusions.

These redistributive actions left taxpayers feeling burdened by rising taxes and business leaders still complaining that the tax code was discouraging savings and investment. With help from a bidding war between House Democrats and the White House, Congress cut taxes so deeply in 1981 that it could distribute substantial relief to all taxpayers. An across-the-board cut of approximately 23 percent was phased in over three years. The proportionality of these reductions meant that they were worth almost seven times more in dollar terms to a family making $60,000 than to one with a $20,000 income. Substantial benefits also were provided to businesses through accelerated depreciation, the opportunity to sell unused tax credits, and many other preferences. When the dust cleared on the 1981 legislation, it became evident that some firms had negative tax rates; that is, they had received preferences that boosted their after-tax income above their pretax earnings.

Special Preferences

The 1981 legislation capped a period in which Congress established or expanded numerous tax expenditures. Table 5.4, drawn from material prepared by the Congressional Budget Office, indicates that many more of these preferences were established in the late 1970s and early 1980s than in the immediately preceding period. As might be expected, many tax preferences were inaugurated during the early decades of the income tax (1909–39) and the World War II period (1940–54), when the income tax was broadened to cover most households. Many early tax expenditures distributed benefits broadly to

Table 5.4 PERIOD IN WHICH TAX EXPENDITURES EFFECTIVE IN 1982 WERE
INITIALLY AUTHORIZED

	1909–39	1940–54	1954–74	1975–81
Number of tax expenditures initiated	37	28	10	29

Source: Congressional Budget Office, *Tax Expenditures: Budget Control Options and Five Year Budget Projections*, November 1982, Table C-1.

most taxpayers. They included the deductability of state and local taxes and interest payments, and the exclusion of fringe benefits and Social Security benefits. The 1955–74 period was relatively quiet with few tax expenditures established during these years. However, there was a resurgence of activity during 1975–81, when twenty-nine preferences were added to the tax code. Most of these later tax preferences were narrowly distributed to businesses or upper-income taxpayers. Congress also enhanced many older benefits. More than half of all the modifications made over the years to the tax expenditures on the books in the early 1980s occurred during the previous decade.[19]

The special preferences tilted the tax structure in favor of upper-income persons and, by narrowing the tax base, contributed to the uptrend in marginal rates.[20] The impact of the distribution of the benefits in the 1981 legislation is reflected in the data assembled in table 5.2. By 1984, when the tax cuts made three years earlier were fully effective, the average tax burden had been much more substantially reduced for families above the median income than for those at or below the median. Compared with 1980, the average tax rate was 11 percent lower for families earning the median income but almost 20 percent lower for those with income five or ten times the median level.

This redistribution made the tax burden less acceptable and Americans less willing to support tax increases to ease the deficit. Despite the big 1981 tax cut, 38 percent of those polled in the 1985 ACIR survey—a higher percentage than ever before—ranked the federal income tax as the worst tax.

GENERATING REVENUE

Having examined some recent objectives of tax legislation, we come now to the purpose that links it most closely to the budget—the production of revenue to finance government. It has been exceedingly rare in American history for the federal government to boost income taxes in peacetime. It has raised taxes during war and then retained some of the added revenue for domestic programs when peace returned. As we saw in chapter 2, the establishment of steep tax rates during World War II was the main factor in financing expanded government after the war.

In view of the rarity of peacetime tax increases, some of the legislation listed in table 5.1 is quite remarkable. Congress raised revenues in three consecutive election years (1980, 1982, and 1984), and it passed a number of other revenue increases in the 1980s. The push to raise revenue was obviously spurred by big deficits. It also was abetted by use of the reconciliation procedures authorized in the Budget Act.

When it was first used in 1980, reconciliation was the instrument for achieving an estimated $8.2 billion in deficit reduction—$3.6 billion in revenue increases and the remainder in outlay savings. In raising revenue, Congress had to maneuver through a minefield of public discontent over the tax burden and the perceived unfairness of the tax system. It succeeded by keeping the amount of tax increase small, relying on an assortment of relatively minor changes to obtain the added income, and imposing most of the increases on business or upper-income taxpayers. Most taxpayers were hardly affected by the revenue increases enacted through reconciliation in 1980 and subsequent years.

The 1980 reconciliation measure left basic tax rates intact. It turned to a variety of "revenue enhancements" instead, including an extension of telephone excise taxes scheduled to expire, limitations on the issuance of certain tax-free bonds, and accelerated payment of some corporate taxes.[21] The pattern was repeated in 1982, but the revenue increases were much bigger this time. In compliance with the instructions issued in that year's budget resolution, Congress passed a reconciliation package that raised an estimated $98 billion in revenue over three years and also included some spending cutbacks. That measure—the Tax Equity and Fiscal Responsibility Act (TEFRA)—was endorsed by Ronald Reagan, who, despite his avowed opposition to tax increases, requested some revenue enhancements in his own budget. Like the 1980 measure, TEFRA drew revenue from an assortment of provisions, including curtailment of some of the preferences enacted in 1981, excise tax extensions, and another round of acceleration in corporate tax payments. It also closed some of the loopholes opened the previous year, such as the "safe harbor" leasing provision, which enabled corporations to sell their tax losses. Once again, Congress refrained from tampering with basic tax rates, and it also rebuffed proposals to delay full implementation of the across-the-board tax cuts enacted in the previous year.

Although TEFRA was enacted with presidential support, it soured relations between the president and Congress and thereby made it even more difficult to enact future tax increases. After TEFRA, Reagan felt cheated because his expectation that each dollar of revenue increase would be matched by three dollars in spending cuts did not materialize. Others who participated in putting together the TEFRA deal denied that there had been any such understanding, but the fact that the additional revenue far exceeded the spending cuts reinforced Reagan's belief that tax increases result in more spending, not in lower deficits.[22]

Nevertheless, the huge deficits compelled the White House to agree to further revenue enhancements. The 1984 Deficit Reduction Act (DEFRA) was part of a package that included an estimated $50 billion in revenue increases over three years and about twice that amount in spending reductions.[23] As explained in the previous chapter, these estimates were measured against the baseline. The basic shape of DEFRA was determined in a "Rose Garden" agreement negotiated by Senate Republican leaders and presidential aides, although the terms were modified in subsequent give- and-take with House Democrats. DEFRA provided for yet another extension of the telephone excise tax, a repeal of exemptions of a portion of interest income from taxation, additional restrictions on income averaging, and several dozen changes in business taxation.

Because it is harder to raise taxes than to lower them, the money added by the three election-year increases did not come close to replacing the revenue surrendered in 1981. Efforts to enact revenue increases also were impeded by growing disenchantment with the federal tax system. The negative attitudes that appeared in the annual ACIR survey were confirmed by other public opinion polls conducted in the mid-1980s and reported in table 5.5. It is especially significant that as the deficit situation worsened, taxpayers became even less supportive of proposals to raise taxes. The percentage of those who agreed that the government should raise taxes to reduce the deficit dropped from 31 percent in 1983 to 19 percent in 1985. Influenced by reports that some major corporations had paid little or no taxes, 59 percent of those polled in the mid-1980s saw the federal tax system as unfair; an equal percentage felt that persons

Table 5.5 PUBLIC ATTITUDES TOWARD FEDERAL TAXES

Question	Year	Agree/Yes (%)
1. Do you think federal income taxes are the worst tax—the least fair? (ACIR)		
	1972	19
	1980	36
	1985	38
	1987	30
2. Do you think our system of federal taxes is basically unfair? (*LA Times*, 1985)		59
People whose income all comes from salary or wages pay too much in incomes taxes. (Roper, 1985)		59
The present tax system benefits the rich and is unfair to ordinary working men and women. (ABC/*Post*, 1985)		75
3. Do you think the government should increase taxes to reduce the budget deficit? (ABC/*Post*)		
	1982	23
	1983	31
	1984	25
	1985	19
4. Do you feel corporations are undertaxed? (Yankelovich/ *Time*, 1984)		52
Should an increase in corporate taxes be very seriously considered to reduce the deficit? (Roper, 1984)		78
Should an increase in personal income taxes be very seriously considered to reduce the deficit? (*Ibid.*)		24
To cut the size of the deficit, would you favor putting a minimum tax on corporate income? (Harris, 1985)		73

Sources: Item 1, Advisory Commission on Intergovernmental Relations, *Changing Public Attitudes on Governments and Taxes*, 1987. All other items, "Opinion Roundup," *Public Opinion* (Feb./Mar. 1985).

whose income comes from wages pay too much in taxes; and 75 percent believed that the tax system was unfair to working men and women.[24]

These attitudes all but ruled out broad-based tax increases to ease the deficit problem. Most Americans felt quite differently, however, about the taxes borne by corporations. More than three-quarters of those polled agreed that serious consideration should be given to an increase in corporate taxes, and 73 percent favored a minimum tax on corporate income.

Revenue Neutrality

Opposition to increases in the individual tax but support for increased corporate taxation provided the political conditions for the revenue-neutral Tax Reform Act of 1986 (TRA). Revenue neutrality dictated that tax benefits given to some groups be paid for by additional burdens on other groups. With the 1982 and 1984 tax increases in mind, conservatives embraced revenue neutrality as a means of blocking the use of tax reform to raise additional funds. Many liberals supported revenue neutrality as a spur to redistributing the tax burden.[25]

Revenue neutrality forced two sets of trade-offs: between individual and corporate taxpayers and between tax rates and tax breaks. An estimated $120 billion in tax liabilities (over five years) were transferred from households to corporations. Without this redistribution, which was endorsed by Ronald Reagan, there would have been no tax reform in 1986. The cost of this shift was eased for some influential corporations by distributing more than $10 billion of preferences in the form of "transition rules."[26] The trade-off between rates and breaks was supported by those for whom lower marginal rates were the key objectives of tax reform as well as by those for whom the curtailment of special tax privileges was the main objective.

Revenue neutrality precluded the imposition of new taxes, and tax reform made such action more difficult than previously. In the afterglow of reform, there was strong sentiment in Washington to maintain the lower rates established in 1986. Politicians understandably took pride in this visible benefit of reform, and they did not want their accomplishment tarnished by tampering with the rates. This consensus might weaken over time, but it did protect the rates in the years immediately following reform. The 1986 legislation also made it harder to pick up additional revenue by closing loopholes. TRA eliminated more than $100 billion in tax expenditures and, by reducing marginal rates, lowered the value of most remaining preferences.[27] After reform, corporations retained less than $40 billion in tax expenditures. Individuals had an estimated $260 billion in tax expenditures in 1989, but more than half of this amount was accounted for by five of the oldest and most popular benefits in the tax code: exclusion of pension contributions and earnings, deduction of home mortgage interest, exclusion of employer-paid medical insurance and care, deduction of state-local income and property taxes, and exclusion of Social Security payments. These and other preferences benefit millions of Americans and are, with the exception of Social Security and Medicare, the biggest middle-class subsidies in the budget.

The postreform difficulty of generating additional revenue was evident in the budget summit occasioned by the October 1987 stock market crash. Despite the anxiety-provoking conditions then prevailing, presidential and congressional negotiators haggled for a full month before agreeing to a deficit reduction package that, among other things, produced only $9 billion in new revenue the first year and $14 billion the second. This was much less revenue enhancement than had been achieved through the 1982 TEFRA and 1984 DEFRA legislation. To achieve even the modest revenue target, Congress made more than three dozen relatively minor adjustments, including numerous accounting changes; another extension of the telephone excise tax; and, perhaps the most significant politically, a limitation on the deduction of home mortgage interest.

The series of tax increases enacted in the 1980s demonstrates that Congress can produce some additional revenue without overhauling the tax code or opening up entirely new tax sources. TEFRA and DEFRA alone added an estimated $83 billion in fiscal 1989 revenue.[28] But these actions have not sufficed to eliminate the structural imbalance between federal revenue and expenditures.

EARMARKING REVENUE

By the late 1980s, there was no groundswell of support for a major tax increase to liquidate the deficit. George Bush had successfully run for the White House on a "no new taxes" platform, and although this pledge still may be overtaken by events, it does not augur well for dealing with the deficit through revenue increases.

The inability to liquidate the deficit occurred during a period of rising public support for expanded programs. But as long as the deficit persists as the major budget issue of the times, it constrains the responsiveness of Congress to program demands. In the past, when deficits were low, Congress could set up new programs without having to be immediately concerned about paying for them. But in an age of high deficits, Congress cannot add significantly to federal outlays without also financing the new programs.

To cope with the contradictions in public demands, politicians have reverted to an old form of revenue behavior and given it increased prominence in recent years. They have earmarked revenue increases to pay for program enhancements. Recent earmarks include the following: (1) The superfund program authorized in 1986 is financed by a package of earmarked taxes on petroleum, chemicals, and U.S. corporations.[29] (2) In 1987, Congress imposed a new tax on vaccine manufacturers to finance a trust fund that compensates persons injured by certain vaccines. (3) In 1988, Congress established a trust fund, financed by an import fee, to assist workers displaced by imports. (4) Also in 1988, Congress expanded Medicare's coverage of catastrophic illness by increasing the premiums paid by elderly Americans into the Medicare trust fund.

Earmarking is an attractive option for revenue-short politicians. First, it enables them to generate additional revenue without raising general taxes. Because most taxpayers are unaffected, opposition to the tax increase is contained. Second, by linking revenue and outlays, earmarking ties the establishment of new programs to agreement on how they should be paid for and may constrain resource demands. The vaccine compensation program, for example, was not activated until earmarked funds were made available to cover the costs. Third, a single set of congressional committees often has jurisdiction over both the outlays and revenues, thereby enabling Congress to balance the blame for imposing taxes with the credit for doing something about the problem at hand. This feature, which has been characteristic of the Social Security program since its inception, facilitates the matching of program income and expenditures.

Some recent earmarks tax a particular segment of the population, not just those who directly benefit from the program. All taxpaying corporations, not only those responsible for pollution, pay Superfund taxes. All persons entitled to the basic Medicare (Part A) program are charged for catastrophic coverage, whether or not they use this service. The added Medicare premium more closely resembles a graduated income tax than a user charge. The premium is levied as a percentage of the individual's income tax payment. The taxlike structure of earmarked revenue reflects the pressure politicians face to generate sufficient money to fully finance program initiatives.

The resort to earmarked revenue, especially in the social and health insurance programs, has been responsible for a progressive deterioration in the government's general fund.[30] The general fund finances all the expenditures of the government except those paid out of trust funds.[31] Table 5.6 shows the trend in general receipts over the past forty years. In 1950, 90 percent of all federal revenue was available for the general purposes of government. This percentage dropped in

Table 5.6 GENERAL FUND RECEIPTS FOR SELECTED FISCAL YEARS

General Receipts	1950	1960	1970	1980	1989 (est.)
As a percentage of total federal receipts	90%	82%	74%	68%	61%
As a percentage of general outlays	92	101	92	81	71
As a percentage of GNP	13	15	14	13	12

Source: Budget of the United States Government, Fiscal Year 1989, *Historical Tables*.
Notes: General Fund receipts correspond to federal fund receipts in the federal budget. The figures in the table are not adjusted for interfund transactions.

each subsequent decade. At present, barely 60 percent of all federal receipts go to the general fund. With the projected growth in Social Security and Medicare premiums, this percentage is likely to decline further in the decades ahead.

As late as the 1970s, general revenue covered 90 percent or more of general outlays. This revenue now provides for only about 60 percent of such outlays. The shortfall has been made up by borrowing from trust funds and other sources. Despite the overall rise in federal taxation, general revenue has declined as a percentage of the gross national product. In fact, it is now a smaller proportion of GNP than it was after World War II, when the scope of federal programs was much more limited than it is today.

These trends point to large, probably rising, general fund deficits and a growing debt burden in the future. CBO baseline projections show that there is likely to be a modest drop in the total budget deficit by the mid-1990s, but almost all of the improvement will be accounted for by a buildup of trust fund balances. The general fund deficit is expected to grow in the 1990s, if current revenue and spending policies are continued.[32]

The shrinkage in general revenues has eroded the capacity of the United States to finance ongoing operations. Even more seriously, the reliance on earmarked sources of revenue is transforming American citizens into shoppers. Whereas a citizen pays taxes in support of government, a shopper pays only for the things he or she buys. As earmarks become more prominent, they make the federal government into a sort of "boutique" in which Americans choose from the array of programs and pay for the ones they select.[33] The boutique is relatively well stocked in programs financed by earmarked revenue, but the supply of some items paid out of general funds is sparse. One of the "goods" in the boutique is "the federal government." The huge general fund deficit tells us that Americans are not willing to pay the full cost of this item. If it persists, this attitude may have profound consequences for the capacity of American government.

BUDGETING FOR REVENUES

At the start of this chapter, I identified several provisions of the 1974 Budget Act designed to link budget and revenue policies. The size and persistence of the budget deficit strongly indicates that the connection has been weaker than intended. Perhaps the main reason for the budget's limited influence is that although it can be an effective tool for deciding how much revenue should be raised, it is not influential in deciding how either tax burdens or tax benefits—two of the principal objectives of revenue legislation—should be distributed.

Using tax policy to control spending—another important objective—brings the budget into play, but not necessarily in the way contemplated by the architects of the budget process. This tactic generates deficits, and because expenditures are sticky and political opposition to cutbacks is strong (as discussed in the last chapter), it often leads to budget outcomes at variance with the intentions of those who wield it. Although revenue denial has undoubtedly constrained spending, it has led to budgets liked by none of their makers and to a breakdown in budget procedures. Earmarking has been another by-product of revenue denial. Whatever its virtues as a means of making those who benefit pay the costs, earmarking breaks the budget, and increasingly the government as well, into financial fiefdoms.

The extent to which revenue and spending policy are integrated depends more on the relationship of the budget and tax committees than on the provisions of the Budget Act. Since the early years of the budget process, the House Ways and Means Committee and the Senate Finance Committee have guarded their independence against encroachment by Congress's budget overseers. These committees have skillfully exploited loopholes in the Budget Act to keep the budgeters at bay. One such loophole is the weaker budget control applied to revenues than to expenditures. Each budget resolution allocates spending resources (budget authority, outlays, and loans) among approximately twenty functions. These functional allocations have made the resolution into a vehicle for debating—and sometimes deciding—federal spending priorities and policies. It should be noted, however, that use of the budget resolution to set spending priorities was weakened in the late 1980s by two developments. First, the appropriations committees increasingly ignored the functional allocations in dividing the portion of the budget under their control. Second, negotiations over the budget (especially between the White House and Capitol Hill) have been conducted in terms of a handful of megacategories, such as defense, nondefense discretionary programs, and entitlements. Except for defense, these categories are much broader than the budget functions. No such breakdown of revenues is made in the budget resolution. Instead, each resolution is limited to decisions on total revenue and on any recommended changes in the total. Attempts by the budget committees in the 1970s to acquire a role in decisions on the sources and composition of revenue, such as the amount of tax expenditures, were rebuffed by the tax legislating committees.[34] As a consequence, the congressional budget says little or nothing about some of the key revenue issues discussed in this chapter—in particular, the distribution of the tax burden.

Another loophole derives from the uneven revenue impact of tax legislation. The influence of the budget process is strongest in the year immediately ahead, but the revenue impact of tax legislation is likely to be greatest in the outyears, the years beyond the one for which firm budget decisions are being made. A glance back at table 5.1 reveals that of all the revenue measures listed there, the 1975 tax measure (which provided temporary tax cuts and a one-time rebate) was the only one whose revenue impact was confined to the single year for which budget decisions were being made. In most of the other revenue measures, the first-year impact was considerably smaller than what was estimated for later years. Efforts by the budget committees to strengthen their influence over the outyears were thwarted by the tax committees in the 1970s. The dispute opened another loophole in the Budget Act, the section 303 bar against consideration of revenue legislation before adoption of the budget resolution. Despite protests by the budget committees, section 303 has been interpreted to preclude early action only on legislation affecting the next year's revenue, not revenues beyond that period.[35]

Several revenue measures enacted in the 1980s illustrate the weak role of the budget process concerning future revenue. The 1980 reconciliation act generated more additional revenue in its first year than in the second. This unusual pattern was caused by the temporary status of some of that year's revenue enhancements. The extension of reconciliation to three years facilitated the enactment of TEFRA, which was debated in terms of the additional revenue to be produced over a three-year period. Yet, the tax committees still resort to temporary expedients of the type identified in chapter 4 to show compliance with the reconciliation instructions. The best example of this behavior is the telephone excise tax, which has been renewed several times in the 1980s. By making the extension temporary, Congress has been able to use it repeatedly to meet the revenue targets, each time taking credit for reducing the deficit without actually levying additional taxes.

Budgetary weakness with respect to future revenue is more than a technical or legal problem. It derives from an attitude encountered a number of times in this book—that the future will take care of itself. The most prominent example occurred in 1981, when budgetary concerns induced the White House to trim back the first-year tax cut but confidence in the future led it, with the support of Congress, to enlarge the outyear tax reduction.

The influence of the budget on revenue matters depends to a considerable degree on regularity in congressional action. Conditions are most favorable for a strong budget role when the budget resolution is adopted on schedule early in the session, after which the tax committees and other affected committees comply with any reconciliation instructions directed to them. The actual sequence of events has differed markedly from the schedule, and it shows evidence of improvisational behavior, which will be investigated in the next chapter. In 1982, the Ways and Means Committee did not consider TEFRA at all; it waited for the Senate to act and then went to conference on the Senate-passed measure.[36] In 1983, months after the original deadline, the Ways and Means Committee reported a revenue bill that fell far short of the increase targeted in the reconciliation bill. House work on the bill was blocked by rejection of the rule under which it was to be considered, and the session ended without any revenue increase. In 1984, Senate Republicans made enactment of DEFRA a precondition for passage of that year's budget resolution. In effect, therefore, the reconciliation bill was passed before the reconciliation instructions were issued. In 1985, the reconciliation bill was stalled by House-Senate conflict over Superfund. In 1986, two reconciliation bills were passed. One was the measure carried over from the previous year, the other provided only minor revenue adjustments. In 1987, action was completed on the reconciliation bill late in the session, only after a budget summit between the president and congressional leaders broke a year-long deadlock. The 1987 reconciliation implemented a two-year deficit reduction agreement, thereby ruling out any revenue action the next year.[37]

The loss of regularity pervades many aspects of budgeting. It does not afflict revenue policy alone. Nevertheless, it does impair the capacity of budget makers to influence the revenue side of the budget.

The record indicates that budgetary influence depends on two conditions: presidential support of a revenue increase and legislative consideration of the increase as part of a deficit reduction package. Both conditions are important because they shelter Congress from the political onus of raising taxes. On the evidence of the 1980s, we must conclude that raising taxes is not something that Congress can do on its own or in defiance of presidential wishes. Every significant tax increase in this decade had the president's approval long before the measure was signed into law. The 1980 reconciliation followed executive-legislative agreement on a revised budget; the door to TEFRA was opened by the revenue enhancements proposed by Ronald Reagan in his fiscal 1983 budget; the 1983 increase in Social Security taxes was devised by a bipartisan commission and endorsed by the president; DEFRA was legitimized in the 1984 Rose Garden agreement between Reagan and congressional Republicans; the 1987 reconciliation was endorsed in the budget summit; and the 1988 boost in Medicare taxes began as a presidential proposal to Congress.

When presidential support has been absent, Congress either has failed to raise revenues or has increased the amount inconsequentially. In 1983, President Reagan repeatedly rebuffed efforts by Senate Republican leaders to put together a large deficit reduction package that would include sizable tax increases. His opposition also contributed to House rejection of the rule allowing consideration of a much smaller tax measure.[38] In 1985, Reagan shifted the debate from tax increases to tax reform, and no significant increases were enacted that year or the next. His insistence that the measure be revenue-neutral effectively protected reform against proposals to turn it into a revenue increase. In 1988, Reagan did not ask for new taxes and Congress provided none.

All of the revenue increases enacted in the 1980s have been packaged with spending cutbacks. The mix of the two has varied from year to year, but, with the exception of TEFRA, the cutbacks generally have been the larger component. Packaging the two components enables Congress to vote for deficit reduction rather than for tax increases. The elements of the package have been made partly interchangeable by a modification in congressional budget rules permitting the Ways and Means and Finance Committees to substitute up to 20 percent of tax increases for spending cuts or vice versa, provided that the total deficit reduction called for in the reconciliation instructions is achieved.[39] Deficit reduction has come to be viewed in the 1980s as a down payment on eliminating the deficit. It signals that the president and Congress are doing something to ameliorate the deficit, but it does not require that they do very much. As long as the budget is projected to be moving in the right direction—toward a smaller deficit—the down payment does not have to be big, and the revenue part can be small indeed. This is why, despite five deficit reduction packages enacted between 1980 and 1987, George Bush found the deficit the nation's most prominent budget issue when he took office in 1989.

Notes

1. The Budget Act originally provided for at least two resolutions each year. The first, to be adopted before Congress acted on revenue and spending legislation, would set targets; the second, to be adopted shortly before the start of the fiscal year, would establish binding ceilings on expenditure and a floor on revenue. The second resolution was dropped in the early 1980s and was formally rescinded by amendments to the Budget Act in 1985. Congress now adopts one binding budget resolution each year.

2. This provision has proved less effective than originally intended. As applied, it does not generally bar changes in revenue legislation effective in the "outyears," the years beyond the one to which that session's budget resolution pertains.

3. The manner in which this process works is described in Allen Schick, *Reconciliation and the Congressional Budget Process* (Washington, D.C.: American Enterprise Institute, 1981).

4. The Gramm-Rudman-Hollings law is, in contrast, asymmetrical in that it looks solely to spending cuts to bring the deficit within preset targets.

5. Although the Budget Act does not prescribe any particular substantial relationship of revenue and outlays, the framers of the act anticipated that forcing Congress to make explicit decisions on the budget totals would lead to smaller deficits.

6. The bipartisan appeal was signed by thirty-seven Republican and thirteen Democratic Senators. Few of the members of the Senate Finance Committee signed the letter.

7. See Congressional Quarterly Inc., *Congressional Quarterly Almanac, 1986* (Washington, D.C.: 1987), p. 515. This stipulation was dropped in conference, and the first-year bulge in revenue due to tax reform was included in computing compliance with the Gramm-Rudman-Hollings deficit target.

8. Milton Friedman, "Why the Twin Deficits are a Blessing," *Wall Street Journal*, December 14, 1988.

9. Daniel P. Moynihan, "Reagan's Bankrupt Budget: The Biggest Spender of All," *New Republic* 198 (December 31, 1983), p. 18.

10. See *Weekly Compilation of Presidential Documents*, 1981, p. 819.

11. "Starting next year, the deficits will get smaller until, in just a few years, the budget can be balanced. And we hope we can begin whittling at that almost $1 trillion debt that hangs over the future of our children." *Ibid.*, p. 815.

12. Shortly after the 1988 elections, Reagan was asked what was the most important thing he had failed to accomplish. He responded: "I could sum that up very briefly— the federal deficit." Quoted in David Kirschten, "Now That A Successor's Picked . . . Professor Reagan's Farewells Begin," *National Journal*, November 19, 1988, p. 2960.

13. See Tax Foundation, *Facts and Figures on Government Finance*, 1988–1989 edition (Baltimore: Johns Hopkins University Press, 1988), table C46.

14. The Treasury Department estimated in 1981 that if the tax structure then in effect were continued, taxpayers earning the median income would experience another 3 percent rise in average rates, and their marginal rates would rise from 24 percent to 32 percent. Taxpayers earning twice the median income would have their average rates move up another 4 percent, and their marginal rates would rise from 43 percent to 49 percent. See *Congressional Record*, July 15, 1981, p. 15792. The Treasury Department data display the same general trend found by Joseph Minarik and reported in table 5.2. However, there are significant differences between the Treasury and Minarik computations.

15. Tax Foundation, *Ibid.*, table C42. Using somewhat different data and assumptions, Joseph Pechman computed the individual income tax at 9.5 percent of personal income in 1975 and 11.3 percent in 1981. See Joseph A. Pechman, *Federal Tax Policy*, 5th edition (Washington, D.C.: Brookings Institution, 1987), p. 366, table B-5.

16. U.S. Office of Management and Budget, *Budget of the United States Government, Fiscal Year 1989, Historical Tables*, table 2.3.

17. Respondents were asked to compare four taxes: the federal income tax, the state income tax, the state sales tax, and the local property tax. See Advisory Commission on Intergovernmental Relations, *Changing Public Attitudes on Government and Taxes: 1987* (Washington, D.C., 1987), tables 5–8.

18. See R. Kent Weaver, *Automatic Government: The Politics of Indexation* (Washington, D.C.: Brookings Institution, 1988), especially chapter 9.

19. See John F. Witte, *The Politics and Development of the Federal Income Tax* (Madison: University of Wisconsin Press, 1985), table 15.2, p. 315.

20. Tax expenditures generally favor upper-income taxpayers for two reasons. They are more likely to itemize deductions, and their higher marginal tax break makes most of the deductions and exclusions worth more to them than to persons in lower brackets.

21. In the 1980s, the term *revenue enhancers* came to mean revenue increases supported by those who were opposed to tax increases. Revenue enhancement would come from closing loopholes, levying user charges, and the like, in contrast to tax increases, which affected rates.

22. The TEFRA issue is discussed in Joseph White and Aaron Wildavsky, *The Deficit and the Public Interest: The Search for Responsible Budgeting in the 1980s* (Berkeley: University of California Press, 1989).

23. Both the revenue increases and the spending reductions were computed in terms of the type of baseline discussed in chapter 4. The extension of expiring taxes was treated as a revenue increase; lowering the future growth path of defense programs was treated as a spending cut.

24. A highly publicized study indicated that in one or more years between 1981 and 1983, 128 out of the 250 large and profitable companies examined paid no federal

income taxes. See Robert S. McIntyre, *Corporate Income Taxes in the Reagan Years: A Study of Legalized Corporate Tax Avoidance* (Washington, D.C.: Citizens for Tax Justice, 1984).

25. The politics of the Tax Reform Act is chronicled in an informative book by Jeffrey H. Birnbaum and Alan S. Murray, *Showdown at Gucci Gulch: Lawmakers, Lobbyists, and the Unlikely Triumph of Tax Reform* (New York: Random House, 1987).

26. Some estimates of the revenue loss from these rules ranged up to $30 billion. See the revealing series of articles on the 1986 transition rules by Donald J. Bartlett and James B. Steele in *The Philadelphia Inquirer*, April 10–16, 1988.

27. See Congressional Budget Office, *The Effects of Tax Reform on Tax Expenditures* (Washington, D.C.: CBO, 1988).

28. See U.S. Government, *Budget of the United States Government, Fiscal Year 1989* (Washington, D.C.: Government Printing Office, 1988), p. 4-4.

29. Part of Superfund financing came from general funds.

30. The federal government does not actually have a general fund. It divides receipts and outlays into federal funds and trust funds. The former are akin to what in state and local governments are classified as general funds. See U.S. General Accounting Office, *Trust Funds and Their Relationship to the Budget*, September 1988.

31. The distinction between special funds and trust funds is not always clear. See U.S. Congress, House Committee on the Budget, *Congressional Control of Expenditures*, Committee Print, January 1977, pp. 111–16.

32. Congressional Budget Office, *The Economic and Budget Outlook: An Update*, August 1988.

33. The author is indebted to William Gorham for the "boutique revenue" metaphor.

34. The relationship of the tax and budget committees is examined in Allen Schick, *Congress and Money: Budgeting, Spending, and Taxing* (Washington, D.C.: Urban Institute, 1980), especially chapter XIII.

35. In 1978, Senator Muskie, who chaired the Budget Committee, raised a point of order that a proposal to phase in tax cuts over a three-year period violated section 303 of the Budget Act. The presiding officer upheld the point of order; the ruling was appealed, but Muskie lost on a 48-38 vote. See *Ibid.*, pp. 551–53.

36. The Senate evaded the constitutional requirement that revenue measures originates in the House by attaching TEFRA to a minor House-passed bill.

37. Congress did pass a tax measure in 1988. Its ostensible purpose was to correct errors made in drafting the Tax Reform Act of 1986. However, the 1988 bill was crafted to be revenue-neutral; the tax increases and cuts were projected to offset each other.

38. The rule was defeated by a 204-214 vote, with 149 Republicans voting against the rule and only 13 for it. The vote was not entirely along party lines. Many Democrats were opposed to a provision of the revenue measure affecting tax-free status of certain bonds, and 65 of them voted against the rule.

39. The Budget Act modification was made in 1985 as part of a package of rules changes included in the Gramm-Rudman-Hollings law. This change appears in section 310(c) of the Congressional Budget Act.

Chapter 6

IMPROVISATIONAL BUDGETING

What happens when, as argued in the two previous chapters, the government does not sufficiently adjust spending demands and revenue capacity to less favorable economic and budgetary circumstances? An obvious result is a chronic budget deficit of the magnitude incurred in the 1980s. But this has not been the only adverse effect. Big, unwanted deficits also have impaired the capacity of the government to budget. Evidence of breakdown can be found readily in the repeated failure of Congress to follow established procedures and to complete its budget work in a timely manner. This breakdown in congressional processes has been highly visible. Less apparent, but no less consequential, has been the deterioration of executive budget roles and practices.

The deficit is only the proximate cause of breakdown. It is symptomatic of other problems, and it cannot be effectively remedied unless more basic issues are attended to. Underlying the deficit and making it intractable are the developments discussed in previous chapters that have impaired the capacity of the federal government to constrain a demand and ration resources. That is, the deficit is the result of a government programmed for strong economic growth and an economy that grows insufficiently to supply expected increments, of a budget driven by mandated expenses that rise by prescribed amounts each year, of claims that can be constrained only by unpopular cutbacks, and of resources that can be added only by unpopular tax increases. If the fundamental imbalance between a budget programmed for growth and an economy that does not grow enough persists, budgetary capacity will not be restored even if Congress and the president have some temporary success in curbing the deficit.

BREAKDOWN AND IMPROVISATION IN BUDGETING

There is an interaction between budget outcomes and budget procedures. When the outcome is welcomed or satisfactory, one should
expect the process to be working reasonably well. When the outcome
is unpalatable, however, one should not be surprised if the process
does not operate in a reliable manner. Wily budget makers seek to
distance themselves from unwanted results, such as huge deficits,
by disregarding schedules and other procedures or by performing
required tasks only after strife and procrastination. They also seek
to shift the blame for the adverse results to others. In the contest for
avoiding blame, stalemate can set in, especially when conflict is
aggravated—as it was in the 1980s—by partisan bickering between
the executive and legislative branches and by deep fissures over tax
and spending policies. Delay, one of the leading indicators of breakdown, is a rational response of politicians to unwanted outcomes.
To put the matter simply, it is much more onerous for members of
Congress and others to act expeditiously when they dislike the policies flowing from the budget than when they like them.

By itself, a budget deficit does not automatically undermine budget
procedures. It is only when the deficit is unwanted and becomes a
matter of intense conflict that budgeting can no longer perform as
expected or required. In the opening chapter, budgeting was characterized as a specialized process for generating, claiming, and rationing resources. Performing these basic tasks in a satisfactory manner
is a sine qua non of effective budgeting. When the deficit is large,
persists during peacetime economic growth, and dominates budgetary debate, it manifests a fundamental inability of the government
to harmonize claims and resources.

Today's budget makers must reckon with the intense policy conflicts and a process that does not work as it should. If the issues were
an elective matter for which doing nothing was a viable option, the
easy and likely way out would be to avoid action. This is not a
realistic outcome in budgeting. One way or another, the budget must
be settled each year, no matter how unpleasant or divisive the chore,
in order to finance the continuing operation of government. To borrow a phrase from a rather different activity, "the budget show must
go on." To continue the flow of money, cross-pressured politicians
have devised jerry-built arrangements that tide the budget through
each year's crisis or impasse. In response to deep policy rifts and a
process in disarray, they have resorted to ad hoc methods that get

the job done. The improvisations have ignored or violated the rules, but they have kept budgeting going, and this has been sufficient justification for them. Politicians have satisfied the government's need for money in much the way that someone might satisfy an immediate need for electricity by stringing together several short wires that connect an appliance to a distant outlet. The mechanism might not be neat or durable, and it probably violates the building code, but it is used when nothing better is available.

So it has been with federal budgeting in the 1980s. Budgeting has become an improvised activity in which each year's rules and roles are adapted to the needs and opportunities of the moment. When improvising, there is one overriding test: Does it work? If it does, it will be used, even if the rules provide otherwise. If it doesn't, some other approach will be sought. As conditions change, so does the form of improvisation. In connecting an appliance to an outlet, one must make do with the material at hand, the skill of the person doing the work, and other variables. It is no different in budgeting, where each year's circumstances are somewhat distinct.

Breakdown and improvisation go hand in hand, and both pervade contemporary budgeting. Because Congress is a transparent institution, it is quite easy to see that its rules have been breached and that each year's budget process has differed from the previous year's. It is well known that during the 1980s, Congress failed to adopt most budget resolutions or to provide most appropriations on schedule. Congress often resorted to continuing resolutions, not merely as stop-gap measures but as substitutes for the regular appropriation bills. Also, as this chapter shows, it made frequent modifications in other budget procedures and operations. What is not as well known is that breakdown and improvisation have spilled over to the executive branch. Although formulation of the president's budget is largely blocked from public view, substantial evidence of breakdown has filtered to the outside. Budgeting is a shared responsibility whose successful performance depends on the cooperation of legislative and executive participants. Failure in one of the branches inevitably radiates to the other. It would be remarkable if the president were able to perform his budget responsibilities without impairment at a time when the congressional side of the process was in disarray.

This chapter focuses on improvisation in federal budgeting. The next section reviews problems and adaptation in presidential budgeting; it is followed by an examination of congressional budget processes. The makeshift arrangements at which the two streams of budgeting have frequently converged in the 1980s—high-level ne-

gotiations between presidential aides and congressional leaders—
are then discussed. The final section of the chapter discusses the
costs of improvisation in terms of budget procedure and substantive
policy.

THE PRESIDENT'S BUDGET: FROM AUTHORITATIVE
POLICY TO OPENING BID

For decades after the executive budget process was established in
1921, the president's budget was an authoritative statement of government policy. It set forth the government's program and financial
recommendations for the year ahead, and these were used by Congress in measuring its own actions. At every step of the way, the
appropriations committees compared their recommendations with
the president's. Vested with the constitutional power of the purse,
Congress typically made many modifications in spending levels, often providing more or less than the president requested. Yet, when
its work was done, Congress's total appropriations usually were close
to the president's recommendation. Authorizing committees also took
their cues from the president's budget and the legislative program
accompanying it. They usually gave serious consideration to presidential proposals and often produced the legislation the president
wanted.

Today, authorizing and appropriating committees exhibit more
independence than in the past. The former still undertake much
legislative activity pursuant to presidential initiative, and the latter
still keep score against the president's request, but his budget is no
longer assured the influence it once had. In some Reagan years—
1981 is the most obvious case—the president's budget virtually dictated congressional actions. It most subsequent years, however, the
budget was pronounced "dead on arrival" by the media and seasoned
observers because there was so little likelihood that Congress would
approve the proposed cutbacks. Yet the "DOA" verdict is not an
accurate assessment of the budget's influence. Even in years when
Congress refused to endorse Reagan's cuts, the president's budget
constrained authorizing legislation and led to lower appropriations
than might have ensued if his requests had been more realistic. Although the budget is not presently an authoritative guide to congressional action, it has evolved into the opening maneuver in a bargaining
process that stretches from submission in January until appropria-

tions and other legislative decisions are made nine or more months later. Unable to impose his budget priorities on Congress, President Reagan crafted his budget policy, as Hugh Heclo has observed, "with an eye to its strategic bearing on Congress. . . . The numbers in the President's budget came to depend not simply on what the executive branch needed but also on what numbers and tactics would move congressional outcomes in the desired direction."[1]

In the 1980s, the White House came to approach the budget as a piece of legislation sent to Congress in the expectation that substantial changes would be made. With this in mind, the president recognized that it would be foolhardy to devise a budget that revealed his actual objectives. Instead, the budget took a hard line that could be softened in an accommodation with Congress. "Results matter," a key OMB aide explained in 1985, "and the real locus of results is what Congress does . . . not just what the President is proposing."[2]

The transformation of the budget from authoritative guideline into opening gambit, has made it difficult to measure the president's impact. His revealed objectives might not be his real ones, so that even when Congress makes substantial changes in the budget, the final outcome might be close to what the White House is targeting. In assessing Reagan's budgets, two opposite conclusions are plausible. First, the president had little success after 1981 because Congress substantially altered budget priorities and consistently refused to go along with most proposed curtailments of domestic programs. Or, second, the president had considerable influence because the budget constrained spending growth and deterred Congress from expanding programs. Interpretations conflict because the budget has become a variable that changes as relationships between the president and Congress unfold. If there is a constant in the president's budget, it is where he wants to come out when Congress is done, but his objective may be veiled by budgetary tactics.

The variability of the budget impelled George Bush to take an unusual tack in February 1989, shortly after he entered office. It is customary for an incoming president to propose revisions in some of his predecessor's revenue and spending plans. The revision issued by Bush left many important matters, such as approximately $10 billion in unidentified cutbacks, blank.[3] The blanks were to be filled in, the president anticipated, through budget negotiations with Congress. By indicating the total he wanted saved but not itemizing the amounts to be taken from specific programs, the president hoped to avoid the DOA label while reassuring Congress to accept cuts in domestic programs.

As a negotiating instrument, the budget is open to revision at any stage of consideration. The prospect of significant change has been enhanced by widespread awareness that the budget is just the opening bid, not firm policy. To protect its budget objectives and to combat legislative initiatives that stray too far from them, the administration must monitor congressional developments closely throughout the year, and it must be prepared to intervene in a timely manner. Effective intervention entails lobbying by OMB officials and other presidential agents, as well as countering congressional actions by putting a new offer or additional demands on the table. These counterproposals substitute for the original budget and become the basis for continuing discussions with relevant members or staff of Congress. Until agreement is reached, any proposal is more in the nature of a probe than a firm commitment, and it can be withdrawn or modified at any time. Many iterations typically occur in the give-and-take of executive legislative discussions, and a suggestion advanced one day might be recast the next, as ideas and arguments flow back and forth. The discussions often move from one venue to another—from the House to the Senate or from one set of committees to another. Several sets of discussions may be going on concurrently, as different congressional committees work on various budget measures. These committee-centered dealings may be supplemented or superseded by summit negotiations at which a broad range of issues are discussed. If the summit produces a comprehensive agreement, its terms likely will require further refinement in piecemeal discussions with particular committees. In sum, the relationship is fluid and unstructured, and executive-legislative bargainers make up the rules of engagement as they go along.

The conduct of negotiations requires sustained attention to, and timely information on, current legislative activities. This absorption in relations with Congress has seriously disoriented the president's Office of Management and Budget, which has long been organized to deal with federal agencies rather than with congressional committees. "In the past," Bruce Johnson has written, OMB's primary role was "as an instrument of presidential control over the bureaucracy. OMB . . . focused its attention on what was going on in the agencies and their specific programs."[4] The examinations divisions in OMB were—and still are—structured along agency lines. Examiners and other OMB staff maintained continuing relations with agencies by reviewing their budget requests, overseeing (closely before World War II, more loosely after the war) the expenditure of funds, and screening agency submissions to Congress to ensure that they were in accord with presidential policy. Examiners were expected to be thoroughly familiar with developments in the agencies for which they were responsible and to spot emerging problems or issues before they became matters of public concern. When OMB made the budget, it judged both the substance of agency requests and the quality of agency management.[5]

In accord with its agency orientation, OMB's budget preparation was decentralized, with ideas and information flowing from the bottom up. Some overall guidance was provided at the Spring preview, which took an early look at the next year's economic and budget situation. After the preview, agencies were given planning marks for the next year's requests. These requests were the basis for discussions in which examiners and agency representatives sought to work out a mutually acceptable spending package that could be recommended to the president.

When the president's budget was finalized, OMB gave agencies allowance letters that spelled out the amounts they could request from Congress and the policies they were to follow. These amounts were entered into OMB's Budget Preparation System (BPS), a computerized database that was updated infrequently during the year.[6] OMB generally withdrew to the background after the budget was presented, leaving agencies with the responsibility for upholding the president's recommendations at appropriation hearings and other contacts with Congress.[7] In fact, OMB did remarkably little to monitor the progress of budget-related matters through Congress. It was positioned to deal with legislative activity principally at two points— when it cleared testimony and other input to Congress, and when it reviewed congressional output awaiting presidential signature or veto. In between, OMB looked mostly to what was happening in executive agencies, not to Capitol Hill.

By the late 1980s, this decentralized, agency-oriented process coexisted with a centralized, Congress-oriented process steered by the OMB director and a corps of political appointees who looked after the president's legislative interests and maintained frequent contact with congressional operatives. In effect, OMB now has two distinct budget processes, one highly structured, the other informal. The two processes converge at various points, but they are driven by different time pressures and data needs. The examiner-agency link has survived, but it is often irrelevant to presidential budgeting. White House agents prepare the budget and negotiate with congressional leaders without wading through the details of agency requests and examiner recommendations. At the same time that they must operate the agency-centered process, examiners must serve the director and others in their ongoing budget dealings with Congress.[8]

More has changed than the centralization of big decisions. The Congress-oriented process is highly volatile, with both the numbers and the relationships subject to frequent and sudden change throughout the year. In their new role as assistants to the OMB director, examiners must turn around requests for information quickly. They cost out the budget implications of the latest proposal or the latest economic news. Accordingly, they come to see the budget as something that is never quite settled but is itself in a continuous state of flux.

It is sometimes said that this transformation of OMB was engineered in the early 1980s by David Stockman to suit his own style and objectives. The image of Stockman, rushing from one meeting to the next, loaded down with budget notebooks and a hand calculator, feeds this notion of an OMB uprooted from its traditional role to a new role of backing up a hyperactive director. But there is much more to this new orientation than Stockman's penchant for bargaining with Congress. True, earlier experience as a congressman sensitized Stockman to the advantages of keeping close tabs on Capitol Hill, but powerful trends, not just a headstrong personality, have been at work making agency-centered budgeting less relevant to presidential purposes and frozen budget decisions less realistic.

A key impulse for the reorientation has been the growing and volatile portion of the federal budget that has little to do with agency spending and operations. Two-thirds of total spending (including interest charges) are in payments that are driven by demographic changes, economic conditions, and other exogeneous factors. To put the matter simply, it is more important for the president's budget makers to be adept at monitoring these outside factors than to be expert reviewers of agency requests. It does not advance the president's interest much to comb through agency budgets to capture some savings by assuming a lower grade average or a higher turnover rate for federal personnel. These calculations still have to be made, which is one reason why agency-centered budgeting has survived. But with billions of dollars in transfer payments hinging on the inflation rate or on the willingness of Congress to reduce cost-of-living adjustments (COLA's) in federal pensions, it is vitally important that OMB know at all times what is afoot in the economy and in Congress. Far more can be saved by a single COLA decisions than by thousands of line-item nicks in agency budgets.

As the economy and Congress are volatile, so must the budget be.

There is not much that OMB can do to smooth out lurches in the economy, but it can organize itself to deal with the budget's vulnerability to independent congressional decisions. The push to centralization within OMB was given impetus by the 1974 Budget Act's establishment of a centralized congressional budget process. The new budget process enhanced Congress's ability to make big changes in the president's budget instead of the piecemeal ones traditionally made through account-by-account decisions on appropriations.

As always, the president faced the risk that his budget would be "nickel and dimed" by the appropriations committees. Now he faced the additional possibility of massive reordering of priorities in budget resolutions as well as the prospect that Congress would decide big budget issues by using its own economic assumptions rather than the president's and that it would rely on a current policy baseline in lieu of the White House's recommendations. By using the baseline, Congress pushed the executive budget aside immediately after it was issued and based its decisions on figures that often were independent of the president's preferences. To protect presidential priorities, OMB had to monitor the baseline and incorporate it into its own database. More importantly, it had to muscle itself into congressional budgeting, an arena in which it had no formal role whatsoever. OMB had to negotiate over Congress's budget, because that was the one that mattered.

In 1981, Stockman improvised the "rec room," a special staff to keep watch over the reconciliation bill and other legislative developments.[9] In calmer moments, he guided establishment of the Central Budget Management System (CBMS), a computerized operation that enables OMB to track budget decisions being made at all levels, in both branches, on a daily or weekly basis. Unlike the standard budget preparation system, CBMS is a rolling data bank that is updated continuously and used to estimate the cost of budget options suggested in negotiations. OMB also established a separate bill-tracking unit, consisting of fifteen persons at the end of the 1980s, to monitor all appropriation bills (and other budget-related measures) at every stage of consideration—subcommittees, full committee, the floor, the conference, and final House and Senate action.[10] The bill-tracking unit feeds up-to-date data to CBMS, to the director and other political officials, and to career examiners.

The changes in presidential budgeting impelled by the growth of transfer expenditure and an independent congressional budget capacity would have evolved even if there were no oppressive budget deficit. The deficit, however, lent greater urgency to this development and undoubtedly sped it up while adding to volatility in presidential budgeting. The deficit meant that there was little or no slack to absorb shocks from the economy or from Congress. It turned budgeting into a continuous activity, as decisions made under one set of expectations had to be reexamined when conditions changed. The deficit also meant that two branches would be fighting over cutbacks rather than over program enhancements and that the situation would be far worse than projected by the president if Congress, by inaction, refused to enact his changes. With emphasis on the deficit, the totals in the budget became much more important in their own right. To protect them, the White House either had to mount a successful campaign to get the president's budget adopted or had to enter into negotiations with Congress. The deficit increased the likelihood that in compressing spending within presidentially acceptable totals, Congress would make big changes in budget priorities.

Intractable deficits indicate, as noted, a breakdown in the balancing of claims and resources. In an era of divided government—which has prevailed since 1981—progress toward a restoration of balance requires heightened cooperation of the president and Congress. Neither branch can do it alone because each lacks the political strength to impose its will on the other or to take full blame for hard choices. Accordingly, deficits have made the two sides more interdependent, adding to the displacement of the president's budget as the guiding force in congressional actions.

The United States has few formal means of bridging differences between the two branches. It must rely principally on the willingness of the two sides to cooperate or on pressures that impel them toward an accommodation. Later in this chapter, we consider an approach that works only through improvised behavior—summit negotiations between presidential and congressional agents. "Subsummit" discussions have been more prevalent, but they, too, have relied on ad hoc arrangements.

Improvisation has led to much more tearing down of executive budget institutions than building them up. With the notable exception of a central data bank and a bill-tracking staff, OMB has not reshaped itself for the new demands on its resources. Neither Stockman nor his successor, the evidence shows, invested heavily in the new processes or tried to counter the destabilizing effects of the changes under way.[11] Presidential budgeting today is littered with remnants of an older, agency-based system—procedures and activities that have withered but not entirely disappeared. This list includes the Spring Preview, allowance letters, and the legislative clearance process. Presidential budgeting has been recast into a process that depends more on fluid tactics than on fixed procedures. Hence, these and other formal practices have been attenuated.

The main casualty has been the most important process of all—the annual cycle of preparing and defending the president's budget. With budgeting transformed into an ongoing stream of moves and countermoves, one year flows into the next. With the annual budget presented as only the opening bid, preparation time has been truncated. The OMB review of agency requests once took more than four months, stretching from early Fall, when agencies submitted their requests, until late January or early February. Now, in election years, much serious work in OMB is delayed until mid-November, but release of the budget has been accelerated to early January. A top-down budget can be made quickly because agency requests are slighted, and OMB examiners are bypassed or turned from program experts into suppliers of data for political operatives.

Yet the time-consuming work of assembling requests inside agencies goes on as if nothing had changed. Agencies still invest prodigious amounts of effort in this activity to ensure that their requests are accurate and effective statements of needs and objectives. The fact that much of the effort is wasted, at least insofar as OMB review is concerned, has hardly made a difference. The old, agency-oriented budget process has not been dismantled or redesigned, perhaps because no one in OMB cares enough to change the procedures or because the well-prepared requests still serve internal management needs and are used by the appropriations subcommittees in their detailed reviews of agency operations.

Yet, another reason for the failure to build new budget capacity must be reckoned with. Improvisation cannot be institutionalized. Presidential budgeting has gone through considerable destabilization in its relationship with congressional budgeting. Rebuilding executive budget institutions will have to go hand in hand with rebuilding congressional capacity. Reforming only one branch's budget effectiveness will not suffice.

CONGRESSIONAL BUDGETING: SAVING THE PROCESS BY CHANGING IT EVERY YEAR

Budgeting in Congress is very different from budgeting in the executive branch, but the two processes have been buffeted by similar pressures, and both have responded with makeshift arrangements. No one in Congress can imprint his or her preferences on the budget the way the president sometimes does. Congress is a fragmented institution that satisfies its political imperative to disperse legislative power by parceling budgetary responsibility among many House and Senate committees. The key split is between revenue and spending measures, which have been handled by separate sets of committees since the Civil War period. Fragmentation is also etched in the distribution of appropriations among thirteen pairs of subcommittees, each with its own appropriation bill. As the scope of government expanded after World War II, the circle of congressional budget participants was widened, principally by the enactment of temporary authorizations and backdoor spending schemes. These developments gave many authorizing committees a more direct and influential role in budget policy.

With many committees sharing power, congressional budgeting is inherently more unstable than its executive counterpart. The relationship between the authorizing and appropriating committees is one destabilizing factor. That between committees and their parent chamber is another. The former generates friction as committees seek to enlarge their legislative jurisdiction or guard against encroachment by others. The latter makes legislative outcomes partly dependent on the skill with which committees anticipate the mood of the House and Senate and shepherd legislation through them.

Despite budgetary fragmentation and instability, Congress must act in a sufficiently cohesive and reliable manner to fiance government, make timely appropriations, and maintain an acceptable relationship between revenue and expenditure. During the postwar period of strong economic growth, Congress could behave in a fragmented manner and still be reasonably confident that the deficit would be of manageable proportions. With weaker growth and big deficits, fragmentation may lead to unwanted outcomes and impede corrective action.

To deal with the deficit, Congress must integrate budget power and constrain the temptation to spend more and tax less. Historically, its budget work has been facilitated by House rules giving revenue and appropriation bills privileged access to the floor.[12] In addition, the work has been eased by the special role accorded to the Ways and Means and House Appropriations Committees as guardians of the treasury.[13] But because legislative discipline is self-imposed, it also must be self-enforced, and this is not always an easy matter. If Congress wants to spend more or to tax less, it will get its way, formal rules and behavioral norms notwithstanding. In fact, the controlling role of the tax and spending committees has been weakened by developments discussed in previous chapters. The pressure to spend more has undermined the grip of the House Appropriations Committee, which now has effective control over less than half of total expenditure, and the drive to decentralize House power has weakened the ability of the Ways and Means Committee to dictate tax policy.

Congressional discipline also depends on relations with the executive branch. In the past, as congressional controllers, the Ways and Means and House Appropriations Committees regularly looked to the White House for guidance. Ways and Means rarely initiated tax legislation, though it usually made significant changes in the President's proposals, and the House Appropriations Committee acted only in response to a presidential budget request. As noted earlier in this chapter, the appropriations committees habitually scored their actions against the president's recommendations, and variances between the two sets of numbers usually were small.

Stresses in presidential budgeting inevitably have spilled over to Congress. With the president's budget more a bargaining ploy than a firm proposal, congress cannot confine its work to fine-tuning appropriations at the margins. It has to be organized to counter the president's bid with its own offer and to make big shifts in spending priorities. It also must be prepared to bargain over the budget as a whole and to enforce the deals it strikes with the White House. In other words, it must act in a sufficiently integrated and consistent manner while still dispersing budgetary power among many committees. Balancing these conflicting demands has not been easy.

The main effort to reconcile budgetary integration and legislative fragmentation came with the Budget Act of 1974, which recognized that Congress, like the executive branch, has two distinct budget processes—one oriented to agency operations, the other to transfers and other mandated expenditure. The agency-oriented process is clustered around the appropriations subcommittees, most of whose jurisdictions correspond to organizations in the executive branch. The transfer budget is dispersed among those authorizing committees that have jurisdiction over entitlements and other mandatory programs. The 1974 act sought to bridge the two processes by means of budget resolutions that cover both types of expenditure, link them to total revenue and the deficit, and establish overall spending priorities.

The Budget Act increased congressional budgetary turbulence. Although this was not the intention, several features of the new processes added to instability. First, an additional set of actors—the budget committees—joined the budgetary roster. The potential for jurisdictional strife was expanded beyond authorizations-appropriations and spending-tax frictions to the budget committees and their relationships with the older committees. Reaching into everyone else's business, the budget committees neither could be walled off from other committees nor could be expected to have the same perspective as the others. Decisions on budget resolutions came to reflect not only congressional attitudes on budget issues but the balance of power in Congress. Sometimes the budget committees were dominant, but more often they could garner sufficient votes to pass the resolution only by accommodating the preferences of others.[14]

Second, the budget resolution confronts the White House on the big budget issues of the day—tax policy, spending priorities, and the deficit. Unlike appropriation bills, which facilitate compromise by breaking contentious matters into discrete items, the budget resolution fuels conflict by aggregating small issues into big ones. Spending priorities, tax policy, and what to do about the deficit are all matters on which Republicans and Democrats can be expected to disagree. Without strong efforts to counter the tendency of the two parties to fight over budget issues, the resolution will be a magnet for partisan strife. Such efforts succeeded in the Senate during the 1970s, but with Republican capture of this chamber and the White House in 1981, partisanship infected the entire budget process and made passage of a budget resolution much more difficult.[15]

Third, from the outset, the budget resolution has been a political orphan. Its need to accommodate the interests of congressional committees makes it a mosaic of many preferences, and a true representation of none. The budget committees are the only committees in Congress that consistently care enough to get the resolution passed. This task is complicated by the resolution's unusual status. It is not quite a budget, though it is much more than a wish list. No money can be raised or spent on its word alone, and nothing in Congress or the executive branch has to stop if the resolution is not adopted. Yet, the process survives because members of Congress believe that adopting the resolution is the right thing to do and that failure to do so would disable Congress from budgeting in a responsible manner. The resolution's ambiguous status leaves members neither so supportive of the process to move the resolution along as if it were "must" legislation nor so fed up by the frustrations of the job as to jettison the process set up in 1974.

Fourth, the resolution process has destabilized Congress by making it take explicit responsibility for some of the most difficult and contentious issues facing American politicians. For nearly two centuries, Congress assiduously avoided voting on total outlays, spending priorities, and the deficit. The absence of votes on these matters was not an oversight. Rather, it was rooted in congressional fragmentation and reinforced by an understandable reluctance to take on tough issues. It was the misfortune of the budget resolution process that it forced votes on these matters just when deficits were growing, discontent over the income tax was rising, and control of expenditures was becoming more difficult.

These conditions made Congress increasingly dependent on the White House for completing its budget work. Despite the president's lack of a formal role in the budget resolution process, the contents and passability of budget resolutions depend to a considerable degree on what the president does. This dependence is political. It rests on the need to share responsibility for tax increases, spending cuts, and big deficits. Perversely, however, in the 1980s, the president often made it more difficult for Congress to deal with these tough issues and to assemble a passable resolution. In transforming his budget into an "opening bid," Reagan took unrealistic positions that complicated Congress' budget work. When the president adorned his budget with unduly favorable economic forecasts, Congress could not effectively riposte with more austere assumptions. Doing so simply raised the deficit and alienated potential supporters. Similarly, when the president endorsed deep domestic cuts, he put Congress in the unenviable position of having to enact the cutbacks, raise the deficit, or take money from other areas. Each of these options was anathema to a sizable contingent of Members.

Collegial institutions such as Congress have a characteristic way of handling difficult or divisive chores. They avoid action. As table 6.1 shows, delays have been common in adopting the budget resolution. Congress consistently failed to adopt the resolution on time during the 1980s. As the decade progressed, the slippage increased, and the resolution was regularly adopted only after the annual appropriations season had commenced. As a result, congressional work on spending bills proceeded without guidance from an adopted resolution. Congress advanced both the executive and legislative timetables in 1985 (effective with the 1987 fiscal year), but instructing itself to act more expeditiously did not enable Congress to do so.

Prolonged delay could be fatal to the resolution process, especially because House rules allow consideration of appropriation bills de-

Table 6.1 ADOPTION DATES OF BUDGET RESOLUTIONS, FISCAL YEARS
1980–87

Fiscal year	Adoption date	Number of days after deadline[a]
1980	05/24/79	9
1981	06/12/80	28
1982	05/21/81	6
1983	06/23/82	39
1984	06/23/83	39
1985	10/01/84	139
1986	08/01/85	78
1987	06/27/86	73
1988	06/24/87	70
1989	06/06/88	52

Source: Robert A. Keith, *Senate Consideration of Regular Appropriations Bills under Waivers of Section 303(a) of the 1974 Budget Act*, Congressional Research Service, January 18, 1989, Table 1.
[a]For fiscal years 1980–1986, the deadline for adoption of the Spring budget resolution was May 15. Since fiscal year 1987, the deadline has been April 15.

spite the failure of Congress to adopt the budget resolution.[16] In the 1970s, the budget committees rallied support for their resolutions by urging members to "vote the process, not the numbers." Their warning that failure to adopt the resolution would doom the new process persuaded enough wavering members to produce a winning majority. But this type of appeal was weakened by repeated use, so that in the 1980s, the budget committees have resorted to other tactics to save the process.[17] Faced with breakdown, Congress improvised by adjusting each year's rules to the legislative balance of power. The following list identifies some of the more prominent and behavioral rule changes made during the 1980s:

☐ *1980.* The reconciliation process was implemented by advancing it from the second budget resolution to the first. The inaugural use of reconciliation was modest, but it paved the way for broader application the next year. Budget summitry also was pioneered in 1980, when President Carter's initial budget was revised in negotiations with congressional leaders.

☐ *1981.* Reconciliation was expanded to three years and to discretionary authorizations funded in annual appropriations. That year's reconciliation bill covered many more committees and had deeper cuts than any other.

☐ *1982.* Congress adopted a single resolution (in the Spring) and

specified that this would become binding if the second resolution was not adopted by the start of the fiscal year. Congress
also passed tax legislation through an unusual sequence in which
the Senate acted first and the House did not consider the measure until the conference.

□ *1983.* Although reconciliation instructions were included in the
budget resolution, Congress did not pass the reconciliation bill.
The bill finally was enacted in the following year. The budget
resolution changed House rules pertaining to the enforcement
of budget totals.[18]

□ *1984.* Congress enacted deficit-reduction legislation before it
passed the budget resolution, thereby reversing the sequence
provided in the Budget Act. The resolution cleared Congress on
October 1, the first day of the new fiscal year, more than four
months after the deadline. The House adopted a blanket waiver,
permitting action on all regular appropriation bills for the next
year before the resolution was adopted.

□ *1985.* Congress passed the Gramm-Rudman-Hollings law establishing deficit targets through the 1991 fiscal year. This law also
made numerous changes in the congressional budget process.
Some of these conformed the rules to prevailing practice (such
as one resolution rather than two); others modified the procedures for making and enforcing congressional budget decisions
in the House and Senate.[19]

□ *1986.* Congress passed two reconciliation bills, one a carryover
from the previous session, the other for the following fiscal year.
Congress also passed a continuing resolution that for the first
time covered all thirteen regular appropriation bills for the entire
fiscal year.

□ *1987.* Congress revised the Gramm-Rudman-Hollings targets and
made a number of adjustments in the deficit reduction process.
The president and Congress negotiated a budget agreement on
revenue and spending for the 1988 and 1989 fiscal years.

□ *1988.* For the first time in the 1980s, the thirteen regular appropriation bills were enacted by the start of the fiscal year. This
also was the only year in the decade during which no work was
done on a reconciliation bill.

This is by no means a full roster of recent adjustments and improvisations. There have been numerous waivers of Budget Act rules
as well as the frequent insertion of provisions into the budget resolution to make it more attractive or the deficit problem appear to

be less formidable.[20] The House Rules Committee has crafted special rules each year to structure floor consideration of the budget resolution. There have also been annual variations in the leadership's role in formulating and mobilizing support for the resolution, in relations between congressional Democrats and Republicans, and in relations with the White House. Some of the changes have strengthened the congressional budget process, in particular, the sixty vote waiver requirement in the Senate and enforcement of the committee allocations made under section 302 of the Budget Act. The general trend has been toward more direct leadership involvement and less budget committee autonomy, greater polarization, and greater interdependence of the two parties, and, as discussed in the next section, increased striving for overall agreement with the White House.

Unlike presidential improvisation, whose main objective has been to seize tactical advantage vis-à-vis the Congress, legislative improvisation has aimed at passing the resolution and related measures. This behavior suggests that budgeting is on shakier ground in Congress than in the executive branch. There is an obvious reason for this predicament. The president can unilaterally decide what to put in his budget, whereas Congress can act only by marshaling sufficient votes to pass the resolution. There has been a measure of desperation in Congress's budgetary antics. The driving force has been to make it through another year by doing whatever it takes to corral the needed votes. What sustains congressional maneuvering is the determination to keep the budget resolution process alive. If Congress were to decide that the struggle was not worth the effort, the resolution and its appurtenances would fade away. Improvisation will not be enough.

RECONCILIATION: AN INHERENTLY UNSTABLE PROCESS

Reconciliation is an inherently unstable process because it violates congressional norms, rooted in the committee system, for the development of legislation. It has the potential to encroach on the jurisdiction of virtually all House and Senate committees and to override normal procedures for considering legislation. This potential led the chairs of sixteen House committees to charge in a 1980 letter to Speaker Thomas P. O'Neill, Jr., that implementing reconciliation in the Spring budget resolution "undermines the committee system, reposing in the Budget Committee authority to legislate substantively with respect to the nature and scope of federal activities.

Such a procedure infringes on the legitimate roles of authority and appropriations processes."[21]

Reconciliation is not a placid, no-feathers-ruffled process. It directs committees to produce onerous legislation—program cutbacks and tax increases—that they would not do on their own initiative, to curtail the very programs they established, and to take back benefits they have provided to various groups. Reconciliation means trimming cost-of-living adjustments and payments to hospitals, narrowing eligibility for transfer payments, and so on. It flies in the face of incremental budgeting.

To survive, reconciliation needs a steady infusion of political support. It operates at the sufferance of House and Senate committees that make it each year into a process they are willing to live with or exploit to their advantage. Evidence of the variability of reconciliation was presented in chapters 4 and 5, where wide fluctuations were reported in its use to raise revenue or reduce expenditure. On the revenue side, the high points have been the 1982 Tax Equity and Fiscal Responsibility Act (TEFRA) and the 1984 Deficit Reduction Act (DEFRA). Only small sums were generated in other years, and none in 1981. On the spending side, 1981 was the year of the "big bang." Since then, savings have been quite modest, and in some years they have been substantially or entirely offset by spending increases enacted in the reconciliation bill.

These variations are part of a broader pattern of instability in the process. Reconciliation bills were enacted in six of the nine years from 1980 through 1988. In two of the other years, Congress failed to complete action on reconciliation, but the measures were enacted the next session. The 1988 legislative session was the only one in which there was no reconciliation activity. The reconciliation bill enacted in the previous year implemented the two-year deficit reduction plan agreed to in the 1987 budget summit, thereby obviating the need for another bill.

The scope of reconciliation is a barometer of committee power in Congress. Reconciliation was applied to conventional authorizations in 1981 but not in subsequent years. An informal understanding, worked out at the insistence of authorizing committees, confines reconciliation to entitlements and some other mandated expenditure. A few of the reconciliation bills, such as the one enacted in 1987, have had caps on total defense and discretionary domestic appropriations, but this has not been standard practice. The appropriations committees would prefer to operate without any externally imposed limits, but they have accepted caps as part of executive-legislative deals that permit higher domestic appropriations than the White House wants. The caps give these committees full flexibility to allocate funds among domestic programs and thereby weaken the role of the rival budget committees in determining spending priorities.

The number of committees drawn into the process has depended on the scope of the reconciliation instructions. Just about every committee with legislative jurisdiction received instructions in 1981. In most subsequent years, however, fewer than half of the committees have been covered.[22] The multiplicity of participating committees has spawned innovations in conference procedures for reconciliation bills and other omnibus measures. The usual practice is for some budget committee members to serve as general conferees and for members of other committees to be conferees for designated portions of the omnibus reconciliation bill. The general conferees oversee the entire process, but they have little or no role in the subconferences at which decisions are made on particular issues. This arrangement gives affected committees control of reconciliation outcomes while enabling congress to act in a coordinated manner.

As reconciliation has accommodated the interests of legislative committees, it has become an effective instrument in challenging the president's budget priorities and in giving Congress the upper hand in maneuvering by the two branches. Both accommodation and confrontation have been facilitated by adding spending increases and unrelated legislation to reconciliation bills. Extraneous legislation, Congressman Leon Panetta acknowledged in urging Congress not to ban the practice "serves to grease the wheels of the reconciliation process and, frankly, attracts votes and support for reconciliation bills. Without this support, reconciliation, and the enforcement of the budget bill, in general, would likely be a great deal more difficult."[23] In 1986, the Senate adopted a rule barring unrelated legislation in reconciliation bills, but this has not stopped the practice.[24] The volume of such legislation reflects both the weakness and strength of authorizing committees. Too weak to move authorizing legislation on their own, but strong enough to insert such legislation into a reconciliation bill or other omnibus measure, the authorizing committees made the best of gridlock in Congress. Through most of the 1980s, freestanding authorizing legislation declined severely, and Congress failed to renew some expiring authorizations.[25] The difficulty in enacting authorizations was largely caused by Reagan's opposition to legislation expanding federal programs. Still, by turning to the reconciliation bill, authorizing committees managed to achieve some of their legislative objectives.

Similar motivations led to the insertion of "sweeteners"—increased spending for selected programs. In utilizing reconciliation to increase spending, authorizing committees challenged the president's budget priorities and pressured him to accept provisions that might have been vetoed if they had been passed separately. Presidential tactics of submitting unrealistic budgets elicited countermoves by Congress to thwart the White House.

Reconciliation is the main legislative instrument for curtailing the deficit, but, as improvised in the mid- and late 1980s, reconciliation had little to do with deficit reduction. Rather, deficit reduction has given cover to the other uses found for the reconciliation process. In fact, as the deficit crisis deepened in the 1980s, the amount of genuine deficit reduction achieved through this process diminished. In 1985, alarm over the deficit moved Congress to pass the Gramm-Rudman-Hollings law. It did not spur Congress to enact a reconciliation bill. The deficit peaked in 1986, but the amount by which reconciliation reduced the deficit that year probably was less than in any other year such a bill was enacted.

Omnibus measures, such as reconciliation, that deviate from normal legislative order cannot be governed by unalterable routines. Testifying a few months after the big reconciliation bill was enacted in 1981, David Stockman argued that reconciliation "should not become an annual omnibus substitute for authorizations and appropriations. . . [It] would be better viewed as a selective action-forcing mechanism.[26] Senator Pete Domenici, then chairman of the Senate Budget Committee, expressed similar views: "I would not like to see the reconciliation process become a routine instrument for establishing federal fiscal policy. Reconciliation is an extraordinary process and should be used only in extraordinary circumstances."[27]

Because budgetary circumstances have been extraordinary through the 1980s, reconciliation has been applied repeatedly. But there is neither a standard set of reconciliation practices nor a single route form instructions to enactment.

MAKING APPROPRIATIONS: FROM INCREMENTAL STABILITY TO DECREMENTAL TURBULENCE

The appropriations process operated like clockwork in 1988. The first of the regular appropriations bills cleared the House on May 17, barely two days after the earliest date permitted by the rules. The last was passed on June 29, one day before the deadline for completion of House action. The Senate also moved expeditiously, passing four regular appropriations in June, eight in July, and the final one in August. All thirteen of the bills were signed by the president before the October 1 start of the fiscal year, making the 1988 session the first time in the decade that stopgap appropriations were not needed.

Orderliness was the exception in the 1980s, but it was normal in most previous decades. In fact, making appropriations had been one of Congress's most routine and predictable activities. Occasionally, some appropriations were held up by legislative glitches or by a flareup of budgetary conflict, and Congress had to provide interim funding in a continuing resolution. When this occurred, the continuing resolution usually was a temporary measure, in effect for no more than a few months. It was a rare session in which all appropriations were not enacted by the time Congress adjourned.

Calming the appropriations process was the incremental behavior depicted in previous chapters. With the president habitually asking for more, and Congress trimming part of the increase, conflict was narrowed to the small band between the previous appropriation and the next year's request. Stability depended, however, on the president playing his expected part by asking for more. When Ronald Reagan asked for less domestic spending in the 1980s, he destabilized the behavior of the appropriations committee and turned the House committee into a wily claimant for increased funding. The ensuing breakdown in appropriations schedules transformed one of Congress's most reliable processes into one of its most unstable.

Just one year before the on-schedule performance of 1988, Congress was unable to pass a single appropriation bill on time, and it folded all thirteen bills into an omnibus measure that sprawled over 450 pages in the *Statutes*. Table 6.2 indicates that this was not the only year in which a massive continuing resolution was the vehicle for providing appropriations. Continuing resolutions have been used for more than a century to finance agencies that lack a regular appropriation at the start of the fiscal year. In the 1980s, however, the function and content of this type of measure was changed. The continuing resolution supplanted the regular appropriations, provided full-year funding for numerous programs and agencies, and was the means of enacting a great amount of substantive legislation. Other than the label, there was little affinity between the final continuing resolutions used in this decade and those passed previously.[28]

Until the 1980s, most stopgap appropriations provided temporary

Table 6.2 CONTINUING APPROPRIATIONS ACTS, FISCAL YEARS 1980–1989

Fiscal year	Number of regular appropriations covered by		Number of regular appropriation acts funded for entire fiscal year in a continuing appropriation	Number of *Statute* pages in lengthiest continuing appropriation
	Initial	Final		
1980	10	7	3	8
1981	13	5	5	9
1982	13	3	4	21
1983	12	8	7	95
1984	9	5	3	19
1985	9	9	8	363
1986	13	7	7	142
1987	13	13	13	389
1988	13	13	13	451
1989	0	0	0	n.a.

Source: Congressional Research Service.

funding at a "continuation" rate, which was typically defined as the lower of the previous year's appropriation, than the president's request, or than the amount provided in the House- or Senate-passed appropriation. The early expiration date and the low spending rate gave Congress a strong incentive to pass the regular appropriations, which usually provided increased funding. In line with the expectation that regular appropriations would soon be enacted, each continuing resolution specified that it would be superseded when the regular appropriation became available.

Unlike pre-1980s stopgap appropriations, recent continuing resolutions frequently have provided more funds for some accounts than were appropriated in the previous year or requested by the president. Moreover, by remaining in effect for the full year, recent continuing resolutions have subsumed many—and in some years, all—of the regular appropriations. Table 6.2 reveals that with the exception of the 1989 fiscal year, the initial continuing resolution enacted in each during the decade covered all or most of the appropriations. The final continuing resolution funded multiple appropriations for the full fiscal year.

These data testify to the widespread breakdown of the appropriations process. Two related factors, which have been a recurrent theme in this chapter, impeded passage of the regular appropriations. One was budgetary conflict, the other was maneuvering in Congress for tactical advantage vis-à-vis the White House. To mold the continuing resolution into an instrument of legislative power, Congress changed it from an interim measure into a full-year appropriation.

Before omnibus continuing resolutions came into vogue, the appropriations process was decentralized. Each appropriation bill came out of its own subcommittee and moved to the floor when it was ready, without waiting for other appropriations and without explicit regard for how the amounts in that bill related to total expenditure or the amounts provided in other bills. Conflict over particular appropriations was confined to that bill alone so that the progress of other bills was not impeded. The establishment of the congressional budget process brought a modest amount of central direction by requiring the House and Senate Appropriations Committees to divide available funds among their thirteen subcommittees.[29] Despite this requirement, the appropriations subcommittees continued to operate in a fairly autonomous manner, and the various bills were considered independently of one another.

In the 1980s, however, conflict between the president and Congress sprawled to the entire budget and made it difficult to complete action on individual bills unless agreement was reached on broad issues such as total spending, overall budget priorities, and the amount and distribution of cutbacks. Passage of the first appropriation was often held up by disagreement on the last one, and it was possible to disaggregate budget conflict by taking up the appropriations one bill at a time.

In this environment, continuing resolutions proved efficient in breaking budget impasses. As "must" legislation, essential for the uninterrupted operation of government, the continuing resolution spurred disputants to come to terms on specific amounts even though they remained apart on budget priorities. As its scope was broadened to include most or all appropriations, the continuing resolution became a key vehicle, along with the budget resolution and the reconciliation bill, in resolving each year's budget battles. Because it determined actual funding levels, the continuing resolution settled contentious issues, such as domestic versus defense spending and the amount of growth provided in discretionary programs, more conclusively than an advisory resolution could.

All participants gained something from the continuing resolution process, including the White House, which frequently railed against it and threatened to veto any omnibus spending measure passed by Congress. The process enabled the president's agents to negotiate a comprehensive agreement that provided more for defense and less for domestic programs than might have been appropriated in separate bills. The White House could assess the total cost, trade off congressional add-ons against one another, avoid a separate floor vote on the usually contentious foreign operations appropriation, and obtain a more binding deal than would be possible in piecemeal appropriations.

Congress also extracted some advantages from a comprehensive continuing resolution. The appropriations committees forced the White House to agree to domestic spending well above the president's requests, obtained assurances that the continuing resolution would not be vetoed, and attached numerous conditions and limitations to the appropriations. Acting on their own initiative or in consort with other committees, the Appropriations Committees loaded the resolutions with legislative provisions, including whole authorization bills, some of which may have had little chance of being enacted on their own.[30] The process of assembling the continuing resolution gave the chairs of the Appropriations Committees an enlarged role in determining final outcomes, but the subcommittees protected their interests and jurisdictions by making the individual appropriations bills the vehicles for the continuing resolution and by having their members serve as conferees on the final bill.[31]

Continuing resolutions are considered at the last minute—days or hours before the start of the new fiscal year or the expiration of the previous stopgap arrangement. To outsiders, the process appears chaotic, with no one sure of exactly what is in the resolution being considered. Items are added or dropped without much discussion or consultation, and it is only some time after the omnibus measure is enacted that its contents can be fully cataloged and assessed. Nevertheless, the process is not as disorderly and frenetic as it sometimes appears. Long before the fiscal year arrives, committees and members sense that they will have one or more continuing resolutions, and they plan accordingly. Some authorizing committees mark up legislation, but take no further action until the continuing resolution comes along. Then, working behind the scenes, they arrange to have pieces of authorizing legislation tucked into the resolution and enacted without drawing floor attention. Appropriations subcommittees work on their bills, position themselves for the end game that will be played out in the continuing resolution. They report individual bills, move them through the House and often through the Senate as well, but stop short of final passage. This enables them to transfer the provisions of the original bill to the continuing resolution without risking a veto. The subcommittees also provide for their report on the individual bills to be applicable to the relevant parts of the resolution.

Although members and committees anticipate the continuing resolution and exploit its opportunities, the scope of these measures varies widely. Among the variables are the number of regular appropriation bills subsumed, the funding levels negotiated with the president, and the extent to which the measure will be open to substantive legislation.

Omnibus continuing resolutions have not been institutionalized. If the conditions that have given rise to them were to abate, Congress might revert to the limited measures that once were the practice. The key factor is interbranch conflict. Through most of the decade, a big continuing resolution was compelled by deep fissures between the White House and Capital Hill on budget policy. In 1988, however, conflicts were papered over by the previous year's summit agreement, and there was no need for any continuing resolution.

GOING TO THE SUMMIT: BUDGETING WITHOUT PROCESS

The disarray in budgeting has altered executive-legislative relationships. Since 1982, the two branches have become more interdependent, because each, as discussed, is highly vulnerable to having its budget preferences blocked by the other. With the president able to gain enactment of only modest cutbacks and Congress only able to get presidential endorsement of modest tax increases, the two sides have been propelled into a bargaining relationship in which each gives in just enough to get an agreement, but not enough to resolve the budget crisis. Interdependence has been fostered by big deficits. It takes combined action by both branches to avoid blame for the deficit by sharing responsibility for the modest spending cuts and revenue enhancements adopted in the decade.

Interdependence breeds frustration and a sense of helplessness. Neither side gets all it wants, and each is apt to feel shortchanged by the compromises it makes to get through another budget crisis. Less than a year after his extraordinary legislative triumphs in 1981, Ronald Reagan lamented: "It's called the President's budget, and yet there is nothing binding in it. It is submitted to the Congress and they don't even have to consider it."[32] Reagan voiced this complaint many times, and he ultimately proposed giving the president a formal role in the congressional budget process.[33]

Lacking such a role, Reagan and his successor nevertheless actively worked the Hill to influence congressional actions. Most of the budget resolutions adopted during the decade were a blend of presidential and congressional policies. Despite the forhal grant of independence by the 1974 Budget Act, Congress could not go it alone in developing its own budget resolutions. The progress of the resolution has often been delayed by presidential opposition, frustrating those in Congress who believe that this measure should reflect legislative priorities.

Budgetary interdependence has spurred the two branches to enter into frequent negotiations. Because of party and policy differences, the discussions have not always ended in agreement. The following list summarizes some of the main budget negotiations conducted during the 1980s:

☐ *1980.* Deteriorating economic conditions induced President Carter to withdraw his budget shortly after it was submitted and to submit a revised plan drawn up in negotiations with congressional leaders.

☐ *1981.* The Reagan blitzkrieg ruled out negotiations in 1981, as the new president dictated most of the terms of the budget resolution, reconciliation bill, and tax legislation. Despite these successes, Reagan faced a recalcitrant Congress late in the year when he sought additional cuts, and the deals worked out by Stockman, on appropriations bills, gave the president little of what he asked for.

☐ *1982.* Negotiations between presidential aides and a congressional "Gang of Seventeen" ended in an impasse when the president refused to accept repeal of part of the tax cuts voted in the previous year and House Speaker O'Neill refused to accept any cuts in Social Security benefits. Congress and the president also squabbled over supplemental appropriations. Reagan vetoed two supplementals, but Congress overrode his veto of a third bill. The year ended with extended negotiations over a continuing resolution, which was passed only after Congress dropped a jobs program opposed by the president.

☐ *1983.* Most interbranch discussions were between the Senate Republicans and the White House. Presidential opposition nearly torpedoed passage of a budget resolution in the Senate and thwarted efforts by the chairman of the Senate Finance Committee to devise an ambitious deficit-reduction plan. A bipartisan supplemental appropriation bill was enacted, but it was trimmed to a level acceptable to the president.

☐ 1984. The White House and Senate Republican leaders negotiated a "Rose Garden" agreement on the budget, but it took another six months of discussions with congressional Democrats to pass the budget resolution. The protracted dispute delayed action on appropriations and led to an omnibus continuing resolution covering nine of the regular appropriations bills.

☐ 1985. Bargaining proceeded on several fronts, beginning in the Senate with efforts by Republicans to put together a passable budget resolution. The White House and Senate Republican leaders agreed to one deal, only to find they lacked the votes to pass it. Senate Republicans then put together another deal that squeaked by with the Vice-President casting the tiebreaking vote. House Democrats passed their own resolution, without involving Republicans in the process. The different House-Senate versions made for a difficult and lengthy conference. The impasse was broken by an "Oak Tree" agreement, hastily put together on the White House lawn, in which the President accepted Democratic demands that Senate cuts in Social Security COLAs be restored, and Speaker O'Neill accepted Reagan's demand that defense be given a full adjustment for inflation.

☐ 1986. The president refused to be drawn into negotiations, fearing that he would be pressured to accept a tax increase and that the tax reform legislation then in the final stages of consideration would be jeopardized. The president did take an active interest in the continuing resolution, however, both because the continuing resolution spanned all thirteen regular appropriations and because it contained provisions limiting his flexibility on arms control policy. After threats of a presidential veto, agreements were worked out on this and other matters in dispute.

☐ 1987. Month-long summit negotiations followed the stock market crash of October and led to a bipartisan agreement that claimed to prune $30 billion from the deficit the first year and $45 billion the second year. The negotiators included key presidential aides— the White House Chief of Staff, the Secretaries of Treasury and Defense, and the OMB Director—and a dozen congressional leaders. President Reagan did not directly participate, but it was clear from the outset that no deal could be struck without his approval. Despite the sense of urgency in financial markets and extensive media coverage, the negotiations proceeded in fits and starts, with one day's confidence that a far-reaching deal would be reached giving way the next day to pessimism that it would not even be possible to get the minimum agreement necessary to avert a Gramm-Rudman sequester. On October 29, the *Washington Post* reported indications that talks would yield more than the minimum $23 billion target set by the negotiators. On November 5, optimism had vanished, as both the *Post* and the *New York Times* described the talks as floundering. Two days later the discussions were back on track, as Republican negotiators proposed a comprehensive framework, and on November 9, a congressional aide said that the "chances are very, very strong" that an agreement would come that day. It took another ten days of haggling before an agreement was announced, however.

☐ *1988.* The previous year's two-year deal obviated the need for high-level discussions, but OMB monitored appropriations to ensure that they generally adhered to the terms of the summit pact. Still, the administration chose to look the other way when Congress exceeded the discretionary domestic target, preferring not to challenge Congress in an election year.

☐ *1989.* Shortly after George Bush took office, Richard Darman, the new Budget Director, initiated discussions with congressional leaders aimed at avoiding a repeat of the bruising budget battles that had plagued the last years of the Reagan presidency. After more than a month of intermittent discussions, the two sides reached an agreement in April that purported to reduce the deficit through equal amounts of revenue increases and spending cuts. The agreement, whose size was the minimum estimated to be needed for avoiding a GRH sequester later in the year, was notable for the extent to which the claimed savings relied on gimmicks and to which the terms of enforcement were spelled out by the two parties.[34] Despite these terms, conflict over how to implement the agreement erupted later in the year, and funds were sequestered.

This summary shows that presidential-congressional negotiations have not been conducted according to a preset schedule and standardized procedures. Each year has had its peculiar features and relationships. Interbranch negotiations cannot be made routine because the relationship is one in which there are no discussions unless the two sides see some advantage in talking. Each year's circumstances determine whether, and when, discussions take place, who participates, the agenda, and the rules of the game. If one or the other side feels disadvantaged by negotiations, it does not have to enter into them. If delay is perceived as advantageous, the talks will be held later rather than earlier. In presidential-congressional negotiations, the procedures are made up as the relationship progresses, and they can be changed along the way.

Political standing and skill have a great bearing on the outcome of the discussions. The negotiations are political events in which more than the budget is at stake. The president's leadership and resolve are tested. To a lesser extent, congressional leaders put their reputations on the line. The media and attentive publics watch the negotiations and rate the performance of the participants. Success or failure in budget negotiations spills over to other policy arenas.

The higher the level of negotiations, the more is at stake to bring the talks to a successful conclusion. When the participants go to the summit, as they did in 1980, 1987, and 1989, some end agreement is assured, but the scope of the agreement is likely to be quite modest. The 1987 and 1989 summits are instructive on this point. In 1987, the claimed savings were substantial—$76 billion over a two-year period. On close examination, however, the amount of deficit reduction was much less than would have been achieved through a GRH sequester. The first year's $30 billion in claimed savings included $5 billion in asset sales that cannot be counted in the Gramm-Rudman process, $1.6 billion from tighter IRS enforcement, $5 billion from holding the increase in defense spending below the inflated baseline, $9 billion in tax increases, $1.8 billion from user fees and similar charges, and $1.2 billion from lower debt service.

The 1989 agreement also was a minimalist package that resorted to financing gimmicks to inflate the reported savings. The total claimed deficit reduction was $28 billion, but a fair accounting of the terms of the agreement suggests that the genuine savings were only about one-fourth of that amount. Two-thirds of the additional revenue was to come from asset sales, user fees, and more money for IRS enforcement. The alleged spending cuts consisted mostly of removing the postal service and some farm credit programs from the budget, early payment of certain farm price supports, cancellation of old (presumably lost) food stamps, the sale of veterans' loans, and the extension of some temporary Medicare provisions.

Summits accomplish little because they are convened when Congress and the president are at an impasse on the budget. The same factors that produced stalemate in the first place carry over to the negotiations. "White House and Congressional negotiators," the *New York Times* reported during the 1987 summit, "remain deeply divided over the same tax issues and military and domestic spending priorities they have fought over since 1981. . . ."[35] The inflated expectations that the summit will conclude with an agreement induces the negotiators to settle for as little as they can get away with.

THE COST OF IMPROVISATION

Breakdown and improvisation are costly because they mean that the routines of budgeting are not operating as they should. As a sequence of steps that are repeated with little variation each year, budgeting prescribes roles for how resources are to be claimed and allocated. It also ascribes roles to those who want and those who ration resources. Out of these rules and roles, stable expectations develop, and budget makers learn to behave in ways that facilitate completion of required tasks.

The routines drain budgeting of much of its potential for conflict. Given the stakes involved, the scarcity of resources, and the diversity of interests and perspectives brought into play, some friction is unavoidable. But stable procedures efficiently confine disagreement to the allocations themselves; participants do not have to wrangle each year over who is to do what or how the decisions are to be made. Stable procedures also simplify budget choices and move the process toward a successful conclusion. Participants know what they have to do to get the job done. They also know what to expect of others. With a stable division of labor, the making of the budget is broken down into many small tasks, and the work can be completed in a reasonably expeditious manner.

Improvisation is both a failure of the process and a sensible response to breakdown. It affords a means of putting together a budget when the process does not work as it should. From this perspective, improvisation has succeeded, inasmuch as one way or another, budget resolutions and appropriations have been approved each year. At best, however, improvisation is a poor substitute for reliable procedures. Improvised budgeting is likely to be fractious and volatile, and its outcomes more uncertain than when decisions are made under stable rules. Improvisation one year begets more of the same in subsequent years because participants constrained by conflict and time pressures have little incentive or opportunity to make durable repairs in the process. With schedules in disarray and budgeting perennially at the brink of collapse, there is not much inclination to build new institutions or to think beyond the crisis of the moment to know the process can be restored to vitality. Structural problems are allowed to fester, and the need persists to muddle through from one crisis to the next.

It is only a short step from making do with improvised procedures to making do with improvised policies. The same conditions and mindset that spur frequent tinkering with the process encourage budget makers to frequently adjust substantive policies as well. When roles and expectations are destabilized and friction intensifies, participants grasp for options that get them out of the crisis, even if it means reopening previously settled issues and favoring short-term expedients. Instead of the cadence and predictability of incrementalism, outcomes become volatile and uncertain.

Improvisation has reached to the substance of policy as well as the manner in which decisions are scored in the budget. Although both annual appropriations and entitlements programs have been destabilized by high deficits and cutback pressures, the latter have been more severely affected by improvisational behavior. Entitlements are ordinarily the most stable part of the budget because they normally continue in effect unless Congress alters the legislation establishing the right to payment from the government. For some entitlements, notably Social Security, Congress usually maintains a hands-off policy, and the program continues from year to year without substantive change. A few programs, however, have been subject to frequent, sometimes annual, legislative change. Table 6.3 reveals that this was the fate of Medicare during the Reagan administration. More than 200 changes were legislated in Medicare during the Reagan years, an average of approximately 25 each year. Legislative action was especially frequent and recurring with regard to provisions directly affecting federal expenditures, such as payments to hospitals and physicians. Not only were legislated changes an annual occurrence but the legislation contained numerous temporary provisions, extensions of expiring provisions, rate increases below the baseline that were scored as cutbacks, and so on.

The frequent changes were not costless. They generated confusion over the rules, made both providers and recipients of health care feel

Table 6.3 MAJOR LEGISLATIVE CHANGES IN MEDICARE, 1981–87

PROVISION	YEAR ENACTED						
	1981	1982	1983	1984	1985	1986	1987
Periodic interim payments	Repeal temporary delay	Delay payments			Increase payments .5%	Eliminate for inpatient services	Extend 2.3% cut[a]
Hospital reimbursement	Limit rate increase	Limit rate increase	Establish DRG system	Limit rate increase	Limit rate increase	Limit rate increase	Change PPS formula application
Physician fees				Freeze 15 months	Extend freeze 8 months	Establish fee schedules	Extend 2.3% cut[a]
Part A and co-insurance	Change deductible formula		Delay rate increase			Change deductible formula	
Part B premiums	Increase deductible	Set at 25% of cost[b]	Delay premium increase	Extend 25%[b] provisions	Extend 25%[b] provision	Extend 25%[b] provision	Extend 25%[b] provision
Secondary payer		Establish for older workers		Extend to spouse	Extend age to 70 years	Extend to disabled	
Capital costs			Exclude from DRG calculations	Limit value increase	Eliminate return on equity	Reduce payments to PPS hospitals	Reduce payments in FY88 and FY89
Number of new provisions	18	27	13	30	51	31	38

Source: Committee on the Ways and Means, *Background Material and Data on Programs within the Jurisdiction of the Committee on Ways and Means*, various years.
[a]Extended through March 1988 reductions of 2.3 percent imposed November 20, 1987, under the revised GRH law.
[b]Temporary.

shortchanged by Congress, and introduced further uncertainties into the budget.[36] On this last point, official statistics claim that about $50 billion was trimmed from Medicare by congressional action, but the accuracy of these statistics is highly questionable. It is impossible to sort through all the temporary provisions, baseline gimmicks, and other ruses to find out what really was done to health care programs during the 1980s. What is certain, however, is that the frequent changes made patients and providers alike feel cheated by the federal government. In the decade during which Medicare spending tripled, patients came to feel that their benefits had been cut; hospitals increasingly felt squeezed by frequent adjustments in the rates; and physicians perceived the practice of medicine as subject to tighter controls. Every time a presumably temporary provision was extended, congressional scorekeepers claimed fresh savings, and providers and recipients felt that promises had again been broken.

Medicare is an extreme case of policy volatility. To this writer's knowledge, no other program has been tampered with so frequently. Nevertheless, Medicare is a useful lesson on the costs of improvisation. It shows that improvised policy generates conflict and confusion, subverts Congress's budgetary objectives, and provides a fertile opportunity for those affected by the legislation to exploit the frequent changes.

Manipulation of the rules for scoring the budget impact of congressional actions has been another by-product of improvisational behavior. When budget procedures are stable, one can be reasonably confident that the same rules for estimating the budget effects of legislative decisions will be continued from year to year. Stability in scorekeeping rules is valued because it facilitates interyear comparisons and enables those making the decisions and those affected by the budget actions to have confidence in what they are doing. Because legislative scorekeeping rules are self-enforced, they are sometimes manipulated for short-term advantage. The machinations undoubtedly escalate when fiscal stress intensifies.

The integrity of budget accounts is at great risk when the scorekeeping rules are made up each year. When one is manipulating budget procedures, there is a strong temptation to manipulate the budget accounts as well. In fact, scorekeeping tricks have become a key tool of improvisation. Without changing a single program or policy, deficits can be made to vanish or savings to materialize by changing the way transactions are accounted for in the budget. Placing items in or outside the budget, delaying or advancing payment dates, and manipulating the sale of assets are old tricks, but one has the impression that they have been used on a broader scale in the 1980s than previously. The baseline is an especially inviting device for improvisation. It is inherently a variable, always in a state of flux as new data become available on inflation, spending rates, and other relevant factors. Hidden assumptions on these variables have been used to inflate the baseline and, thereby, the claimed savings.

What is new about the scorekeeping gimmicks is their unabashed use. With the single-minded attention on driving the deficit numbers down, budget makers now openly boast of their "smoke and mirrors" chicanery. Hardly any effort was made to veil the scorekeeping tricks improved in 1987; and none was made when the 1989 summit invented almost $20 billion in false savings. These days, the budget's new scorekeepers inoculate themselves against criticism by confessing to the scorekeeping sins they have committed. Their defense is that it is all in a good cause—to avert a worse fate, sequestration of funds under the Gramm-Rudman-Hollings law. The law encourages budget improvisation by requiring only that lower deficits be promised, not that they be realized.

Improvisation is a creature of big deficits. But it also has assured that deficits will remain big. Improvised rules avert genuine deficit reduction today by promising chimerical reductions tomorrow. When tomorrow comes, the deficit is still troublesome, so another round of improvisation is needed. And so it was that the fiscal 1988 deficit was bigger than 1987's, and 1989's bigger than 1988's. No funds were sequestered in either year. Only one budget rule survived intact, and it was sufficient: When you can't, improvise.

Notes

1. Hugh Helco, "Executive Budget Making," in *Federal Budget Policy in the 1980s*, ed. Gregory B. Mills and John L. Palmer (Washington, D.C.: Urban Institute Press, 1984), p. 271.

2. Donald W. Moran, Executive Associate Director, Office of Management and Budget, quoted in Jonathan Rauch, "Stockman's Quiet Revolution at OMB May Leave Indelible Mark on Agency," *National Journal*, May 25, 1985.

3. See *Building a Better America*, Message of the President to Congress, February 9, 1989.

4. Bruce Johnson, "OMB and the Budget Examiner: Changes in the Reagan Era," *Public Budgeting and Finance* 8 (Winter 1988), p. 5. OMB's changing role is also discussed in Bruce E. Johnson, "From Analyst to Negotiator: The OMB's New Role," *Journal of Policy Analysis and Management* 3, no. 4 (1984), pp. 501–15.

5. Heclo depicts the traditional role of OMB examiners as follows: "To a young budget examiner just joining OMB, the traditional ethos of the organization went something like this. 'The president's budget is a statement of value about every program the federal government runs. You are joining an organization that has to be able to respond competently to any issue. . . . That means knowing something of the history, the law, the happenings in the agency, and the academic studies, so that when called upon, you can judge the worth of a program.' " *op. cit.,* p. 279.

6. See Bruce Johnson, "The OMB Budget Examiner and the Congressional Budget Process," *Public Budgeting and Finance* 9 (Spring 1989), p. 7.

7. The number of appearances on Capitol Hill by the OMB Director and other political officials increased significantly during the 1960s and beyond. Most of these appearances were at overview hearings on the budget and the economy conducted by the budget and appropriations committees or on major legislative issues. To this day, the OMB Director does not normally testify on particular appropriations.

8. "During the Reagan administration," Bruce Johnson writes, "OMB has faced conflicting demands between its traditional role as the analyst, formulator and enforcer of the president's budget priorities and its new roles as advocator and negotiator for the president's budget policies. These conflicting demands have overburdened and confused the budget examiners and weakened their ability to perform their traditional role." In "OMB and the Budget Examiner: Changes in the Reagan Era," *op. cit.,* p. 3.

9. The "rec room" refers to the staff put together by Stockman in 1981 to monitor congressional action on the reconciliation bill. This monitoring function was institutionalized in 1982 by the establishment of the Central Budget Management Branch in OMB as the focal point for the exchange of budget information between Congress and OMB.

10. Peter T. Kilburn, "Expert Behind Budget Tells a Tale of Change," *New York Times,* April 18, 1989.

11. Heclo concludes his study of executive budgeting with a warning about the erosion of OMB's institutional capacity. "The experience of the last three years [1981–84] leaves more open than ever the question of what kind of organization the Office of Management and Budget is to be. . . . The attenuated two-way communication between the larger political layers and career staff has the same effect of undermining institutional capabilities. As career officials are less expected to understand the uses to which their information is put in the front office, so they become less able, and ultimately less interested, in understanding the larger picture. In this sense, OMB's political power may have increased while its institutional strength has eroded." In Heclo, *op. cit.,* pp. 290–91.

12. The House Ways and Means and the Appropriations Committees rarely exercise privilege in taking their bills to the floor. The Ways and Means Committee usually gets a rule protecting its legislation against floor amendments, and the Appropriations Committee gets a rule waiving points of order for unauthorized appropriations or other violations of House rules.

13. Mayhew labels the House Ways and Means Committee and the Appropriations Committee as "control committees" whose function has been to constrain the House from responding to the political pressures buffeting members. See David R. Mayhew, *Congress: The Electoral Connection* (New Haven: Yale University Press, 1973).

14. See chapter VIII, "The Accommodating Budget," In Allen Schick, *Congress and Money: Budgeting, Spending, and Taxing* (Washington, D.C.: Urban Institute, 1980), pp. 307–56.

15. The problems of governing in an age of divided government are discussed in James L. Sundquist, "The New Era of Coalition Government in the United States," *Political Science Quarterly* 103, no. 4 (1988), pp. 613–35.

16. The 1974 Budget Act originally barred consideration of appropriation bills for the next fiscal year until the Spring budget resolution was adopted. This was changed by the 1985 Gramm-Rudman-Hollings law (PL 99-177) to permit the House to consider regular appropriation bills after May 15 even if the budget resolution has not been adopted.

17. Nearly a decade ago, this author warned that the "vote the process" argument "loses force in repetition. Members cannot be expected to forgo their substantive interests endlessly, just to keep the budget process alive. As budgeting becomes less novel on Capitol Hill, members may become less willing to vote for resolutions that do not reflect their budget priorities. The long-term health of the congressional budget process cannot be secured by frantic, last-minute appeals to vote against one's political interests or views." Schick, *op. cit.*, p. 250.

18. This provision, known as the "Frazio exception," permits the House to consider a measure that would cause total spending to exceed the ceiling in the budget resolution if the committee with jurisdiction over the measure has not exceeded the allocation of new discretionary budget authority or new spending authority made to it pursuant to section 302 of the Budget Act. There is no equivalent exception in the Senate.

19. See Robert A. Keith, *Changes in Congressional Budget Process Made by the 1985 Balanced Budget Act (PL 99-177)*, CRS Report no. 86-713, Congressional Research Service, May 23, 1986.

20. During the 97th and 98th Congresses (1981–82 and 1983–84), for example, the House adopted 140 rules granting more than 200 waivers of Budget Act provisions. Some recent data on waivers is presented in Robert A. Keith, *Waivers of the 1974 Budget Act Considered in the Senate During the 100th Congress*, CRS Report no. 89-76, Congressional Research Service, February 3, 1989.

21. The letter, dated March 27, 1980, is reprinted in U.S. Congress, House Committee on the Budget, *A Review of the Reconciliation Process*, Committee Print, October 1984, p. 19.

22. Data on the coverage of reconciliation bills is provided in Allen Schick, *The Whole and the Parts: Piecemeal and Integrated Approaches to Congressional Budgeting*, U.S. Congress, House Committee on the Budget, Committee Print, February 1987, p. 31.

23. See U.S. Congress, House Committee on Rules, Subcommittee on the Legislative Process, Hearing on *The Budget Reconciliation Process: The Inclusion of Unrelated Matter*, 99th Cong., 2d sess., July 30, 1986, p. 13.

24. The rule, known as the Byrd amendment, was first adopted as section 20001 of the Consolidated Omnibus Budget Reconciliation Act of 1985 (enacted in 1986). The Byrd amendment requires a three-fifths vote to waive the bar against extraneous provisions in reconciliation bills. The House does not have a comparable rule.

25. See Louis Fisher, "The Authorization-Appropriation Process in Congress: Formal Rules and Informal Practices," *Catholic University Law Review* 29, no. 5 (1979), pp. 52–105; also "Annual Authorizations: Durable Roadblocks to Biennial Budgeting," *Public Budgeting and Finance* (Spring 1983), pp. 23–40.

26. Quoted in *A Review of the Reconciliation Process*, *op. cit.*, p. 33.

27. *Ibid.*

28. Congress often adopts several continuing resolutions each year. All but the last are temporary; hence, they have to be renewed. The comments concerning the coverage of the continuing resolution pertains to the final one adopted for the fiscal year. For a fuller discussion of the evolution of continuing resolutions, see *The Whole and the Parts: Piecemeal and Integrated Approaches to Congressional Budgeting*, *op. cit.*, p. 33–39.

29. Section 302 of the Congressional Budget Act of 1974 establishes a two-stage process for the allocation of the budget authority set forth in the adopted budget resolution among House and Senate committees, including the appropriations committees. In the first stage, each committee is allocated its share of total budget authority; in the second, each committee subdivides the amount allocated to it among its programs or, in the case of the appropriations committees, its subcommittees.

30. Two features of the continuing resolution open it to substantive legislation. First, the prohibition in congressional rules against legislation in an appropriation bill applies only to "general" appropriations. Because the House does not deem the continuing resolution a general appropriation, the rules do not apply to this measure. Second, the continuing resolution is usually considered under time pressures and other rushed conditions that diminish the knowledge that members and executive officials have of its contents.

31. In some recent years, all members of the Senate Appropriations Committees and most House Appropriations Committee members have participated in the conference. The conferees break up into subconferences corresponding to the regular appropriations bills included in the continuing resolution.

32. Quoted in John Herbers, "President Denounces Budget Process," *New York Times*, May 29, 1982.

33. Reagan's proposal, which was endorsed by George Bush shortly after he took office, would convert the budget resolution into a statutory measure that could be signed or vetoed by the president.

34. "Negotiators Agree on Budget Targets," *Congressional Quarterly Weekly Report* 47, no. 15 (April 15, 1989), p. 804.

35. "Elusive Spirit of Compromise on Budget," *New York Times*, November 5, 1987.

36. See Allen Schick, "Health Policy: Spending More and Protecting Less," in *The Future of Health Care in the United States*, ed. Marion Ein Lewin (Washington, D.C.: American Enterprise Institute, 1989).

Chapter 7

RESTORING THE CAPACITY TO BUDGET

The federal government is awash in good ideas for reforming the budget process.[1] Dozens of reform measures have been introduced in recent sessions of Congress, calling for a two-year budget cycle, revised impoundment rules, the realignment of committee jurisdictions, new deficit reduction procedures, and other changes.[2] Ronald Reagan's final budget charged "that the federal budget process is fundamentally flawed," and it recommended eight modifications "to instill budget discipline throughout the legislative process."[3] George Bush's first budget endorsed all of Reagan's proposals and added four of his own.[4]

The case for reform is amply supported by the material presented in previous chapters. Established procedures have broken down, budgeting has become a contentious, unstable process; the reliability of data has deteriorated; and efforts to curtail the deficit have had little success. This concluding chapter takes the position that achieving significant improvement requires confronting the underlying factors that have contributed to breakdown and devising suitable remedies for these problems. It does not suffice to draw up lists of possible reforms or to suggest modifications that may have some merit but would do little to cure contemporary budget ills. The three underlying causes identified in this book are the persistence of high deficits, erosion of the government's capacity to ration resources, and a failure to sufficiently adapt budgeting to the changed composition of federal expenditure. The three problems are linked, but for purposes of proposing improvements in budgeting, each is considered separately here.

The number one question stalking contemporary budgeting is this: Why has a process, which worked so well in the past, failed recently? All roads in budgetary analysis lead to the conclusion that the massive deficits that have beset the federal government in the 1980s are the chief cause of breakdown. The recent history of budgeting would have been much more favorable if the deficit had been much smaller. Another way of making the point is to state that no reform will cure budgeting's ills until substantial progress is made in reducing the deficit.

Once the deficit has abated, it should be possible to adjust budgetary practices to discourage a recurrence. The key issue is restoration of a balance between the budget's capacity to generate claims and its capacity to ration resources. The leading factors of imbalance were identified in previous chapters: the programming of the budget for growth, the advent of less buoyant economic conditions, the rising share of the budget consumed by mandatory payments and other sticky expenditures, and the unwillingness of the government to raise taxes to keep up with the rise in spending. The first development opened the budget to incremental claims. The second made it less capable of financing these claims. The third permitted many claims to rise despite the lack of adequate increments to pay for them. Together, these conditions have fostered high deficits, intense conflict, and budgetary breakdown. To be effective, budget reform must come to grips with this imbalance between the claiming and rationing capacities of budgeting. Each proposed modification in budget practice should be assessed in terms of whether it would bolster claims or facilitate the rationing of resources.

In the course of restoring budgetary balance, it will be necessary to deal with the changed composition of federal expenditure. In the past, budgeting was mainly an administrative process for managing the expenditures of government departments; it has evolved over several decades into a process that also allocates resources to firms, households, and other recipients. To state the argument succinctly, the federal government has a budget process designed for managing agency operations but spends the bulk of resources on transfer payments. This mismatch between the capacity of the budget process and the character of federal expenditure has rendered agency submissions largely irrelevant, disoriented the Office of Management and Budget, uprooted the president's role in budgeting, and complicated Congress's ability to control expenditure. In becoming more of a transfer process, budgeting cannot become less of an expenditure management process. It must meld the two types of budgeting into an integrated process.

The stresses of big deficits, budgetary imbalance, and changing expenditure patterns have revealed deficiencies in the institutional arrangements of budgeting. Improvisation is not a satisfactory substitute for reliable procedures. One can expect some stabilization of executive and legislative roles once deficit pressures ease and an acceptable balance is achieved in claiming and rationing resources. Nevertheless, the growth of transfer expenditures and other changes in budgeting make established patterns of behavior inadequate. Budget summits are the leading edge of emerging shifts in the relationship between the president and Congress. In suggesting ways of countering the underlying problems, we will also comment on how institutional roles might be adjusted.

The three criteria identified here are not the only ones that might be considered in devising an agenda of budget reforms. Others have been suggested elsewhere by this author.[5] The ones selected here flow from the issues examined in previous chapters. In the sections that follow, each of the criteria is explained and proposals are advanced for dealing with the problem at hand.

DEFICIT REDUCTION IS THE KEY

Ending the crisis in budgeting depends on significant, genuine, and durable reductions in the deficit. As long as massive deficits persist as the dominant fact of budgeting, they will distort behavior and debilitate established rules and procedures.

Four years after the Gramm-Rudman-Hollings law was enacted, it is apparent that although this control has induced some expenditure constraint and small tax increases, it has not made a deep enough dent in the deficit. The year after GRH was enacted, the deficit dropped some $70 billion, a steeper decline than ever before. Approximately half of this reduction was accounted for by nonrecurring factors, such as the timing of the 1986 tax reform and asset sales. After 1987, the deficit resumed its upward march. In the 1988 fiscal year, it was higher than in the previous year, and in 1989, it was about the same. If the enormous Social Security surpluses were removed from the calculation, the annual deficit at the end of the 1980s would be higher than it was before the enactment of GRH. What is most remarkable about the stubborn deficit is that it has persisted despite the longest peacetime expansion in American history. Thus far, therefore, neither sustained growth nor fixed deficit targets have resolved the deficit problem.

The long expansion has spurred vigorous debate concerning the economic effects of the deficit. Some economists have countered alarm about the deficit with the argument that the imbalance would be much lower than reported if appropriate adjustments were made for capital investment and inflation.[6] Others have presented elegant theories that claim that the impact of the deficit and other government fiscal actions is discounted in advance by the rational expectations of households and entrepreneurs. Some critics take comfort in the stabilization of the public debt relative to GNP and in reduction in the relative size of the deficit to about half of what it was earlier in the decade.[7] Finally, the deficit has been welcomed by those who see it as one of the few constraints on the rise in public expenditure.

Whether the deficit portends economic ruin is a question that will be debated for many years. But it is already apparent that the deficit has brought considerable political difficulty. This is the facet of the problem that requires attention to restore budgeting to health. As the dominant political issue of the 1980s, the deficit has taken a heavy toll in governmental competence. The political bill of particulars against outsized deficits is quite formidable. It includes the collapse of budget regularity, the encouragement of deceitful accounting practices, a premium on gimmicks that produce short-term improvement but do not ease the structural problem, strained relationships between the president and Congress, the attenuation of the president's role in budgeting, congestion and frustration in Congress, the overloading of the political will of elected leaders, the crowding out of attention to other important national concerns, and the lack of resources to respond to emerging issues and priorities. The deficit is not the only debilitating condition facing American government, but as long as it persists, one should not expect a high degree of budgetary competence.[8]

The deficit will not go away by itself. CBO projections referred to in the opening chapter point to chronically high deficits well into the 1990s, even if economic growth continues. To restore budget capacity, it is not necessary to liquidate the entire shortfall. The federal government managed to function reasonably well in the past, when deficits ranged between 1 and 2 percent of GNP, and it can probably do so again in the future.[9] Arguably, a zero deficit target, such as has been prescribed by GRH, is so unrealistic that striving for it would do more harm than good. As long as a zero deficit objective is on the books, any deficit will be seen as a policy failure, even if it is modest compared with experience in the postwar era.

In setting an appropriate target, there are no compelling political reasons for excluding the Social Security funds from the computation. By lowering the reported deficit, these funds ease political pressure. Rather than facing a shortfall in the vicinity of $250 billion by the mid-1990s, politicians have to deal with a problem that is made $100 billion smaller by the rising Social Security balances. One can envision a time in the next century when the annual drawdown in the Social Security balances and the regular budget shortfall will combine to make a truly gargantuan deficit problem. It would be prudent for the government to address this issue long before the upsurge in the retirement population occurs, but, at a time when politicians have difficulty coping with the overall budget deficit, it does little good to urge them to tackle the task of eradicating the much larger on-budget deficit.[10]

Reducing the deficit to manageable proportions will be a difficult task, for it runs afoul of the preference of Americans for more program benefits and lower taxes. The paltry sums saved through the 1987 and 1989 summits attest to the challenge that lies ahead. The following subsections suggest a course of action that might ease the task.

Presidential-Congressional Cooperation

Substantial amelioration of the deficit requires the active cooperation of the president and Congress. In an era of divided government, neither branch has the political will to go it alone or the political leverage to force the other side to act. What is required is not simply a willingness to meet at the bargaining table but a willingness of each side to make it easier for the other to offer significant concessions.

Effective negotiations require the sharing of both credit and blame. Unfortunately, in today's budget environment, there is not much credit to go around. For this reason, it is vital that neither branch try to outmaneuver the other so that one bears the onus for the bad things, such as a tax increase, and the other garners the credit for the good things, such as saving programs. Nor would it do much good for the two sides to conspire to give each what it wants the most. In recent summits, the Republican president protected defense and the Democratic Congress protected domestic programs. With each side coming away a winner, the resulting deficit was probably about as high as it would have been had the two branches gone their separate ways and settled the budget without high-level negotiations.

What is necessary is that the president and Congress each yield on something of value. One side's concession may make the other's more forthcoming. The 1986 tax reform is instructive on this point.

The road to enactment was lined with extraordinary policy reversals in which Republicans and Democrats abandoned salient positions. A Republican president endorsed the shift of an estimated $120 billion in tax burdens (over a five-year period) from individuals to corporations, and congressional Democrats accepted a steep drop in marginal tax rates on high-income persons. A comparable deficit-reduction strategy would have the Democrats accept genuine cuts in domestic spending, the president accept deeper cuts in defense, and both share the blame for needed tax increases.

Negotiations would be facilitated by behavior in which each branch protects the other's political position. Perhaps this is too much to ask of politicians operating in today's contentious environment. Yet, neither branch can take the political risks of cutting programs or raising taxes if it remains vulnerable to attack by the other. In our political system, one of the unwritten roles of the president is to shelter Congress—that is, to make it easier for legislators to take unpopular actions. It is not hard for the president to score political points by bashing Congress as fiscally irresponsible and as culpable for the deficit. Americans relish the potshots taken at Congress. The president complicates Congress's life when he submits budgets built on questionable economic or program assumptions. Unrealistic budgets and a confrontational relationship with Congress may produce summit agreements, but they do not lead to deep inroads into the deficit. Congress must also ease the president's task by looking to the White House for budgetary leadership. After two decades of chipping away at presidential power, it is untoward for Congress to complain about the president's failure to lead.

We shall have more to say later about the institutional roles and relationships of the two branches. For the present, it should be noted that if the two branches do not work in concert to substantially curtail the deficit, the case for a more fundamental overhaul of American government will be strengthened. The plea for cooperation is premised on confidence that divided government can work. If it can not, stronger measures may be needed.

Spending and Tax Policies

The three essential ingredients of any successful deficit-reduction package have already been mentioned: reductions in defense and domestic spending and a boost in tax revenues. Refusal to negotiate on any of these means either no deal or an inadequate one. On the spending side, recognition of the government's financial straits compels a vigorous search for savings in both defense and nondefense programs. Obviously, those who clamor for more defense or domestic money would find major cutbacks unpalatable. But one must raid these big budget categories with the same frame of mind with which Willie Sutton robbed banks—"go where the money is." To get a deal, it is important that defense cuts not be used, as they have been in the recent past, to finance domestic program enhancements. Defense savings must be allocated directly to deficit relief, and any wanted expansion in domestic programs should come from reallocations within that sector.

Foreseeable savings on the expenditure side will not add up to sufficient deficit reduction. Hence, the search will have to turn to taxes for a big chunk of the package. The case for a sizable tax increase rests on an important strand of evidence presented in chapter 5— the relative decline in the general revenues of the federal government. General revenues are now a smaller percentage of GNP than at any time since World War II. They are lower, relative to the economy, than they were before the postwar expansion of federal programs. The plain fact is that the government is not generating sufficient revenue to finance general expenditure. In fact, general revenue now covers less than 75 percent of general outlays. Part of the shortfall is made up by trust fund surpluses, but even after these are included, a sizable deficit remains.

To achieve a normal deficit in the vicinity of 1 to 1.5 percent of GNP would require a combination of about $75 to $100 billion in tax increases and spending cuts. It would be prudent to spread the effects of a sizable deficit reduction package over a few years. But if serious actions were stretched out too long and only minimum inroads made at the start, the package probably would come apart before significant abatement of the deficit was achieved.

In devising a target, one must reckon with the possibility of a recession in the next few years. Any recession would bring a halt to deficit reduction. A deep or prolonged downturn would propel the deficit substantially upward. As the 1980s draw to a close with a deficit pegged in the vicinity of $150 billion, there is considerable risk of much higher deficit levels in the next decade unless corrective action is taken while there is still opportunity to do so.

Honest Accounting

Efforts to rein in the deficit must come to grips with the assortment of gimmicks used to overstate the amount of relief that is being achieved. If all the reductions in the deficit claimed between 1982 and 1989 were legitimate, the federal government now might be running a surplus, and budgetary order would be restored. During this period, the reliability of the claimed savings deteriorated greatly. Early in the decade, most of the claimed reduction in the deficit was legitimate. By the end of the decade, the true savings were far outweighed by the fabricated ones. The 1989 summit had only one part legitimate to three or more parts falsified deficit reduction.

Politicians have demonstrated considerable creativity in exaggerating the claimed reductions. Their repertoire of tricks includes removing expenditures from the budget; advancing payments to the current years, or postponing them to the year after next; renewing temporary provisions or enacting new ones; selling federal assets or accelerating the payments of loans; estimating higher revenue from tougher enforcement of the tax laws; and taking credit for canceling payments that would not be made anyway. Many of these deceptive practices add to future deficits, but they are applied because of the favorable impact on the deficit for the current or next fiscal year.

If the truth be told, deception has been fostered by the interbranch cooperation urged earlier. Anything goes in federal budgeting these days, as long as it is agreed to by the White House and congressional leaders. When the two sides conspire to substitute gimmicks for legitimate savings, the budget process loses credibility, and the deficit persists. The incentive to lie is great because each dollar of deceit means that one less dollar of deficit reduction has to come from paring expenditures or boosting taxes.

Political deceit has also been encouraged by the Gramm-Rudman-Hollings process, about which more will be said in the next subsection. Well-meaning politicians dissemble because other options are either unavailable or less attractive. To discourage budgetary gimmicks, the advantages of deception must be curtailed. One way of doing so would be to enforce scorekeeping rules that count only structural changes in revenue or expenditures as deficit reductions. One-time savings, taking items off-budget, and all other fabrications do not contribute one dollar toward genuine deficit reduction, and, therefore, they should not be counted.[11] A further required step would be to give responsibility for scoring deficit reductions to an independent body that would be relatively free of political influence.

The Gramm-Rudman-Hollings Process

The GRH law has been a mixed blessing for deficit reduction. Trend data indicate that the deficit targets and the threat of sequestration constrained expenditure growth and the deficit in GRH's first year or two, but the impact wore off as politicians became bolder in gaming the process to avoid sequestration. At present, GRH brings only modest deficit relief while exacting a high price in budgetary integrity. GRH might regain effectiveness in the future, if the targets set in 1987 are retained, but there is a strong possibility that they will be modified before their real bite is felt.

When the original GRH law was enacted in 1985, controversy swirled over its automatic procedures. Some critics thought it was unwise to put the federal government on automatic pilot and to permit across-the-board cuts regardless of program needs or economic circumstances. After four years of experience, it is clear that this concern was misplaced. There is hardly anything automatic in the GRH process. Whether sequestration occurs depends substantially on the discretionary actions of the law's custodians. Political tactics can override the GRH targets and neutralize the automatic sequester.

GRH started out as a process for reducing the deficit and has become a means of hiding the deficit and running away from responsibility for it. The process has been twisted into something quite different than what was intended because it requires trimming only the projected—not the actual—deficit. The projection is made shortly before, or at the start of, the fiscal year. Once the final projection is issued on October 15, 350 days still remain in the fiscal year, but the GRH process is mothballed, and no action has to be taken regardless of the outturn in the deficit. No adjustment has to be made if, as happened in the 1988 and 1989 fiscal years, the deficit surges well above targeted levels. This feature of GRH gives politicians a strong incentive to issue fanciful projections that are then superseded by the force majeure of budgetary developments. Worse yet, it gives politicians a strong incentive to schedule increased spending in the current rather than the next year's budget. After October 15, additional spending cannot trigger the GRH process, no matter what it does to the deficit.

GRH purports to be a multiyear process for purging the deficit. In fact, it puts a premium on one-year-at-a-time behavior. All that matters is the single year for which projections are being made. Any maneuver that purports to lower that year's estimated deficit is welcomed, even if it has the effect of worsening the deficit outlook in future years.

The acid test of GRH is whether it has delivered on its promise to curtail the budget deficit. A comparison of the fiscal 1986 and 1989 deficits suggests that the modest reduction—about $70 billion—achieved during this period might have been realized if budgeting had been permitted to run its own course. This was a period of uninterrupted economic growth and a sharp reversal in the defense buildup, yet the drop-off in the deficit was approximately half of what was targeted by the original GRH law. To achieve a balanced budget by 1993, the fiscal year for which the current GRH law promises a zero deficit, would require three to five times more deficit reduction in the next four years than was achieved in the previous four.

Perversely, the failure of GRH to live up to its notices has stimulated political support for the process. After the Supreme Court invalidated an important feature of GRH, Congress enacted a fix that gave the process new life. It did so because GRH gives politicians the best of both worlds—the appearance of doing something about the deficit and the reality of not having to do very much.

GRH should be overhauled or scrapped altogether. There is some advantage in preset deficit targets, but only if the distortions GRH has generated are eliminated. At the least, steps should be taken along the lines suggested earlier to create a tamperproof process. Furthermore, no revenue or spending action should be scored as a saving unless it would reduce the deficit both in the year for which sequestration is pending as well as in the outyears.

CLAIMING AND RATIONING RESOURCES

Large and persistent deficits are evidence of an imbalance between the budget's capacity to generate claims and to ration resources. It is harder to guard the treasury today than it was in the past, and it is easier to advance claims independently of the financial environment in which budgeting is practiced. Many factors affect the relative strength of claims and rations. The list is long because budgeting is an open system subject to all the influences and vagaries of politics. Just about any change in political circumstances can affect the vigor and effectiveness with which resources are claimed and rationed. The proximity of campaigns and election returns and the latest public opinion polls and economic reports, the activities of interest groups and the organization of government—these and many more political changes sway budgeting in one direction or another. As a result, budgeting changes even when its procedures appear not to. The same reconciliation process used to retrench spending in 1981 foiled presidential cutbacks later in the decade. What changed? Not the rules. The larger political environment in which budgeting proceeds induced Congress to alter the manner in which the rules were applied.

Throughout modern budget history, changes in policy and in process have moved in tandem. Favorable economic conditions after World War II led to expansive spending claims and the relaxation of controls. As the government expanded, the budget took on a more programmatic orientation. Recent fiscal stress has led to constrictive policies, such as the GRH targets, as well as to restrictive procedures, such as tough points of order in the Senate. The interplay of policy and process is not simply one of cause and effect but one of the two facets of budgeting responding to the same conditions. When the environment of budgeting changes, procedural adjustments facilitate changes in policy outcomes.

The key variable in these adjustments is the financial condition of the government. When increments are ample, budgeting is not practiced the same way as when money is scarce, nor are the results likely to be the same. When resources are plentiful, budgeting is conducted in ways that encourage claims. When they are scarce, expansive behavior is discouraged, and the rationing of resources is strengthened. A simple example illustrates the adaptability of budgeting. When the budget is expanding, issues tend to be defined in program terms. Decisions on education will focus on the additional courses offered, improvement in student-teacher ratios, and other program benefits. Some of the attention to program issues will be filtered through budget procedures, such as the form of the requests submitted by spending agencies. Much will come from behavioral influences, such as awareness that money is available for expansion and receptivity to good ideas for spending it. When contraction is the order of the day, however, education decisions will tend to be made in financial terms, such as the amount saved by percentage cutbacks or by a freeze on filling vacant positions. The shift in focus from program to financial categories may seem to be inconsequential, and it may not entail modifications in formal procedures, but it facilitates adjustment of the budget to changing conditions and the achievement of acceptable outcomes.

This example of policy and process interacting on the claiming and rationing capacities of budgeting is not an isolated case. Constrictive outcomes depend on procedures that dampen claims or bolster controls. Attainment of expansive objectives hinges on relaxing the grip on resources and stirring up demands for additional funds. Of course, these are not the only propellants of change in budgeting, but they explain many of the modifications made over the years and are the factors most relevant to the theme of this book.

Budgeting is efficacious when the policy and the process are in harmony—that is, when they advance the same ends. Ideally, claiming and rationing resources would be balanced through self-correcting adjustments in expectations and behavior. Self-correction goes a long way toward explaining why budgeting produced acceptable outcomes in the past. Contemporary deficits and the strains in the process tell us that self-correction no longer suffices. Entrenched claims are insensitive to changes in fiscal conditions and policy expectations. Hence, one must reform budgetary practices to bring claims and resources back into alignment.

Reform has to reach both presidential and congressional budgeting. There seems to be a pronounced bias in budgeting that recognizes the problems afflicting the congressional side of the process but ignores comparable difficulties in the executive branch. But although the impairment of budgeting is more visible in Congress, it is no less a problem for the president.

In our fragmented governing arrangements, claims pour in from all directions. One should not take the simplistic view that it is the president who prudently guards the purse while Congress behaves in a spendthrift manner. When the budget is driven by growth, both branches spur claims and degrade their rationing capacity. Reform of congressional practices will not amount to much if they are not accompanied by improvements in presidential budgeting. To restore a balance between the claims and available resources, it is necessary to strengthen guardianship in both branches.

Controlling Entitlements

The most potent move in this direction is also the least feasible. Claims on resources would be greatly weakened and the capacity to control their allocation would be strengthened by deindexing transfer payments. Each year's rise in expenditure is dominated, data presented in chapter 4 reveal, by sticky expenditures such as entitlements and the payoff of past commitments. Some of the updrift is due to demographic trends and other developments over which the government has little or no say. Nevertheless, a substantial portion is attributable to the indexation of various benefits.

Deindexation would signal a more austere budget posture. It still would allow discretionary adjustments in payments, and these probably would keep pace with inflation when resources were plentiful. There is a possibility that pressured politicians would provide adjustments in excess of inflation, as happened to social security before it was indexed. But that behavior occurred when the government's financial condition was more favorable than it is today. In a harsh fiscal environment, the government would have the option of fine-tuning the adjustments by, for example, giving increases to some recipients but not to all, or by delaying their effective date.

The political costs of removing the automatic adjustment of payment would be enormous. There also would be formidable social costs, such as the potential for hidden attrition in the standard of living of vulnerable sectors of the population. Deindexation will not occur because spending control and budgetary balance are not the only values pursued in a democratic society. The United States, along with other industrialized democracies, has made it high national policy to mitigate the loss of income due to aging and infirmity, to provide economic support to dependent persons, to protect the real value of assistance to the elderly against erosion by inflation, and to enable workers to confidently prepare for retirement. Throughout the 1980s, the goal of deficit reduction has given way to these values, and there is no reason to believe that the contest will turn out otherwise in the future.

Some savings can be achieved by chipping away at entitlements at the margins. Eligibility rules can be altered to withdraw benefits to those with a weaker claim for assistance or to give them smaller payments. But a frontal attack on the entitlement state or on protections against inflation just is not going to work, nor would proposals to adjust payments by a fixed percentage below the indexed rate, such as inflation minus 2 percent. As long as indexation is on the books, providing anything less than a full adjustment tells beneficiaries that they are being cheated out of money that is rightfully theirs. A more promising approach would be to provide full benefits but to subject them to income taxation, as is now done for a portion of the Social Security payments received by persons earning above a prescribed threshold. Another approach that has been applied recently would be to dampen demand for additional benefits by making the pool of recipients pay for them. The enhancement of Medicare's catastrophic illness program enacted in 1988 has this characteristic. One would do well to proceed cautiously because special taxes further erode the general revenue base and may distort budget priorities.

Moreover, as the Medicare catastrophic legislation has demonstrated, taxing beneficiaries to finance their benefits can provoke a backlash that compels politicians to withdraw or curtail the new program.

Countering the Distortions of Baselines

The foregoing paragraphs mean that sticky expenditure is here to stay. How government adapts to this budgetary fact of life affects the balance between claims and controls. As chronicled in chapter 4, the prevailing practice is to project future expenditures on the basis of expected inflation and mandated workload changes. All policy changes are computed against this baseline, so that any action that lowers estimated future expenditures is recorded as deficit reduction.

Baseline budgeting strengthens the claims on, and weakens the control of, incremental resources. Budgeting, Wildavsky and many others following him have demonstrated, generally concentrates on distributing incremental resources. Although control of the base is weak, incrementalism enables budget makers to apportion spending increases according to the availability of funds. When the increment is small, increases over the previous year's level also are small.

The baseline, however, gives claimants a strong grip on the increment before any allocations have been made, whether or not additional resources are sufficient. With inflation built into the baseline and the provision of anything less than the full amount characterized as a cutback, budgeting has become a process that spends money the government does not have.

Currently, many key budget documents, especially those used in Congress, refer only to the baseline. They do not even mention the current or previous level of expenditure. The fact that allocations are being increased is veiled from politicians, who are told that if they provide less than the baseline, they are cutting the program. It is not hard to see that classifying the increase as a cutback complicates the control of expenditures.

This point was driven home at a 1989 activity in which this writer participated. The occasion was a deficit reduction exercise involving twenty-five members of a congressional committee. The briefing material prepared for the exercise presented a number of options for cutting Medicare and other federal programs against the baseline. Participants were asked to see whether they might agree on about $2.7 billion in Medicare cutbacks, the amount set in that year's summit agreement between the president and congressional leaders. The task proved difficult because the issue was framed in cutback terms. Had it been defined in terms of how much Medicare spending should be allowed to rise, participants might have been able to suggest ways of reaching the target without bearing the same political onus they faced in cutting back. Only after this phase of the exercise was completed were participating members advised that the CBO baseline had projected a more than $70 billion increase in Medicare spending between 1989 and 1994. At no time during the exercise were they asked to decide how this additional money should be spent.

The baseline also distorts perceptions because of the questionable assumptions embedded in it. One reason the Medicare baseline shows such a steep rise in spending is that it assumes a much higher uprating of hospital and physician payments than has occurred in recent years. Moreover, the baseline assumes that all temporary provisions will expire, and it therefore projects a much higher spending level than is likely to ensue. The treatment of temporary provisions overstates both the size of the baseline and of cutbacks, and it thus gives wily politicians a powerful incentive to substitute temporary expedients for genuine savings.

Remedying the expansionary bias of the baseline will not be easy. President Bush tried in his inaugural budget but failed. His budget rejected the baseline "as a habit of mind . . . [that] has unfortunate and misleading effects," and it urged that "next year's budget must be framed in relation to last year's actual spending—and in relation to available resources and deficit targets—not in relation to some hypothetical, perpetually expanding 'current services' baseline."[12] This position was untenable and it was abandoned in the president's budget as well as in the summit agreement negotiated shortly after Bush became president.[13] There are legitimate reasons for baseline projections, especially for indexed entitlements whose expenditures are driven by participation and inflation rates. With Social Security adding half a million recipients each year, it is not useful to budget solely on the basis of the previous year's allocation. The case for baselines is much weaker in discretionary programs, but it can be argued that they should be treated the same way as the rest of the budget. If they are not, the budget's already-formidable bias in favor of mandatory expenditures would become even more pronounced.

Some mitigation of the baseline's expansionary thrust might be achieved by several small changes in the display and computation of budget data. First, as a rule, baseline projections should be displayed alongside current spending levels, not as a substitute for them. Budget users then would have ready comparisons of current spending, next year's request, and outyear projections.[14]

Second, baseline projections should itemize their underlying assumptions, such as inflation rates and workload changes. Where a new provision is to take effect or an existing one is to expire, it should be identified, along with a detailed explanation of the impact on projected revenue or expenditure. Special program characteristics, such as a special price index, should be justified. For complex entitlements, the baseline should disclose each factor contributing significantly to the projected rise in spending. Thus, instead of lumping all Social Security or Medicaid into a single projection, the baseline should provide sufficient program detail for budget makers to be able to decide intelligently whether to make any changes. The Medicare baseline would, for example, show changes due to increases in beneficiaries, general inflation, medical inflation, increased volume of services, the introduction of technology, hospital construction, special payments for particular services, and so on.[15]

Third, the baseline rules should be revised to remove the distorting effects of temporary provisions and gimmicks on the projection of future revenue and outlays as well as on the computation of savings. Provisions that are temporary in appearance only, such as the repeated extension of the telephone excise tax and frequent adjustments in Medicare payments, would be treated as permanent. If Congress decided not to renew the telephone tax, its inaction would be scored as a revenue loss. Similarly, if Congress allowed the limitation on reimbursement for capital expenses to expire, its inaction would show up as a spending increase.

Finally, the baseline should incorporate a savings factor for productivity improvements. It is not unreasonable to expect agencies to achieve a 2 percent annual productivity gain in personnel expenditure. Thus, if the projected pay increase were 4 percent a year, the baseline would have only a 2 percent rise. Forced savings may appear arbitrary, but they are already being extracted from the many agencies compelled to absorb a portion of the annual pay increase. Linking the savings to productivity has been applied recently with success in Sweden and in a number of other democratic countries.[16]

The net effect of the various proposals would be a somewhat flatter baseline and a clearer understanding of what is behind the projections. Budget makers would have more data and options to choose from. Those who want to portray any level of spending below the baseline as a cutback still would be able to do so. Those who want to show it as an increase would have an easier time making their case.

Bolstering the President's Rationing Power

Strengthening the government's willingness to ration resources will entail making adjustments in both presidential and congressional budgeting. It will not suffice to look for relief to only one of the branches. If the president or Congress were hell-bent on pumping up budget demands, it would be hard for the other branch to effectively countervail. We first suggest a few changes in presidential budgeting and then turn to congressional behavior.

The president has a dual role in federal budgeting. He is the most potent claimant for funds and the most potent guardian of the treasury. Balancing these conflicting tendencies entails reconciling the parts and totals of the budget and exerting a constraining influence on congressional actions.

From the New Deal to Ronald Reagan, the president was often in the vanguard of the drive to expand federal programs. Most of the budgets sent to Congress during this half century called for major spending boosts in one or more areas. Although it is probably impossible to compute the portion of expenditure growth attributable to presidential initiative, a fair reckoning certainly would give him the lion's share of the credit or blame. When the president took the initiative, Congress typically responded with more money, though often with less than the chief executive wanted and sometimes with more. Ronald Reagan continued the president's role in policy initiation, but instead of asking more for domestic programs, he wanted more for defense.

The president cannot only be a claimant, however; he also must give attention to the adequacy of the resources at hand. As much as he may want to spend on roads or schools, the president is constrained in his appetite for more funds by his responsibility for the budget's totals. Over the years, the president has taken the lead in this regard, usually defining for Congress how high spending would be permitted to rise and what an acceptable deficit would be. Congress conceded the lead to the White House because its principal interest was in the parts, not in the aggregates. This division of labor generated frequent flareups, as the president sought to hold the line on his budget by inveighing against congressional add-ons.

The president's role as guardian of the totals is now shared with Congress, which, through its annual budget resolution, also goes on record with respect to total revenue, spending, and the deficit. Judging from recent performances, expanding the circle of participants has diluted responsibility for the totals. The evolution of the president's budget from an authoritative policy into a legislative gambit has encouraged the White House to be less than forthright in its forecasts and assumptions. Recent presidential dissimulation leads one to wonder whether the important task of forecasting economic conditions and the budget's totals might be entrusted to an independent group of experts. Before moving in this direction, one should carefully consider whether stripping the president of a vital feature of his budget power would have deleterious side effects and weaken him in other ways as well. A shift in responsibility for the budget's assumptions from politicians to experts should be tried only as a last resort and only if improvement in the deficit situation does not engender greater honesty in budgeting.

The president has always shared influence over the budget's parts with Congress. Over the course of two centuries, the relationship has often been turbulent, with the two branches vying for primacy and the ascendancy of one branch marked by the relative decline of the other. Recently, Congress appears to have had the more powerful voice. It has skillfully packaged provisions into omnibus legislation to counter the president's veto threat, and it has disabled his impoundment power. Both Ronald Reagan and George Bush have countered with a set of proposals to restore the president's budget lead by giving him an item veto, a formal role in the congressional budget process, and a stronger impoundment power.

Over the years, many presidents have asked for an item veto to counter Congress's proclivity to spend more on favored projects or activities. Congress has resisted these demands because it sees the item veto as having more to do with the distribution of budgetary power between the two branches than with the level of federal spending. There is no foreseeable prospect of Congress granting an item veto. Asking for this power is more a way of bashing Congress on the budget than doing something about the problem.

Enabling the president to sign or veto the budget resolution would transform it from a set of guidelines into a statutory decision. Yet, even as a statute, the resolution would not be self-enforcing. Implementing its revenue and spending policies would still depend on other legislation.[17] Making the resolution into a statute would enhance its status and possibly that of the overall congressional budget process as well. By giving the president a voice in the outcome, this reform might spur timely budget negotiations with Congress. But one should not lose sight of the possibility that when the president and Congress share responsibility, they still may not be able to resolve their differences. The odds of an impasse are not insignificant, in view of the political division between the two branches and the strong disagreements between them on budget priorities. Unless this change were accompanied by other changes that would make it into "must" legislation, converting to a statutory resolution would substantially escalate the risk of breakdown in the congressional budget process. In any event, Congress is likely to view a statutory resolution as putting the president in a stronger position to impose his preferences or to block those of Congress. On the plausible assumption that Congress would not be enthusiastic about bolstering the president's budget power at its expense, one should not expect it to act favorably on this idea.

Strengthening the president's impoundment power might also run into congressional opposition. One version of the "enhanced rescissions" concept floated by the White House would require a vote of Congress to overturn a proposed rescission. In contrast to the current rules, which compel the release of funds unless the rescission is approved within a brief period, the enhanced rescission authority would provide for the funds to be withheld unless Congress voted to release them. The rescission rules would be reversed—the president, not Congress, would prevail in case of legislative inaction. The president also would gain from expedited procedures that compel Congress to act and bar it from terminating proposed rescissions passively.

In assessing the erosion of the president's once-commanding budget position, it would be more fruitful to look at his behavior than at that of Congress. True, there has been a growing assertiveness of Congress in budgeting and in other areas of national policy. But this has been accompanied by a pervasive failure of recent presidents to protect their power. If the president does not look after his own interests, no one will do so for him.

The restoration of presidential budget clout depends more on political behavior than on legal rules. An adroit president can have an effective voice in congressional budget decisions even if he does not get to sign the resolution. He can constrain congressional spending demands even if he does not possess an item veto or an assured vote on rescissions. Lacking these powers, past presidents still were effective. Today's chief executive has a more complicated task because he must bridge differences not only between the two branches but between the two parties as well. To act as a brake on spending claims, the president must be seen as a fair and realistic guardian of the treasury, not as someone who disproportionately favors some claims over others or who sends up "dead on arrival" budgets whose purpose is to out-maneuver Congress.

Recasting the Congressional Budget Resolution

Congress has much more experience deciding the budget's parts than the totals. Since the beginning, it has made allocations to particular items of expenditure, but it has been setting budget totals only since 1975. Congress generally concedes leadership on the totals to the president, and it tries to approve outlay totals and the deficit pretty much in line with his recommendation. If the president applies fanciful assumptions to show lower spending or a smaller deficit, Congress cannot effectively riposte with more reliable numbers of its own.

Whether or not the president fabricates the totals, Congress often has difficulty fitting the parts into them. Congress is inherently a distributive institution whose members have a political imperative to provide concrete benefits for their constituencies. Whatever interest members have in voting appropriate budget totals, they also must think about their particular states or districts. There is nothing new about this behavior, as a look back at old rivers and harbors and postal roads legislation would show.

Over the years, Congress kept these particularistic claims on the budget reasonably small by making them in bite-size portions. Federal largesse was typically parceled out in appropriation bills and in the reports accompanying them. Members of the appropriations committees were especially well situated to "bring home the bacon," but distributive politics cut a broader swath through Congress, and many other members managed to garner money for back-home projects. The "pork" may have been of questionable quality, but it rarely was as prominent a factor in federal spending as the media portrayed. As the federal budget expanded in the postwar era and entitlements became more prominent, the money distributed in this fashion also rose, but it certainly declined as a portion of total spending.

The process of distribution played out in appropriations is an order of magnitude smaller than that associated with the budget resolution, however. The ante is much bigger in voting on budget resolutions because decisions are made at a higher level of aggregation, and the benefits tend to be spread across the country. Unlike appropriations, where the items can be as small as members make them, the minimum decision on a budget function is $50 million in the House and $100 million in the Senate. Another difference that pushes up the size of the budget logroll is that appropriations can be targeted to particular functions, whereas budget allocations are by function. Any additional funds budgeted for education are likely to be distributed among many school districts. Hence, there has to be enough money to make the effort worthwhile.

Some proposals have been made to strip functional allocations from the budget resolution and to limit it to decisions on the aggregates. However, totals lacking any backup might prove unenforceable. An alternative might be to restructure the categories in the budget resolution. Rather than allocating funds among the various functions, decisions might be made on a number of cross-cutting categories, such as those used in recent summits: defense, discretionary domestic programs, means-tested entitlements, and other entitlements.

In budgeting, the totals have to constrain the parts. One way of giving the budget aggregates more influence would be to adopt the two-step budget procedure advanced by House Republicans several years ago. In the first step, Congress would decide the totals. Only afterward would it move to the second step, which would be approving functional allocations. At this stage, Congress could revise the totals only through a new vote on them. This procedure has a potential drawback that might undermine the viability of the congressional budget process. If separate votes were required on the whole and the parts, members of Congress might take a restrictive posture in setting the size of the deficit and total outlays and an expansionary one in allocating funds among functions. One advantage to the current arrangement is that by allowing the total to be the sum of the allocations, the budget process makes it easier for members to adopt an arithmetically consistent resolution.

Controlling Budget Authority and Outlays

Federal budgeting operates with two currencies—the resources available for obligation (budget authority) and the funds actually spent (outlays). Both have to be controlled to maintain a balance between claims and resources. But because the government has an obligations-based budget, the budget authority figures are usually the decisive ones. They provide the main opportunities for decision and control in both the legislative and executive branches. Outlays are the final step in a chain of financial transactions culminating in the issuance

of a check. With the important exception of trust-funded entitlements, they normally cannot be controlled directly.

The fact that the government exercises weak control over discretionary outlays is an advantage. Because of this, it has less incentive
to manipulate the timing of payments to show a lower deficit. The
outlay chips can be permitted to fall when they are due. Because
entitlement payments can be directly controlled, their timing has
been manipulated frequently, as evidenced by the many efforts in
the 1980s to reduce Medicare spending without lowering program
levels.

Recent concern over the deficit has boosted the prominence of
outlays and the result has been a weakening of budget control. The
1974 Budget Act provides for outlays as one of the key aggregates in
the budget resolution, and it also requires allocating total outlays
among the various budget functions. At the time the Budget Act was
under consideration, the appropriations committees successfully rebuffed proposals for specifying outlay limits in each of the annual
appropriation bills.

Emphasis on outlays also has been reinforced by the GRH deficit
targets. The only way to meet the targets by spending action is to
reduce outlays, either indirectly, by adjusting budget authority, or
directly, by reducing entitlement payments. Because the outlays ensuing from discretionary budget authority depend on the rate at which
the resources are spent, they are subject to considerable manipulation. One can show lower outlays and a smaller deficit merely by
projecting a lower spendout rate or by switching funds from high
spendout to low spendout programs. The switch will not save any
money in the long run, but it will make it appear that spending has
been reduced. This situation invites politicians to trade-off between
budget authority and outlays, adding money to the former and taking
money from the latter. They then can claim that the deficit has been
lowered. Of course, what poses as a reduction in expenditures is
actually an increase, albeit one whose outlays will not enter the books
until some time in the future.

The budget-authority/outlay trade-off was made after the 1987 and
1989 budget summits. Pursuant to the 1987 summit, Congress found
itself with extra money for defense budget authority but in a tight
situation on defense outlays. It solved the dilemma by allocating $7
billion for the construction of two aircraft carriers. This money had
a negligible impact on the current deficit because shipbuilding has
an extremely low spendout rate, but it did add $7 billion to outyear
spending. In 1989, the budget summit sought to constrain outlays

tightly to avoid a GRH sequester, but it permitted a rise in discretionary budget authority. This time, the additional money was spread among domestic programs, but the result was the same as two years earlier. Under the guise of reducing the deficit, spending control was weakened.

It is important to restore the emphasis on budget authority. Rules changes are not necessary because there already are sufficient controls on budget authority. What is required is a lessening of the incentive to make the trade-off in the first place. To do so, direct controls on outlays and their contribution to short-term deficit reduction should be lessened. Here is a case in which less control might mean more effective control.

ADJUSTING TO CHANGES IN FEDERAL EXPENDITURE

There is a mismatch between inherited budget practices and the composition of federal expenditure. Budgeting came of age in the United States as a means of controlling administrative expenditure. The complex routines of budgeting revolve, as they have for many decades, around the preparation and review of agency requests. Operational expenditure, however, accounts for a declining share of total expenditure, and it is the portion of the budget in which spending is most controllable.

Rules and procedures that make sense for operating expenditure may have little application to mandated transfer payments. It does not add much expenditure control for agencies to go through the motions of preparing detailed budgets for these transfers. Their cost can be more efficiently estimated by a central staff, as can the impact of major changes in policy. Changes in transfer programs require political decisions. At the top levels of government and in Congress, to be effective, budgeting must be organized to facilitate such decisions and to reduce the political costs of making them.

Budgeting for Multiyear Policy

A key distinction between administrative and transfer expenditures is that the former are controlled by annual appropriations and the latter generally operate under permanent authority that continues in effect until Congress changes it. Because of this distinction, budget makers concentrate on the part of the budget that requires the least attention. Administrative expenditure, which poses few control problems, is reviewed annually. Transfer payments, which pose difficult problems, typically escape regular scrutiny.

One way of redressing this anomaly would be to install a multiyear budget. But as long as the concept of multiyear budgeting is promoted as a replacement for annual appropriations, it stands no chance of adoption. There is no prospect in the near future of the appropriations committees surrendering their annual review of agency requests. A more plausible approach would be to have multiyear authorizations and budget resolutions coexist with annual appropriations. Within the framework of annual appropriations, it might be possible to phase in a system similar to the one being introduced in Sweden. The Swedish approach frames annual appropriations within a three-year budget cycle. At the start of each cycle, an in-depth assessment is conducted of each spending agency's past performance and an understanding is negotiated on policies and resources for the next three years. In the intermediate years of the cycle, agencies would obtain annual appropriations, but these would be subject to a less intensive legislative review unless major departures were made from the agreed to resources and objectives.

Obviously, the Swedish system of government is considerably different than the American, and reforms that may be acceptable in one setting may not be in another. Nevertheless, the federal government has already moved significantly in the direction of multiyear budgeting, even for discretionary expenditure. Sizable chunks of the budget are appropriated in no-year money that is available for future use. Moreover, upward of one-third of annual outlays are derived from budget authority provided in prior years.

Reformers generally focus on the advantages that would accrue to Congress from a multiyear approach. It would suffer less congestion and legislative committees would benefit from having a more certain and stable budgetary environment, more breathing space to look ahead and examine policies, and a less grating relationship with Congress.

Budgeting for Entitlements

The budget is an inherently weak instrument for governing mandatory entitlements. We have already commented in this chapter on the broad social values that drive this part of the budget and consign financial consideration to secondary influence. Yet, the built-in escalation in entitlement spending during a period of fiscal stress has compelled increased budgetary attention to this problem.

When the budget is used to constrain entitlement spending, it tends to favor adjustments that save some money in the short run without opening up larger questions about the direction and future costs of the program. The reconciliation process is especially prone to short-term tinkering, both because it focuses on the amount to be saved in the period immediately ahead and because the affected committees are given little time to come up with recommendations. If the baseline and scorekeeping rules suggested earlier were implemented, reconciliation would have a somewhat longer horizon because committees would get credit only for savings that were generated by structural changes. In addition, the savings would be computed on a fully implemented basis so that less emphasis on the first year in which the adjustments occur and more would be placed on the long-term impact.

Structural changes require time to develop, enact, and implement. Here is where the previous suggestion of a multiyear budget could be put to good use. A biennial budget would provide more lead time for committees to delve into the possibility of major changes.

The relationship of entitlements and discretionary spending has generated some controversy. Clearly, the budget has to span both types of expenditure, but should overruns in mandated programs be cordoned off from above-budget spending in discretionary accounts? The House and Senate have taken different positions on this question. The former operates under the Fazio exception, which protects discretionary accounts against points of order due to an unbudgeted increase in mandatory spending. The Senate does not have a comparable exception, and it allows points of order on discretionary appropriations when entitlements cause the budget's spending totals or a committee's allocation to be exceeded. The position taken here is that remedies should be sought through more effective budgeting for entitlements, not by bleeding the discretionaries.

The Budgetary Relationship of the President and Congress

The basic division of labor, in which the President assembles a national budget to which Congress makes appropriations, was forged at a time when almost all federal spending was for administrative operations. The president's role in formulating the budget reinforced his role as chief executive and strengthened his ability to manage federal operations.

This division of labor spawns difficulties when it is applied to transfer programs. The salience and visibility of entitlements makes it difficult for either branch to take them on unilaterally. Doing so would entail serious political risks, as Ronald Reagan found out early in his presidency, when he proposed cutbacks in Social Security. Controlling the upward climb in entitlement payments requires more than the routine cooperation of the president and Congress. It has to be a joint venture in which both move in tandem.

Summits and other high-level negotiations offer occasional opportunities for joint action. But regularizing these events in the budget calendar would consign them to routine matters. In budgeting, as in international diplomacy, summits should be exceptional occasions, undertaken only when the stakes and probability of success are high. Consideration might be given to a two-stage process, which could be accommodated in a multiyear budget cycle. In the first stage, the president would present a framework for the next two years. Rather than having all the details crammed into contemporary budgets, the framework would concentrate on the aggregates and a small number of cross-cutting categories, including one or more for entitlements. Congress would debate the framework, and it would be at this stage that a decision could be made to activate the reconciliation process. At this stage, also, the president and Congress would have the option of entering into negotiations or devising alternative means for settling on an approved framework. After adoption of the framework, budgeting would move into the second stage, and the president would submit a detailed budget, following which Congress would act on appropriations and other budget legislation.

Regardless of the methods used, presidential-congressional cooperation is likely to become more regular in the future. Although they have not been institutionalized and cannot be made a regular feature of budgeting, the recent summits were not aberrations. Rather they were harbingers of changing relationships between the two budgeting branches of government.

BUDGETING AND GOVERNING

The opening paragraph of this book stated that the capacity to govern depends on the capacity to budget. We conclude the book with brief reflections on how budgeting and governing affect each other.

A persuasive case can be made that budgeting is hostage to larger political forces that create imbalances between claims and resources and deter the government from remedial action. If the government cannot effectively allocate resources, it may be because the basic institutions of government are inadequate, not because the machinery of budgeting is faulty. As a problem in governance, budget reformers must look to the quality of presidential leadership and congressional operations, as well as to the relations between the two branches and the behavior of office holders. It is to these matters that one should go for an explanation of why big policy mistakes were made in 1981 and why sufficient corrective action was not taken when the extent of the problem became known.

Democratic governments do a better job distributing benefits than redistributing resources. They do not find it easy to parcel out losses, and for long stretches of time, the federal government did not have to. When economic and budgetary circumstances changed, they found it difficult to adjust to the new conditions. There is reason to believe, however, that the weakening of American governing institutions is largely due to nonbudgetary factors, such as erosion of confidence in government, political and policy frictions between the two branches, and overloading the government.

Yet budgeting also merits study on its own, not just as a subfield of politics. Judging from the attention given to the process over the years, one would conclude that the procedures of budgeting do materially affect policy outcomes. The manner in which budgeting is conducted does affect the balance between the mobilization of claims and the rationing of resources. Anyone who ignores this reality will contribute neither to the vitality of government nor the capacity to budget.

Notes

1. See Rudolph G. Penner and Alan J. Abramson, *Broken Purse Strings* (Washington, D.C.: Urban Institute Press, 1988), chapter 7, and Allen Schick, "Proposed Budget Reforms: A Critical Analysis," in U.S. Congress, Senate Committee on Governmental Affairs, 100th Cong., 2d sess., *Proposed Budget Reforms: A Critical Analysis*, 1988.

2. See Edward Davis, *Congressional Budget Reform: 101st Congress*, Issue Brief IB89022, Congressional Research Service, 1989.

3. U.S. Office of Management and Budget, *Budget of the United States Government, Fiscal Year 1990* (Washington, D.C.: Government Printing Office, 1989), p. 1–13.

4. Message of the President, *Building a Better America*, February 9, 1989, p. 19.

5. Schick, *op. cit.*, sets forth five criteria for assessing budget reforms: the impact of proposed changes on the size of the budget deficit, the budgetary powers of the president and Congress, the distribution of budgetary power in Congress, the timely completion of congressional budget actions, and the enforcement of budget policies in Congress.

6. The leading spokesman for this school of thought is Robert Eisner, *How Real is the Federal Deficit?* (New York: Free Press, 1986). See also Robert Heilbroner and Peter Bernstein, *The Debt and the Deficit* (New York: W.W. Norton, 1989).

7. After dropping from a peak of 127 percent of GNP in 1946 to a low of 33 percent in 1981, the gross federal debt climbed to 54 percent of GNP in the 1988 fiscal year. The debt held by the public was 114 percent of GNP in 1946, 26 percent in 1981, and 43 percent of GNP in fiscal 1988. The deficit peaked at 6.3 percent of GNP in the 1983 fiscal year and declined to 3.2 percent of GNP in fiscal 1988.

8. For a broader view of the contemporary problems of governance, see John E. Chubb and Paul E. Peterson, eds., *Can the Government Govern?* (Washington, D.C.: Brookings Institution, 1989).

9. Assuming that the economy averages annual growth in excess of 2 percent, a deficit in this range would lead to a steady reduction in the public debt relative to GNP.

10. The March 1989 report of the National Economic Commission recommended that the entire on-budget deficit be eliminated. But in urging the liquidation of more than $250 billion of deficits, the Democratic and Republican members of the Commission were unable to agree on where the first billion in reductions should come from.

11. The 1987 Gramm-Rudman-Hollings amendments sought to counter deception by providing that extraordinary asset sales and prepayments would not count in determining compliance with the annual deficit target. Nevertheless, the fabrications have continued since then.

12. *Building a Better America, op. cit.*, p. 23.

13. The Bush budget used baseline figures when it was expedient to do so, for example, in arguing for a full adjustment inflation for defense, *ibid.*, p. 137.

14. As a longtime budget watcher, who has reviewed the budget documents of hundreds of governments in the United States and elsewhere, this writer has found the practice of publishing only the baseline or variances from it to be highly unusual. The near-universal practice is to display the estimated levels for the current year alongside the requests for the next year, thereby facilitating interyear comparisons.

15. This suggestion follows along the lines of proposals made by Timothy Muris, whose penetrating analysis has stripped away many misunderstandings about how baselines are constructed and used. See Timothy J. Muris, "The Uses and Abuses of Budget Baselines," unpublished paper, January 1989. Muris acknowledges that publishing detailed data on baseline assumptions would be more complex than current practices, but, he notes, "Medicare and many other government programs are not simple. Understanding and making intelligent decisions about those programs requires knowing why the program is growing. If the technical budgetary display of these programs is anything less, it tends to hide important information about the program and indirectly influences outcomes," p. 71.

16. The use of productivity targets and savings in the allocation of resources is discussed in Organization for Economic Cooperation and Development, *Measuring Performance and Allocating Resources* (Paris, 1989).

17. Several years ago, Rep. David Obey proposed an arrangement in which a statutory resolution would be part of an omnibus budget measure that would also include

appropriations and changes in entitlements and revenue legislation. In his scheme, enactment of the omnibus measure would have been the means of implementing the budget resolution contained in it. The Obey proposal is discussed in Allen Schick, *The Whole and the Parts: Piecemeal and Integrated Approaches to Congressional Budgeting*, U.S. Congress, House Committee on the Budget, Committee Print, February 1987.

ABOUT THE AUTHOR

Allen Schick is a professor of Public Policy at the University of Maryland and a visiting scholar at The Urban Institute. He previously served at the Congressional Research Service and the Brookings Institution and taught at Tufts University. Schick is the founding editor of *Public Budgeting and Finance*, a professional journal that covers matters affecting government finance. He is the author of more than 100 publications. His book *Congress and Money: Budgeting, Spending, and Taxing* was published by the Institute in 1980; it won the Hardeman Prize for the best book on Congress and the Brownlow Award for the best book on American Political Institutions. In 1989, Schick received the Waldo Prize from the American Society of Public Administration for lifetime contributions to the literature of public administration. Schick's studies of budgeting have covered all levels of American budgeting and many other democratic countries. He has conducted research or lectured in more than 40 states and more than 20 countries, and was the lead consultant for *The Control and Management of Public Expenditure*, a report published by the Organization for Economic Cooperation and Development (OECD).